READERS' GUIDES TO ESSENTIAL (

CONSULTANT EDITOR: NICOLAS TREDELL

Published

Lucie Armitt	George Eliot: *Adam Bede – The Mill on the Floss – Middlemarch*
Richard Beynon	D.H. Lawrence: *The Rainbow – Women in Love*
Peter Boxall	Samuel Beckett: *Waiting for Godot – Endgame*
Claire Brennan	The Poetry of Sylvia Plath
Susan Bruce	Shakespeare: *King Lear*
Sandie Byrne	Jane Austen: *Mansfield Park*
Alison Chapman	Elizabeth Gaskell: *Mary Barton – North and South*
Peter Childs	The Fiction of Ian McEwan
Christine Clegg	Vladimir Nabokov: *Lolita*
John Coyle	James Joyce: *Ulysses – A Portrait of the Artist as a Young Man*
Martin Coyle	Shakespeare: *Richard II*
Sarah Gamble	The Fiction of Angela Carter
Jodi-Anne George	Chaucer: The General Prologue to *The Canterbury Tales*
Jane Goldman	Virginia Woolf: *To the Lighthouse – The Waves*
Huw Griffiths	Shakespeare: *Hamlet*
Geoffrey Harvey	Thomas Hardy: *Tess of the d'Urbervilles*
Paul Hendon	The Poetry of W.H. Auden
Terry Hodgson	The Plays of Tom Stoppard for Stage, Radio, TV and Film
Stuart Hutchinson	Mark Twain: *Tom Sawyer – Huckleberry Finn*
Stuart Hutchinson	Edith Wharton: *The House of Mirth – The Custom of the Country*
Betty Jay	E.M. Forster: *A Passage to India*
Elmer Kennedy-Andrews	The Poetry of Seamus Heaney
Elmer Kennedy-Andrews	Nathaniel Hawthorne: *The Scarlet Letter*
Daniel Lea	George Orwell: *Animal Farm – Nineteen Eighty-Four*
Philippa Lyon	Twentieth-Century War Poetry
Carl Plasa	Toni Morrison: *Beloved*
Carl Plasa	Jean Rhys: *Wide Sargasso Sea*
Nicholas Potter	Shakespeare: *Othello*
Berthold Schoene-Harwood	Mary Shelley: *Frankenstein*
Nick Selby	T.S. Eliot: *The Waste Land*
Nick Selby	Herman Melville: *Moby Dick*
Nick Selby	The Poetry of Walt Whitman
David Smale	Salman Rushdie: *Midnight's Chidren – The Satanic Verses*
Patsy Stoneman	Emily Brontë: *Wuthering Heights*
Susie Thomas	Hanif Kureishi
Nicolas Tredell	F. Scott Fitzgerald: *The Great Gatsby*

Nicolas Tredell	Joseph Conrad: *Heart of Darkness*
Nicolas Tredell	Charles Dickens: *Great Expectations*
Nicolas Tredell	William Faulkner: *The Sound and the Fury – As I Lay Dying*
Nicolas Tredell	The Fiction of Martin Amis

Forthcoming

Peter Dempsey	The Fiction of Don Delillo
Michael Faherty	The Poetry of W. B. Yeats
Matthew Jordan	Milton: *Paradise Lost*
Merja Makinen	The Novels of Jeanette Winterson
Stephen Regan	The Poetry of Philip Larkin
Nicolas Tredell	Shakespeare: *Macbeth*
Angela Wright	Gothic Fiction

Palgrave Reader's Guides to Essential Criticism
Series Standing Order
ISBN 1–4390–0108–2
(outside North America only)

You can receive future titles in this series as they are published by placing a standing order. Please contact your bookseller or, in the case of difficulty, write to us at the address below with your name and address, the title of the series and the ISBN quoted above.

Customer Services Department, Palgrave Macmillan Ltd
Houndmills, Basingstoke, Hampshire RG21 6XS, England

The Fiction of Ian McEwan

EDITED BY PETER CHILDS

Consultant editor: Nicolas Tredell

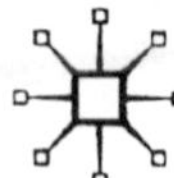

First published in 2006 by
PALGRAVE MACMILLAN
Houndmills, Basingstoke, Hampshire RG21 6XS and
175 Fifth Avenue, New York, N.Y. 10010
Companies and representatives throughout the world.

PALGRAVE MACMILLAN is the global academic imprint of the Palgrave Macmillan division of St. Martin's Press, LLC and of Palgrave Macmillan Ltd. Macmillan® is a registered trademark in the United States, United Kingdom and other countries. Palgrave is a registered trademark in the European Union and other countries.

ISBN-13: 978–1–4039–1909–0 hardback
ISBN-10: 1–4039–1909–7 hardback
ISBN-13: 978–1–4039–1908–3 paperback
ISBN-10: 1–4039–1908–9 paperback

This book is printed on paper suitable for recycling and made from fully managed and sustained forest sources.

A catalogue record for this book is available from the British Library.

A catalog record for this book is available from the Library of Congress.

10 9 8 7 6 5 4 3 2 1
15 14 13 12 11 10 09 08 07 06

Printed and bound in China

CONTENTS

A Note on References and Quotations x

Acknowledgements xi

Introduction 1

Outlines McEwan's life and career, then situates him among contemporary British writers, and provides a brief summary of the contents of the Guide.

CHAPTER ONE 8

The Fleshly Grail: *First Love, Last Rites* (1975)

Considers the reception of McEwan as a macabre writer of 'literature of shock' on the evidence of his first collection of short stories. After noting the contemporary press response, the chapter discusses McEwan's own reflections in interview on the writing of the stories before examining the perspectives of Kiernan Ryan, David Malcolm and Jack Slay, all of whom concentrate on the focus, themes and scope of the stories, followed by Lynda Broughton, who adopts a feminist perspective.

CHAPTER TWO 21

Underworld: *In Between the Sheets* (1978)

Discusses the reviews of the British and American press of this second collection of stories, and in particular the analysis of V. S. Pritchett in the *New York Review of Books*. After considering McEwan's discussion of the collection with John Haffenden, the chapter surveys the responses, in terms of the stories' presentation of male sexuality, sadism and masochism, of Angela Roger and Christina Byrnes, before considering the readings of Kiernan Ryan, who compares McEwan with his contemporary Martin Amis, and Richard Brown, who looks at McEwan's first representation of America in 'Psychopolis'.

CHAPTER THREE 33

A Lovely Sleep: *The Cement Garden* (1978)

Looks at the different initial responses to McEwan's first novel, from those that found it unsympathetic in its portrayal of isolated children to those who thought it announced McEwan as one of the finest British novelists of his generation. In terms of longer readings of the novel, Christopher Williams looks at the lineage of representations of the adolescent in fiction, Randall Stevenson ponders the claustrophobic feel of the narrative, and Carmen Callil and Colm Tóibín examine the story in terms of its contemporary setting. The chapter also includes two extracts from interviews with McEwan in which he explains the genesis of the novel as well as its concern with Oedipal conflict and incest – a concern also explored by Jack Slay. Angela Roger concentrates on the gender relations in the novel, while David Sampson examines the book's implications for types of reading in the light of the theories of Roland Barthes.

CHAPTER FOUR 46

The Desire to be a Victim: *The Comfort of Strangers* (1981)

Delineates the spectrum of reactions, frequently characterised by outrage, to McEwan's second novel. By contrast, Malcolm Bradbury views the narrative as a fable about sexual feelings and gender roles, aspects of the novel explained by McEwan in a discussion with John Haffenden of the novel's origins and the reactions it received from some feminists. Both Kiernan Ryan and Judith Seaboyer examine the book's take on desire and gender roles in their analyses. Finally, Angela Roger indicates how the novel is occupied throughout with victimhood and the principled passivity that 'allows' aggression, male violence and patriarchy to be perpetuated.

CHAPTER FIVE 59

True Maturity: *The Child in Time* (1987)

Opens with a discussion by McEwan of how he came to conceive the novel and the significance of the other projects with which he was concerned in the years between this novel and his previous one. Malcolm Bradbury and D. J. Taylor are then both interested in McEwan's decision to place the narrative in the future: Bradbury sees this as an indication of the direction of McEwan's fiction in the ensuing decade, while Taylor believes it in fact indicates McEwan's inability to deal with wider social settings than were prominent in his earlier writing. While Allan Massie sees the novel's success lying in its central depiction of the character of Stephen, Adam Mars-Jones attacks the book as an appropriation of feminism – by Stephen and by McEwan. Next, Ellen Pifer analyses the aspect of the novel that has probably received most comment, its depiction of adults' relationship with childhood, while Jack Slay discusses its other key element: time. Dominic Head then examines the book's interest in the new physics, but Ben Knights, by contrast, sees the book as a 'green parable'. Finally, Paul Edwards offers a reading of the third chapter of the novel in the context of British literary responses to modernity.

CHAPTER SIX 76

No Different From You: *The Innocent* (1990)

Starts by noting that critics were again divided in their reception of McEwan's fiction. Merritt Moseley then reviews the triangle at the centre of this new novel, before Michel Deville notes how its oscillation between different ontological positions apparently leaves the novel without a consistent value system. Wendy Lesser offers a more refined analysis, concentrating on the narrator Jeremy, while Christina Byrnes scrutinises McEwan's symbolisation of evil, a central concern of the narrative. Developing on from Deville's concerns, Marc Delrez proffers a sustained critique of the values and contradictions that appear to underlie the story, while Jago Morrison is more interested in the ways in which Jeremy attempts to make sense of the past through his piecemeal narrative, a facet of the novel taken up by David Malcolm in his discussion of the relationship between public and personal histories.

CHAPTER SEVEN 90

Ça Suffit: *Black Dogs* (1992)

Begins, after an exegesis of the novel's content and concerns, with Michael Wood's review of the principal themes of deception, ignorance, aggression and the loss of innocence. Richard Brown then considers the novel in terms of the relationship between Britain and the USA, illustrating how McEwan has broadened his social and political concerns since his early novels, while Mark Ledbetter concentrates on the novel's set piece, the dismemberment of Otto as a metaphor for the division of Berlin, and Tamás Bényei discusses the significance of the central image of 'the tunnel'. After an extract from an interview with Rosa González-Casademont in which McEwan explains the novel's setting and provenance, Jack Slay analyses the way in which the novel presents several different kinds of initiation for its innocent protagonist, Leonard. Finally, Kiernan Ryan explains how the spy genre lends itself to McEwan's particular kinds of exploration of human experience.

CHAPTER EIGHT 104

Rationality Is Its Own Kind of Innocence: *Enduring Love* (1997)

Records the polarised reactions to the novel on its publication, with reviewers varying considerably in their pronouncements, from those who saw it as 'brilliant' to those who concluded it was 'half-baked'. After interventions by McEwan on the novel's opening chapter and the book's beginnings elsewhere, Adam Mars-Jones explains why he feels the novel is undermined by Joe Rose's development as an unreliable narrator, and James Wood berates the narrative for its over-reliance on a hackneyed plotline, a view counterposed with McEwan's own explanation of the story's development. David Malcolm explores the novel's interest in reason and rationality, while Roger Clark and Andy Gordon discuss the role of Jean Logan, whose central position in the novel's subplot shows how McEwan is concerned with perspective and juxtaposition. Finally, Christina Byrnes provides a useful review of the history of de Clérambault's syndrome, while Jago Morrison considers the degree to which Jed Parry is presented as the product of Joe's own obsessions.

CHAPTER NINE 118

Their Reasonable Laws: *Amsterdam* (1998)

Notes the variety of responses to the novel, but also the problem reviewers had with placing the novel in McEwan's *oeuvre*, in terms of genre as much as merit. McEwan explains the novel as a farewell to nearly two decades of Conservative government, and, in some ways in keeping with this, David Malcolm concludes that *Amsterdam* is in part a psychological study and a morality tale. For John Brannigan, the novel is most concerned with mid-life crises and the spectre of mortality, but William Pritchard places it in the tradition of satirists such as Evelyn Waugh and Kingsley Amis, and Nicholas Lezard also sees it as an exposure in comedy of a cynical heartlessness at the heart of the British ruling classes. Finally, Christina Byrnes examines the novel in terms of sadomasochistic dynamics, maturational crises and depression.

CHAPTER TEN 129

Storytelling as Self-justification: *Atonement* (2001)

Surveys the almost universally positive reviews of McEwan's first novel of the new century before McEwan himself explains both his purpose in the narrative and its relation to the tradition of the English novel. Frank Kermode then explores McEwan's use of point of view in the novel, while Claire Messud discusses in particular the presentation of Briony's perspective. For John Updike, the descriptive richness of the novel addresses in terms of form the content of Briony's attempt at atonement, while Martyn Bedford is exercised by McEwan's abiding concern with the theme of the storyteller's difficulty of imaginative empathy, and Geoff Dyer chooses to foreground stylistic elements which are still underdiscussed in McEwan criticism. Hermione Lee considers the novel's relationship to both its literary precursors and European history before James Wood argues that the novel works best as a detailed evocation of English life in the mid-twentieth century. John Mullan concludes the chapter by examining one typically English preoccupation of McEwan's in the novel's long opening section: the weather.

CONCLUSION 144

And Now, What Days Are These?: *Saturday* (2005)

Summarises McEwan's contemporary reputation and analyses *Saturday* before providing a short consideration of McEwan's novel for children, *The Daydreamer* (1994).

NOTES 152

SELECT BIBLIOGRAPHY 159

INDEX 162

A NOTE ON REFERENCES AND QUOTATIONS

Page references to Ian McEwan's fiction are given in brackets in the main text of the Guide. All other references are in the notes; full details can be found in the bibliography. In the extracts in this Guide, insertions by the editor are in square brackets and standard type. Definitions of words, where provided by the editor, are taken from the *Collins English Dictionary*, unless otherwise stated in the notes. Insertions in square brackets and bold type in the extracts are by the authors of the extracts themselves. Editorial ellipses are enclosed in brackets.

ACKNOWLEDGEMENTS

The editor and publishers wish to thank the following for permission to use copyright material:

Richard Brown for material from 'Postmodern Americas in the Fiction of Angela Carter, Martin Amis and Ian McEwan', in Anna Massa and Alistair Stead, eds, *Forked Tongues? Comparing Twentieth-Century British and American Literature*, Longman (1994), pp. 104–5, 107, by permission of Pearson Education Ltd.

Christina Byrnes for material from *The Work of Ian McEwan: A Psychodynamic Approach*, Pauper Press (2002), pp. 57–8, 143–9, 242–3, 265–7, by permission of the author.

Marc Delrez for material from 'Escape into Innocence: Ian McEwan and the Nightmare of History', *Ariel*, 26:2 (1995), pp. 18–20, by permission of the Board of Governors, University of Calgary.

Geoff Dyer for material from 'Who's afraid of influence?', *Guardian*, 22.9.2001, p. 8, by permission of the author.

Paul Edwards for material from 'Time Romanticism, Modernism and Modernity in Ian McEwan's *The Child in Time*', *English*, 44:178 (1995), pp. 48–51, by permission of the English Association.

Dwight Garner for material from 'The Salon Interview – Ian McEwan', *Salon*, 31.3.1998. Copyright ©2003 Salon.com, by permission of *Salon*.

Rosa González-Casademont for material from 'The Pleasure of Prose Writing vs Pornographic Violence: An Interview with Ian McEwan', *The European English Messenger*, 1:3 (1992), pp. 42–3, by permission of the author.

John Haffenden for material from *Novelists in Interview*, Methuen (1985), pp. 169–73, 177–81. Copyright © John Haffenden, by permission of Curtis Brown Ltd, London, on behalf of the author.

Frank Kermode for material from 'Point of View', *London Review of Books*, 4.10.2001, pp. 8–9, by permission of the *London Review of Books*.

Mark Ledbetter for material from *Victims and the Postmodern Narrative or Doing Violence to the Body: An Ethic of Reading and Writing*, Macmillan/ St Martin's Press (1996), pp. xii, 99–102, 159, by permission of Palgrave Macmillan.

Hermione Lee for material from 'If your memories serve you well ...', *Observer*, 23.9.2001, by permission of the author.

Wendy Lesser for material from 'Black Dogs', *The New Republic*, 11.11.1992. Copyright © 1992 The New Republic LLC, by permission of *The New Republic*.

Nicholas Lezard for material from '"Morality Bites": Ian McEwan's five-finger finesse', *Guardian*, 24.4.1999, by permission of the author.

Adam Mars-Jones for material from *Venus-Envy: On the Womb and the Bomb*, Chatto & Windus (1990), pp. 24–8, by permission of PFD on behalf of the author.

Jago Morrison for material from 'Narration and Unease in McEwan's Later Fiction', *Critique*, 42:3 (2001), pp. 258–60, Heldref Publications, by permission of the Helen Dwight Reid Educational Foundation; and *Contemporary Fiction* by Jago Morrison, Routledge (2003), pp. 75–7, by permission of Taylor & Francis Books Ltd.

John Mullen for material from 'Elements of Fiction: turning up the heat', *Guardian Review*, 22.3.2003, by permission of the author.

Jonathan Noakes for material from 'An Interview with Ian McEwan', in Margaret Reynolds and Jonathan Noakes, eds, *Ian McEwan: The Essential Guide*, Vintage (2002), pp. 11, 13, 19–20, 22–3, by permission of the Random House Group Ltd.

Ellen Pifer for material from *Demon or Doll: Images of the Child in Contemporary Writing and Culture*, University of Virginia Press (2000), pp. 201–3, by permission of the University of Virginia Press.

William H. Pritchard for material from 'Book Review – Ian McEwan's *Atonement*', *New York Times*, 27.12.1998, p. 4, by permission of the *New York Times*.

V. S. Pritchett for material from 'In Between the Sheets', *The New York Review of Books*, 24.1.1980, pp. 31–2. Copyright © 1980 NYREV, Inc., by permission of *The New York Review of Books*.

Angela Roger for material from 'Ian McEwan's Portrayal of Women', *Forum for Modern Language Studies*, 32:1 (1996), pp. 12–8, by permission of Oxford University Press.

Kieran Ryan for material from *Ian McEwan*, Writers and Their Work Series (1994), pp. 7–9, 58–60, by permission of Northcote House Publishers; and 'Sex, Violence and Complicity: Martin Amis and Ian McEwan', in Rod Mengham, ed., *An Introduction to Contemporary Fiction*, Polity Press (1999), pp. 209–11, 213, by permission of Polity Press Ltd.

Judith Seaboyer for material from 'Sadism Demands a Story: Ian McEwan's *The Comfort of Strangers*', *Modern Fiction Studies*, 45:4 (1999), pp. 959, 961, 965–7, by permission of the Johns Hopkins University Press.

Jack Slay for material from *Ian McEwan*, Twayne's English Authors Series (1996), pp. 18–20, 46–8, 135–8, 123–5. Copyright © 1996 Twayne Publishers, by permission of the Gale Group.

James Wood for material from 'The Trick of Truth', *The New Republic*, 21.3.2002. Copyright © 2002 The New Republic LLC, by permission of

The New Republic; and 'Why it all adds up', *Guardian*, 4.9.1997, p. 9. Copyright © 1997 Guardian Newspapers Ltd, by permission of Guardian Newspapers Ltd.

Michael Wood for material from 'Well done, Ian McEwan', *London Review of Books*, 10.5.1990, pp. 24, 26, by permission of the *London Review of Books*.

Material from 'An Interview with McEwan', from the internet [www.randomHouse.com/boldtype/1298/mcewan/interview.html]. Copyright © Random House, Inc., by permission of Random House, Inc.

Every effort has been made to trace the copyright holders, but if any have been inadvertently overlooked the publishers will be pleased to make the necessary arrangement at the first opportunity.

Introduction

At the start of his career, Ian McEwan appeared to reviewers to be one of the *enfants terribles* of a new kind of writing that was emerging in the 1970s. He took this title along with Martin Amis (born 1949), who was himself one of the rebellious sons of the old guard. McEwan has said of the literary climate in the UK when he began writing:

> The published writers then seemed a sort of postwar generation – Kingsley Amis [1922–95], Angus Wilson [1913–91] – the latter I came to know and respect enormously. They showed me a world that seemed to be too tied to a form of social documentary. Too concerned with those things that the English novel has often done well – the nuances of class, the perils and attractions of social mobility, the furniture well-described. I think I was trying to make a strength out of my ignorance. I didn't know that world. I was a very déclassé sort of young man. I'd been tucked away in a country boarding school where most of the boys were from a working-class background in central London, but the idea was to give them the kind of education that wealthier kids would have had. I was there because there was a small intake of army brat kids. (Dwight Garner, 'Salon Interview', 1998)[1]

Though the postwar generation that McEwan mentions had opened up literary fiction to a new breed of writers – lower middle-class, provincial, and socially disaffected – twenty years later those novelists inevitably appeared to be backward-looking, addressing issues that were primarily of historical interest to a succeeding post-imperial generation that grew up with a sense of new youth movements, Americanisation, and popular culture.

While Martin Amis produced one comparatively conventional rites-of-passage novel before publishing *Dead Babies* (1975), a book that would help delineate a shocking new transatlantic world of sex, drugs and violence, Ian McEwan's first published fiction was met from the start with as much outrage as praise. *Dead Babies* and McEwan's debut collection, *First Love, Last Rites* (1975) came out in the same year and garnered similar outraged reactions. As the mavericks of a new generation, which is how they are retrospectively positioned, Amis and McEwan's emergence heralded the arrival in the 1980s of the writers who are now the best-known contemporary British novelists, such as Julian Barnes (born 1946), Kazuo Ishiguro (born 1954), Graham Swift (born 1949),

Salman Rushdie (born 1947), Jeanette Winterson (born 1959) and Pat Barker (born 1943). Yet none of these writers, not even Rushdie, has been considered shocking by critics and reviewers in the same way as McEwan and Amis. While Amis has continued to gain headlines through his celebrity status and his more provocative novels, such as *Money* (1984) and *London Fields* (1989), McEwan has developed in the 1990s into a serious and contemplative novelist, whose first book of the new century, *Atonement* (2001), places itself firmly in the mainstream literary tradition running from Samuel Richardson (1689–1761), through Jane Austen (1775–1817), to Henry James (1843–1916) and beyond.

Born on 21 June 1948, Ian Russell McEwan grew up in Aldershot and in military stations abroad such as Singapore and Libya. His mother had two much older children from an earlier marriage, but McEwan had no other siblings, and so has always considered himself very much 'an only child'. After an army childhood he attended Woolverstone state boarding-school in Suffolk from 1959 to 1966. Subsequently, he read English and French at the University of Sussex for three years before enrolling for the modern fiction MA degree at the University of East Anglia. Here, as part of his degree, he took a course in creative writing, principally under the tutelage of Malcolm Bradbury (1932–2000). Finishing this one-year course in 1971, he spent part of the following year on a trip to Afghanistan and the North-West Frontier Province.

McEwan's first book was a collection of short stories he had worked on at East Anglia. As I've mentioned, *First Love, Last Rites* immediately won him a reputation for writing literature to shock, mainly because of its seeming preoccupation with sordid sexuality, abused children and violent relationships. Its concerns seemed to reviewers at once to be bleak and compelling, squalid and unconventional, yet recognizably and disturbingly human. It won the Somerset Maugham Award for 1976.

That year, McEwan travelled to the USA before his next publications: *In Between the Sheets* (1978), another collection of short stories, and *The Cement Garden* (1978), his first novel. If only because it lacks the impact of a debut, McEwan's second set of short stories is less striking than his first, though it received the same slightly hysterical reaction from some quarters. For the most part, the stories are concerned with unconventional sexual relationships and adopt a number of different narratorial perspectives. Subjects vary from a woman who keeps an ape as a lover to a two-timing man who is castrated by the nurses he is deceiving. By contrast, McEwan's first novel is an introverted first-person narrative of burgeoning adolescent sexuality that builds on the themes and insights that made *First Love, Last Rites* such a powerful first book.

The first of McEwan's several film and television scripts was aired in 1976: 'Jack Flea's Birthday Celebration', a half-hour confrontational dinner-party drama directed by Mike Newell. McEwan has said he thinks of it as a part of the stories assembled for *First Love, Last Rites*. In 1979, an adaptation of one of his best short stories, 'Solid Geometry', was halted by the BBC following concerns over its subject matter, but in the new decade McEwan saw his second original TV script produced: *The Imitation Game* (1980, published 1981), a World War II story of sexual politics within English patriarchy, set at Bletchley Park, directed by Richard Eyre as a BBC *Play for Today* (the title comes from the test by mathematician and Enigma-code-breaker Alan Turing (1912–54) of whether a machine can think). McEwan also adapted his story 'The Last Day of Summer' for television in 1983, but his subsequent scripts have been for film: *The Ploughman's Lunch* (1983), an anti-Thatcherite story set at the time of the Falklands, again directed by Richard Eyre; *Soursweet* (1988), a faithful adaptation of the 1982 novel *Sour Sweet* by Timothy Mo (born 1950) about a Chinese family in 1960s Britain, and *The Good Son* (1993), an original script that shares similar themes, from different angles, with many of his novels.

McEwan's second novel, *The Comfort of Strangers* (1981), was shortlisted for the Booker Prize. It is more clearly amenable to categorization as 'literature of shock' than even his other novels, but it also leans towards conventional genre fiction. Set in Venice, it tells the story of a tourist couple who become involved with a local man who proves to be a sadistic murderer. The book seems to take Blanche DuBois's assertion in Tennessee Williams's (1911–83) *A Streetcar Named Desire* (1947) that she has always relied on the kindness of strangers and turn it on its head to explore the ways in which travellers are at the mercy of others when holidaying in alien surroundings.

The following year McEwan married Penny Allen and in 1983 their son William was born. That year, McEwan's oratorio about the threat of nuclear war, *or Shall We Die?*, was performed at London's Royal Festival Hall with a score by Michael Berkeley (born 1948). He was also included that year along with Martin Amis, Salman Rushdie, Julian Barnes, Kazuo Ishiguro and others as one of the Book Marketing Council's twenty Best of Young British Novelists. In 1984 he was elected to the Fellowship of the Royal Society of Literature.

McEwan's third novel displayed some considerable changes from his earlier two. Informed by the experience of writing for television and film, *The Child in Time* (1987) has a far broader social and political canvas. For many critics this book revealed McEwan to be one of the foremost novelists of his generation, though for others it showed that he was best writing about couples and families in small-scale, almost claustrophobic situations. The novel, set in a future ten years away from its time of writing, deals with a couple who become estranged after the disappearance of their only child and then become reconciled with the birth of a new baby. The second string plot concerns the writing of a government childcare manual, and the two strands of narrative are brought together not just through the characters but through their concern with the idea that a generation or society can be appraised by its attitude towards the nurturing and education of children. *The Child in Time* won the Whitbread novel prize. McEwan also travelled to the Soviet Union as part of a delegation from European Nuclear Disarmament (END) in 1987, and this trip arguably marks the turn towards European perspectives in his writing.

The gap between McEwan's previous two novels had been six years, but it was only three years before *The Innocent* (1990) appeared, the first of four novels McEwan published in the 1990s. It is again possible to consider the narrative as consciously working with a specific genre, as it is ostensibly a Cold War spy story about the Anglo-American attempt in the mid-1950s to build a surveillance tunnel through to the Soviet sector of Berlin. *The Innocent* was his most successful book to date and McEwan adapted it for film in 1993. Two years later, *Black Dogs* (1992) was published, McEwan's most thematically ambitious book. The novel uses the dogs of its title as an emblem of an evil that may appear at any time in the world, and the narrative is concerned with questions of the redemptive power of love and the possibility of the supernatural or divine, as well as the provenance of good and evil. *Black Dogs* was the second of his novels to reach the Booker Prize shortlist.

McEwan's next novel, *Enduring Love* (1997), is both a meditation on love's endurance and on an individual's endurance of unwanted, misdirected love. It again has a marriage in crisis at its centre: a loving couple whose union is threatened by a fanatical stalker. Following their meeting at an intense emotional event, the attempt to hold down a hot-air balloon in danger of flying away with only a small child aboard (one man dies in the attempt), Jed Parry latches on to the novel's narrator, Joe Rose. The reader is never quite sure, until late on, whether Parry is indeed stalking Joe, or, as Joe's partner Clarissa believes, Joe is making up most of the story.

Amsterdam (1998) won the Booker Prize in 1998, and perhaps secured McEwan the CBE he was awarded in 2000. The novel is a little different from his previous ones. Read as another serious exploration of themes of responsibility and warped love, it fails to live up to the standard of his previous work. However, read as a black comedy, the novel's faults (predictability, melodrama, over-coincidence) appear to be entirely within the genre in which McEwan is working and to reveal a new strand to his writing. The plot centres on three men gathered together at the funeral of a woman to whom they have all been lovers. Through a series of bizarre plot-twists and a willed lack of understanding, two of the men, best friends, travel to Holland, where each plans secretly to kill the other by exploiting the Dutch euthanasia laws. The third man, husband to the dead woman, appears at the end to rise from being a foolish cuckold to the orchestrator of their doom. Unlikely to be regarded as one of his best novels, *Amsterdam* nevertheless shows McEwan's continuing skill at providing macabre twists to debates over contemporary social issues.

McEwan has also published a novel for children, *The Daydreamer* (1994): a collection of seven interconnected stories about imagination and transformation: the bodily metamorphoses envisaged by a young boy. Unlike its content and style, the themes of *The Daydreamer* complement McEwan's eighth novel, *Atonement*, an artful study of the moral and aesthetic considerations of storytelling, in the context of a woman's attempt to atone for a catastrophic childhood mistake through a blend of truth and fiction. It narrowly missed out on the Booker Prize, but won the 'People's Booker' and was the first of McEwan's works to escape fully the usual charge of being macabre or bizarre.

Since the publication of *Atonement*, McEwan has said in interview: 'After the events of 9/11, I wrote a piece for the front page of *The Guardian*, in which I expanded on [the main character of *Atonement*] Briony's thought in relation to those events: that the hijackers probably could not have committed their acts of cruelty if, for a moment, they had been able to (feel) what it meant to be their captives on the plane.'[2] He goes on to say: 'That power we have of empathy really lies at the foundation of our morality. So it's not simply a matter of curiosity or vague interest to know what other people are like, or to feel what it is to be someone else. I think it is the cornerstone of a moral system.'[3] Most importantly, what McEwan asserts is something that the novel has frequently been used to argue: that the exercise of the imagination enables individuals to modify, or at least better comprehend, their actions. He wrote in the *Guardian* after the 9/11 terrorist attack on the Twin Towers of the World Trade Center in New York that most people on 11 September 2001 found themselves in a daydream or fantasy, empathetically projecting themselves into the situation of the victims as the hijacked planes were flown in to the towers. McEwan argued that this moment was what the hijackers had blocked themselves from imagining, because cruelty relies on refusing to place oneself in the position of one's victim: imagination is linked to morality because imagining oneself as another is at the core of compassion.[4]

McEwan was particularly interested in this point because it was at the heart of his intention in *Atonement*. Like many novelists, McEwan has been taken to be an amoral writer, when in fact his interest in the marginal and the perverse has always aimed precisely at defining ethical limits. Michèle Roberts wrote about him in a review of *Enduring Love* that he is always thought by reviewers to be studying horror and nastiness, paedophiles, severed penises and perverse machismo. Against this, she argues that McEwan is in fact more concerned with inner states and in ways of loving, between men, women, parents and children, in naturalistic but also metaphorical settings.[5] This seems to be a helpful appraisal of McEwan's writing, though it is an assessment that most reviewers only arrived at with the publication of *Atonement*. As McEwan is perhaps no more than halfway through his career, there is strong reason to hope that his reputation will develop still further.

As Roberts notes, early stories like 'Solid Geometry' secured McEwan a certain notoriety for producing seedy, shocking fiction. This was a response that soon homogenized all his work into one category; when it is more helpful to see his career in three phases. McEwan's subsequent three books were to meet with similar reactions to those that greeted *First Love, Last Rites*. Which is to say, they appeared to reviewers again to be concerned with masculinity and feminism, with violence and perverse behaviour, the bizarre and the macabre. Understandably, therefore, the early short works up to *The Comfort of Strangers* earned McEwan the reputation for writing claustrophobic, brutal stories of sexual and psychological hinterlands. But, as McEwan himself has said, the later books from *The Child in Time* to *Enduring Love* are different kinds of works, in terms of form and content, though they have some similar preoccupations: 'novels of a sort of crisis and transformation, rites of passage of great intensity for characters'.[6] Both *Amsterdam* and *Atonement* have, then, taken McEwan in new formally experimental directions, the first towards satire of the sort practised by Evelyn Waugh (1902–66) or Kingsley Amis, the second towards self-reflexive historical fiction of a kind that mixes the styles of realist and experimental approaches to the novel, drawing on a host of intertexts from Jane Austen to Elizabeth Bowen (1899–1973). What remains constant throughout McEwan's writing is less an interest in the macabre than in both delineating individual reactions to moments of crisis and presenting the tenderness and brutality of relationships without sentimentality. McEwan's most recent novel, *Saturday* (2005), is written in the same clear, direct prose as *Atonement*. It suggests that McEwan has found, for the moment, a new style and confidence in his twenty-first-century work. *Saturday*, like *Atonement*, alludes to selected literary predecessors of McEwan's, perhaps most obviously James Joyce (1882–1941) and Matthew Arnold (1822–88), whose poem 'Dover Beach' (1867) is a touchstone at the end of the novel. McEwan's style also draws on the meditative, elegiac style of Arnold and the Joyce of 'The Dead' from *Dubliners* (1914). Though set in the contemporary world, *Saturday* has much in common thematically with *Atonement* through the connections traced above to 9/11, which features as a subject of reflection in the later novel: for example, the equivalent in *Saturday* to the Twin Towers is London's Post Office Tower, behind which in the first few pages a stricken aeroplane descends from the sky; the tower looms over the central character Perowne's home and would quite possibly crush the house if it fell in that direction after an attack like that of 9/11.

In the Guide that follows, each of McEwan's books of fiction will be treated chronologically. The chapters consider the responses of reviewers and summarise some of their representative comments, with reference to the occasional extreme view which is of interest. The majority of each chapter is devoted to a consideration of extracts from the best McEwan criticism to date, linked together by the editor's commentary. The reader will find selections from over thirty books and articles included in the Guide, amounting to a comprehensive overview of the essential criticism to date on a writer whose impressive body of fiction over thirty years has earned him a place in the front rank of British fiction.

CHAPTER ONE

The Fleshly Grail: *First Love, Last Rites* (1975)

As well as winning him the 1976 Somerset Maugham Award, Ian McEwan's short stories in *First Love, Last Rites* earned him the reputation of a macabre writer of 'literature of shock'; this was not least because the title itself plays menacingly on the famous 1860 autobiographical story by Turgenev (1818–83), 'First Love' (*Pervaya lyubov*).[1] Yet several reviewers were also able to discern the importance of the author's style and humour. On its publication in the summer of 1975, *First Love, Last Rites* was enthusiastically received by John Mellors in the *London Magazine* as 'a brilliant and devastating début' because of its blend of comedy and perversity, its paradoxically absurd yet logical plots, and its style, observation and grotesque detail.[2] In the *New York Review of Books*, Robert Towers went further when he reviewed McEwan's work up to 1979, by concluding that over the previous thirty years, *First Love, Last Rites* was perhaps the most 'brilliantly perverse' and 'sinister' short-story collection to emerge from England.[3]

Generally, reviews of this first book were positive but focused on the sensational and sexual aspects of the stories. McEwan himself has said that he was taken aback by the extreme reactions to his work in some, perhaps most, quarters. John Haffenden discussed this with him in interview:

■ [John Haffenden:] *You are on record as saying that you were surprised when critics chose to emphasize the shocking and the macabre aspects of your early stories, their concern with degenerate or dislocated behaviour.*

[Ian McEwan:] I honestly was very surprised. My friends, most of whom had had a literary education, seemed to take for granted the field of play in the stories; they had read Burroughs, Céline, Genet and Kafka [William Burroughs (1914–97), American novelist; Louis-Ferdinand Céline (1894–1961), French novelist; Jean Genet (1910–86), French novelist and dramatist; and Franz Kafka (1883–1924), Austro-Czech novelist], so that lurid physical detail and a sense of cold dissociation did not stun them. I was not aware of any pattern, and each story seemed to me at the time of writing to be a fresh departure, often with very trivial rhetorical ambitions like writing a story in the present tense ('Last Day of Summer'). They often proceeded out of doodles that had a certain kind of automatic quality.

I was quite surprised, for example, when the BBC banned 'Solid Geometry' [days before it was due to be filmed in March 1979], but then TV is so safe and dull. It doesn't put on anything funny about sex. I've never seen good sexual jokes on TV.[4]

What was the especial significance for you of the bottled penis that figures in 'Solid Geometry'?

On the most basic level it was playful, to show a man working on his great-grandfather's diaries with a preserved penis on his desk. It had to be an erect penis, because that's apparently how they're preserved. By extension, the fact that he won't make love to his wife suggests that his own penis is bottled up, as it were, and it provides her with a splendid opportunity (which would have been great fun to do) to bust it open: it's an appropriation, since she quite reasonably wants his cock. But once the penis is out of the jar he goes and buries it and carries on with his work. There's no stopping him. [...]

Was 'First Love, Last Rites' in any way written as an allegory of your own experience? It is perhaps your most heavily symbolic story; it's about a relationship and a pregnancy, and it includes fishing for eels, which you have at some time done.

Oddly enough I had no sense of its symbols when I was writing it, none at all. I certainly wasn't inserting symbols into the story. I was remembering and changing certain events in my own life. I think the story is about pregnancy. The narrator has a sure sense of the girl's power as she kneels by a dead rat. I've always thought it was an affirmative and tender story, as I do 'In Between the Sheets', and that was part of the source of my astonishment at the sensational copy reviewers made out of the stories. Reviewers seemed to be fixated by things that weren't central.

I agree with you there: 'First Love, Last Rites' seems to me to concern the characters purging themselves of false images of an as yet unsatisfactory relationship. Whatever is macabre in the story works towards a positive resolution.

I also had a simple-silly desire to end the story with the word 'Yes'. I was dazzled by the end of *Ulysses* [1922, by James Joyce]. My problem was how to get to this 'Yes'. The problem almost preceded the content, and when you concentrate on that sort of trivial puzzle you find yourself drawing quite freely and unconsciously on surprising material: you come upon an eel in a bucket and it's not a symbol – it's a *memory*. When the eel is set free, I was not thinking of it as a thinly disguised phallus, nor did I think of eel traps as vaginas. One doesn't think about symbols, though there comes a time when one can't deny that they are there.

But another story. 'Butterflies', concerns a man abusing and finally killing a child, and that is an appalling subject.

Yes, 'Butterflies' is appalling; it's a story written by someone who had nothing to do with children. I couldn't possibly write that story now, it would frighten me too much. As children come more into your life the possibility of their death is not something you can play with lightly. □

(John Haffenden, *Novelists in Interview*, 1985)[5]

In an earlier interview, with one of his mentors, the poet, critic, editor and biographer Ian Hamilton (1938–2001), McEwan described the influences on the stories in *First Love, Last Rites* and the importance of pastiche to his early approach to writing.

■ [Ian Hamilton:] *'Solid Geometry' was ... very ingeniously put together, rather more planned out than some of your other stories of the same period.*

I suppose it's the most anecdotal. It had different sources. I'd been reading Bertrand Russell's diaries, which had just come out in paperback and I suddenly wished that I had a grandfather or a great-grandfather who had been as interesting or as literate, who had written about his own life in the way that Bertrand Russell [1872–1970] had – those were the origins of the narrator obsessed by his great-grandfather's diaries. I had had some lengthy and fascinating conversations with an Argentinian mathematician. I also wanted to write about the kind of people I'd gone to Afghanistan with [in 1972]. So I wrote in a woman, or a girl, in that world, a kind of hippy girl. The narrator is rather a nasty person, cold, sexless, self-obsessed and yet the girl he has married, whatever her warmth and obvious sexuality, is sadly self-deceiving. The story is really about the kind of confusions I felt about where I stood. I was coming down from being someone who'd spent long months in that girl's world and yet I had some wistful nostalgia for it too.

Did you have any view of the 'kind of story' you wanted to write, in the way that poets often have very defined ideas about the kind of poem that's 'needed' at a given time?

No, I don't think I ever had any really clear concept of what I was up to. I think I had an idea that each story I wrote was a kind of pastiche of a certain style and even if after a page or two into the story I began to take it seriously, its origins were always slightly parodic.

Of what, what sort of thing?

Either a particular writer or a particular style. 'Homemade' when I started it was, I thought, an elaborate send-up of Henry Miller [1891–1980]. But then I got into it and felt that this was at least going to be an amusing story. But still by the time I finished it I still felt it was about the absurdities of adolescent male dignity.

The narrator in 'Homemade' is looking back on his first sexual experience. How old is he now, at the time of telling the story?

Well, I suppose he's meant to be a sort of Henry Miller-ish age, a wizened sixty. It's really about sexual aggrandisement. I mean, I had noticed that people, men especially, when they recount episodes of sexual failure, are frequently indulging in a kind of self-regard – in other words, so successful they can afford to admit failure. And I wanted to write a story about *total* sexual failure. I know it's fairly common for writers to write 'my first fuck' stories but I wanted to write a first fuck story where the actual fuck would be abysmally useless and yet its narrator would foolishly still derive huge satisfaction from it. The bleak satisfaction being simply that he'd got his cock into a cunt and come.

The narrator, though, has in the fullness of time become a rather poised, knowing man of the world.

Yes, that poise is integral to the self-regard I mentioned. I suppose the tone came mostly from Miller and a little bit from [Norman] Mailer [born 1923], both of whom I enjoyed but thought were totally bogus, and I wanted to send them up.

What other stories started as pastiche?

Well, I very much admired *The Collector* [1963, by John Fowles, born 1926]. I still do, I think it's Fowles's best book. In 'Conversation with a Cupboard Man' I wanted to do the kind of voice of the man in *The Collector*: that kind of wheedling, self-pitying lower middle-class voice. That was the starting point for the story. What tended to come out in the end was some mixture of what I'd read and my own experience. It was just that at that stage I was a bit of a counter-pointer and material from my own life didn't suggest itself immediately. Pastiche seemed a short cut, the line of least resistance. □

(Ian Hamilton, 'Points of Departure', 1978)[6]

The writers that McEwan mentions here – Miller, Mailer, Fowles – might suggest two qualities of the early stories, each of which is discussed in one of the two extracts that follow. On the one hand, these are writers deeply concerned with masculinity and sexuality; authors who have been considered at times 'masculinist' or 'macho' in their stances. McEwan's debt to them is therefore interesting in his own presentation of male rites of passage, but also in the degree to which his pastiches differ from the source material. Kiernan Ryan, in his book on McEwan, discusses the presentation in *First Love, Last Rites* of the fragility of masculine identity in the pre-teenage years:

■ The passing childhood of 'Last Day of Summer' [...] is suffused with an eerie sadness and overshadowed by the deaths with which the narrative concludes. The opening sentence immerses us at once in the mentality of the juvenile narrator: 'I am twelve and lying near-naked on my belly out on the back lawn in the sun when for the first time I hear her laugh' (p. 41). The sustained present tense simulates the artless idiom of the boy, creating a poignant tension between the limits of his language and the momentous events whose implications he intuitively apprehends [...] 'Last Day of Summer' draws its power from leaving its narrative unplaced and replete with unforced significance. [...]

'Last Day of Summer' is a parable about the cruel cost of turning into a man. Becoming masculine means a murderous denial of the dependency and need for intimacy evoked by the mother and the female body. Learning to fear the feminine and deep-freeze the emotions is a condition of fashioning the kind of adult male identity most cultures promote. But the self forged by this act of repression is fragile, and constantly assailed by insurgent drives to restore the very state masculinity must repudiate. In 'Conversation with a Cupboard Man' we meet the first of McEwan's many studies in infantile regression, as our interlocutor recounts the events which warped him into a reclusive freak curled up in his womb-like wardrobe. It is the hidden emotional history of many men, grotesquely caricatured as the confession of a madman. Until he is seventeen his widowed mother forces her only child to remain a baby, making him sleep in a crib, tying a bib round his neck, leaving him helpless and retarded: 'I could hardly move without her, and she loved it, the bitch' (p. 76) But his mother's remarriage terminates his childhood overnight and tosses him out into the cold to fend for himself as a man. The upshot is a volatile mixture of loathing for his mother, from whose oppressive nurture he was so cruelly divorced, and a consuming hunger to return to that blissful state of coddled impotence recovered in the cupboard: 'I don't want to be free. That's why I envy these babies I see in the street being bundled and carried about by their mothers. I want to be one of them. Why can't it be me?' (p. 87)

The frailty of masculine identity is also the subject of the last story in the collection, 'Disguises'. Like 'Homemade', this story revolves round the sexual abuse of a child, but in this case the victim is a ten-year-old schoolboy called Henry and the predator is his flamboyant aunt Mina – a thespian paedophile with a taste for transvestism. After his mother's death, Mina becomes what she calls 'a Real Mother' (p. 100) to her orphaned nephew, who is at first enchanted by her eccentric theatricality and her fantastic dressing-up games. But their relationship takes a sickening turn when Mina forces him to dress as a sweet little girl in party frock and wig, while she molests him in the uniformed guise of a dashing, drunken officer. As Mina presses the boy's face 'against the faintly scented corrugated skin of her limp old dugs', which 'appear grey and blue the way he imagined a dead person's face' (p. 116), his mind glimpses in the repulsive flesh of his surrogate mother the corpse of the mother he has lost.

Through the love of his schoolfriend Linda, however, Henry learns to translate the oppression of his costume into a source of pleasure and a refuge from guilt. His masculine shell dissolves and he becomes 'invisible inside this girl' (p. 114), blissfully released from the burden of identity and hence from the blame that a fixed self incurs: 'all disguised and no one knows who you are, anyone can do what they want because it doesn't matter (pp. 117–18). The horror of letting go is coupled with a dionysic delight in the effacement of borders and the violation of deep-seated taboos. The confounding of sexual difference and the suspension of liability are as enticing as they are frightening, and McEwan taps straight into our aptness to be torn by both emotions. □

(Kiernan Ryan, *Ian McEwan*, 1994)[7]

McEwan's representation of masculinity in 'Disguises' arguably parodies its presentation in the first story, 'Homemade', with its influences from Mailer and Miller. The concern with masculinity is one notable aspect of McEwan's literary role models for the stories, but on the other hand a second common observation by critics was that the stories in *First Love, Last Rites* were narrowly focused in terms of content, a point taken up by David Malcolm.

■ Some critics suggest that the subject matter of McEwan's stories is quite limited. This is not entirely true. Several, but by means all, of those in *First Love, Last Rites* are concerned with adolescents, children and young adults. In 'Homemade', an adult narrator recounts how as a fourteen-year-old he achieved sexual initiation of a sort by having sexual intercourse with his younger sister. 'The Last Day of Summer' is narrated by an orphaned twelve-year-old boy, who observes the life of the adults around him and also undergoes further experiences of loss and death. 'Conversation with a Cupboard Man' presents the psychologically traumatic experiences and their consequences of a young man's treatment by his obsessive and then indifferent mother. The subject matter of 'Disguises' is similar. Here a young boy who is being brought up by his aunt is dragged into the aunt's fantasy world, including her transvestite games. 'First Love, Last Rites', on the other hand, is told by a narrator at the brink of adulthood, whose relationship with his silent, guarded girlfriend becomes strangely stagnant and then seems to rekindle after an encounter with a pregnant rat. 'Butterflies' also involves a child, but the centre of the story is rather the unhappy and isolated young man who sexually abuses and murders her, while 'Cocker at the Theatre' (perhaps the weakest of the stories) has adult protagonists, actors in a sex show, two of whom, instead of only simulating intercourse on stage, actually have sex during a rehearsal, much to the consternation of the director and choreographer. The protagonists of 'Solid Geometry' are also adults, although the chilly self-absorbed husband who destroys his wife physically, emotionally, and finally by magic has a certain immature egoism which recalls adolescence. [...]

In a 1979 interview with Christopher Ricks, McEwan, discussing his interest in adolescents, argues that they fascinate him because they are close to childhood and yet are constantly 'baffled and irritated by the initiations into what's on the other side – the shadow line, as it were'.[8] This comment is revealing on two connected accounts. It suggests the nature of many of the central events depicted in McEwan's short fiction, and it also, by the allusion to Joseph Conrad's [1857–1924] famous short story 'The Shadow-Line' (1917), indicates the literary tradition within which he is operating. Most of the stories in *First Love, Last Rites* can be described as stories of initiation. If the initiation is obscure in the title story (what do the narrator and his girlfriend learn from the dead rat's pregnant body?), it is certainly there, as it is in the narrator's first experience of sexual intercourse in 'Homemade', in the narrator's first sexual experience in 'Butterflies', in Henry's induction into the confused world of adult games and sexuality, and also in childhood friendship in 'Disguises'. Even 'Last Day of Summer' depicts a further initiation for the protagonist-narrator into the world of sadness and loss. Of all the stories in this volume, only 'Solid Geometry', 'Cocker at the Theatre' and 'Conversation with a Cupboard Man' do not show initiations of some sort. □

(David Malcolm, *Understanding Ian McEwan*, 2002)[9]

Malcolm's concentration on the initiation of narrators is illuminating but could also be said to obscure the concomitant and often more violent 'initiations' of other characters in the stories, especially girls in 'Homemade' (Connie), 'Butterflies' (Jane) and 'Last Day of Summer' (the neglected Alice possibly ends the story drowned). The initiation of McEwan's male narrators frequently involves the abuse of females in a way that anticipates the later novels, where women are violently sexually abused in *The Comfort of Strangers, Black Dogs, The Innocent* and *Atonement*; it is also relevant here that in *The Child in Time* Stephen's rite of passage as a parent is based on his daughter Kate's disappearance, and in *Enduring Love* the narrative begins with a child in peril, while in *Black Dogs* Jeremy's fascination with violence is begun by the abuse suffered by his niece Sally. This presentation of women entangled and injured in the process of male rites of passage also applies to the final story in *First Love, Last Rites,* 'Disguises', discussed by Jack Slay:

■ The disrupted family, a favourite subject of McEwan's, is again encountered in 'Disguises' (first published in *American Review* in September 1973). Young Henry, the protagonist, at the death of his parents is delivered into the hands of his aunt Mina, a woman who is, in turns, very strange and frighteningly abnormal. Henry is taken, then, from a normal life and a mother who is 'solid and always sane' [p. 105: the text actually reads 'solid and always the same'] and placed into the custody of a 'surreal mother' (p. 100). Henry soon learns that living with his aunt includes partaking in her 'hobby' – dressing for dinner in various costumes. Having been an actress and lived the life of the theatre, Mina continues her charades and role-playing with her sole companion, providing him with an array of disguises and personas. When she forces him to dress in the garb of a young girl, however, Henry finds himself in dire circumstances.

Through her games, Mina attempts to draw Henry into the tainted world of adulthood, but in doing so she also corrupts his innocence. From the beginning, the relationship between aunt and nephew is anything but normal. Immediately upon his arrival, Mina seems peculiarly, even incestuously attracted to Henry: for instance when she relates the events of her day, she is 'more wife [...] than aunt' (p. 102); likewise, in one of their cross-dressing games, she makes a pseudo-pass at him, groping under his dress, pressing his face to her breasts, all the while singing 'a soldier needs a girl, a soldier needs a girl' (p. 116). For the most part, Henry finds his identity suppressed, even trapped, in Mina's world. At school, away from his aunt, he is different, freer; there he lives an ordinary life, finding joy in the precocious, carefree world of a young boy rather than suffering the pressure of providing companionship to a much older, extremely eccentric woman.

The dressing game, 'the motif of this story' (p. 101), rapidly develops from one of Mina's idiosyncrasies into something that truly horrifies Henry. At first dressing up is simply a daily chore, something done merely to appease his aunt; Henry obeys the whims of Mina and parades through his new life in an array of costumes: a soldier, an elevator operator, a monk, a shepherd. Although he recognises the bizarreness of the situation, initially it is also 'somehow to Henry ordinary' (p. 104). Only when he is forced against his will to don the dress of a girl does he realise that these rituals are 'games which are not really games' (p. 117). Confronted by the costume, 'all flounces and frills, layer on layer with white satin and lace edged with pink, a cute bow falling at the back' (p. 104), Henry is at once sickened and horrified; to him 'it was wrong to be a girl' (p. 105). Nonetheless, he finds himself literally forced by Mina to assume the role, becomingly 'a sickeningly pretty little girl' (p. 106).

Part of his repulsion at dressing as a girl stems from his typical boyhood attitude toward the opposite sex [cf. *The Cement Garden*, pp. 46–8], the seeds of the latter, more detrimental patriarchal mind-set: 'Like the best of Henry's friends at school he did not care for girls, avoided their huddles and intrigues, their whispers and giggles and holding hands and passing notes and I love I love, they set his teeth on edge to see' (p. 105). Soon after suffering the humiliation of cross-dressing, Henry comes face to face with Linda, a new girl in his class who immediately violates his space by being assigned a seat at his desk. Henry, however, finds himself curiously drawn to her, attracted by her young beauty, by her feminine mystique [the title of a work of analytical feminism by Betty Friedan]. It is with Linda that he experiences, upon touching hands with her, his first sexual awakenings. Unlike most of McEwan's characters, though, Henry allows these new feelings to remain unexplored; even when the two children lie naked in bed together, their alliance remains innocent, unhampered by sex. His new bond with Linda, in part, helps Henry cope with the tyranny of Mina.

Henry learns to control his fear of his aunt, as well as his repulsion of dressing as this strange blonde girl, by projecting himself into the image of Linda. Dressing in the disguise, he becomes 'Henry and Linda at once, closer than in the car, inside her now and she was in him' (p. 114). He copes with this bizarre situation by placing it in the context of what he can consider ordinary, identifiable. Ironically, Henry finds himself released from the horror of dressing as a girl by imagining himself *to be* a girl. His association with Linda, a pure and innocent friendship, the sole *normal* relationship in his life, provides him with an escape from the tainted, perverted relationship he endures with Mina.

The relationship that develops between Henry and Linda at first seems to provide a hint of optimism; their friendship is innocent, affirming. In the final scene, however, Henry unwittingly drags Linda into the trap of Mina's unnatural world. At a party in which all the guests are 'disguised as ordinary people' (p. 122), Linda becomes a bewildered Alice in Wonderland, lost in a world she does not, cannot understand.

Henry watches as she falls prey to one of the guests, and as the story closes, he slowly, drunkenly makes his way towards her; McEwan, however, leaves us with the distinct impression that his intervention will make no difference. Just as the relationship between Jenny and the narrator of 'Last Day of Summer' was not enough to sustain them in their world, neither is the friendship of Henry and Linda ultimately strong enough to protect them from the evils of Mina's adult world. Rather than providing protection, Henry's alliance with Linda ultimately results in an inadvertent betrayal. As in 'Homemade' and 'Last Day of Summer', the outside world closes upon its adolescents, stealing from them the innocence that creates the shadow line between youth and adulthood, between purity and corruption. □

(Jack Slay, *Ian McEwan*, 1996)[10]

Lynda Broughton is also concerned with notions of 'purity and corruption' in her feminist reading of the first story in the collection, but her primary interest is in its construction of gender differences. Identifying 'Homemade's' allusions to the male-sexual-quest tradition of writing which stretches from Edmund Spenser (?1522–99) to Norman Mailer, Broughton shows how the story contains a critique of its own working, through its literariness and its self-ironizing word-play. Broughton finishes her analysis by asking how far a text like 'Homemade', which still reads as 'a rather nasty piece of pornography', can be ironized or self-ironizing. She asks if the story emerges as both a feminist and an anti-feminist story, one in which the pastiche of writers like Mailer, perhaps inevitably, becomes an example of the genre it is parodying.

■ In 'Homemade', the subject of the story presents himself, within the context of a series of literary allusions, as the Romantic hero whose quest is the search for the 'fleshly grail' of adult knowledges, the last and most desirable of which is the female body, the 'last fur-lined chamber of that vast, gloomy and delectable mansion, adulthood' (p. 12). The 'fleshly grail' he seeks, it is revealed, is cunt – the hero does not yet know what it is, but he knows that, like Everest, it is there. It is the unknowability of the dark gothic mystery, woman, which makes it desirable; once incestuously known, the female body is no longer desired and is left, ten years old and weeping, on the edge of the bath while the 14-year-old hero celebrates the success of his quest in glorious self-absorption, alone.

Thus the story appears to reproduce the familiar textual strategy of glorifying the notion of the hero as a man alone – singular, complete, unified; the integrated, inviolable 'I' elevated to mythic status – while at the same time ironizing it. The hero's introspection, his celebration of his separateness from the society in which he finds himself – the world of petty domestic routine, of meaningless competition and ill-paid, repetitive and ultimately futile work – belongs to the tradition of high romance which the literary allusions in the story reinforce. The story is told from a self-consciously literary perspective, and is peppered with allusions to other texts which similarly celebrate male quests, the acquisition of knowledges and specifically male journeys from innocence to experience. This is the boy as hero of his own narrative, the male self celebrated as conqueror. And yet there are ironizing devices within the text which turn it back on itself; or rather, they produce an internal distancing effect. There is, admittedly, in this text, a narrative voice which is consistently aware of the ironic spaces in its discourse; a double irony which opens up the making of the text as it opens up the making of the subject.

The story traces the hero's progress from innocence to experience under the tutelage of his friend Raymond, who is a year or so older and confers on the hero a series of knowledges which, ironically, he himself cannot use. Raymond introduces the hero to the pleasures of an adolescent version of the adult world – alcohol, dope, crime, dirty stories, horror movies, masturbation – all of which the hero takes to with considerable pleasure and success while poor Raymond finds only discomfort and boredom. The hero despises and rejects the realities of adult life in the repressed, 'respectable' social class from which he comes: dull and unrewarding work, loyalty to exploitative employers, petty family responsibilities. His father's gifts of pocket money and homespun wisdom are pathetic in the face of the hero's growing knowledge and economic power, since by selling stolen books – stolen knowledges – to a second-hand dealer in the Mile End Road he can earn more than his father and uncles can after a week's backbreaking work. Most of all, he despises the stupefying dreariness of domestic life, represented in the story not so much by his parents' lives (as in many children's stories the parents are conveniently absent or ignored throughout except when a point is to made), as by his little sister's fantasy game of 'Mummies and Daddies'.

As he gains experience of the 'adult' pleasures provided by Raymond, the hero acquires, through his own detachment from it, a knowledge of human futility. There is a sequence in the story when, as the detached and superior spectator at a school cross-country race, he takes pleasure in waiting until the final stragglers – one of whom, of course, is Raymond – are painfully finishing the race, long after the winners have gone home:

> [...] and then suddenly [...] discern[ing] on the far side of the field a limp white blob slowly making its way to the tunnel, slowly measuring out with numb feet on the wet grass its micro-destiny of utter futility. And there beneath the brooding metropolitan sky, as if to unify the complex totality of organic evolution and human purpose and place it within my grasp, the tiny amoebic blob across the field took on human shape [...] just life, just faceless, self-renewing life to which, as the figure jack-knifed to the ground by the finishing line, my heart warmed, my spirit rose in the fulsome abandonment of morbid and fatal identification with the cosmic life process – the Logos. (p. 17)

This futile struggle, analogous at once to conception, birth and death, becomes, within the story, a metaphor for life itself as most people he knows will live it – painful, without reward, noble and at the same time profoundly comic: ' "Long before I knew it" ', the narrator says, ' "I was a student, a promising student, of irony" ' (p. 15). The narrative constantly operates on this double level, recounting the events which constitute the hero's progress from innocence to experience with the detached, adult literariness of the narrator.

The last of the knowledges the hero is to acquire is, of course, sexual knowledge, the knowledge of woman; for him and for Raymond the most terrifying knowledge of all, and yet from the point of view of the narrator the most comic, absurd and ultimately squalid. The boy already knows the theory, from sitting in cafés listening to men talking about their sexual encounters. These stories of male sexuality, overheard without understanding by the boy but recalled with relish by the skilled adult narrator, are told in terms of 'an unreal complex of timeworn puns and innuendo, formulas, slogans, folklore and bravado' which the hero stores away for future reference and out of which he constructs, 'augmented by a quick reading of the more interesting parts of Havelock Ellis [1859–1939] and Henry Miller' a reputation as a juvenile 'connoisseur of coitus [... and] all this after only one fuck – the subject of this story' (p. 14). Promised an encounter with a girl called Lulu Smith, whose reputation for sex is of legendary proportions:

> [a] heaving, steaming leg-load of schoolgirl flesh who had, so reputation insisted, had it with a giraffe, a humming-bird, a man with a iron-lung (who had subsequently died), a yak, Cassius Clay, a marmoset, a Mars Bar and the gear stick of her grandfather's Morris Minor (and subsequently a traffic warden). (p. 13)

in the course of which he will be allowed to 'see it for a shilling', the hero decides to make a preliminary reconnaissance, to increase his prior knowledge, by seducing his ten-year-old sister. He lures her into his parents' bedroom as part of her favourite game of 'Mummies and Daddies' and attempts, without success, to have sex with her with the only humiliating result that she laughs both at the idea and at him – or rather at his signifier, his ineffectual penis, '"*So silly, it looks so silly*"' – until, as he is about to give up, she touches him on the elbow: '"I know where it goes"', she says (p. 23). In this shocking moment the child Connie acquires a different kind of significance; from being a petulant, unattractive little-sister figure, she assumes in that moment the mythic, symbolic status of woman – the idea of woman as the terrifying, knowing, unknowable other which informs 'male' fictions. Connie both has knowledge and is herself the embodiment of knowledge – *con/naissance*.

Thus in the text sexual difference becomes word-play, a matter of conning. To 'con' is both to learn and to trick someone by supplying them with false meanings, as in 'con-man'. The translinguistic pun on *connaissance* reminds us that *con* is French for cunt; used in France as an insulting epithet, as well as a pejorative term for the vulva and the vagina, as it is in English. 'Knowledge' has well-known sexual connotations in English, in which 'to know' has a double meaning. Thus, among its other literary allusions, the story includes an echo of the mythology of the Fall of Man, in which both knowledge and sex are placed in the province of Woman, whose misuse of them caused Man to be thrown out of paradise and thereby brought suffering and death into the world, and the punishment of eternal subordination upon herself. *Con/naissance* is both knowledge, and birth (*naissance*) through knowledge: birth through the *con* and birth of a *con*. The story of the Fall shows that this birth is also death: the death of the body, the 'death' of orgasm, the cosmic beginning and end of everything. It is the universal rite of passage of all humanity, all (with superhuman, mythic exceptions) experiencing birth through that fleshly access route to life. This final, carnal *connaissance*, this 'dawning of his sexual day', this birth of the hero triumphant, literalizing his phallic subjectivity into his erect penis, joining 'that superior half of humanity who had known coitus and fertilized the world with it', is thus a kind of *con/naissance* of the subject – the birth of the hero-as-a-man takes place through the con/quest of Con/nie; at once the knowing little girl and the innocent 'inter-galactic-earth-goddess-housewife' (p. 20), who is both desired knowledge and abstract, feared, unknown cunt; both desire itself and its object. [...]

On the surface the story appears to be the unproblematized recounting of a particularly unpleasant domestic crime (incest, child abuse), from a subject position within a disordered version of patriarchal authority: the events of the story are described with shocking detachment and chillingly good-humoured affection from an adult perspective which appears to invite the reader to share both its misogyny and its celebratory tone, both of which are presented unproblematically. The shock of this 'adult' detachment – the coolness with which the narrator remembers the torture of birds in the park, for example; the roasting alive of a budgerigar, feeding glass splinters to pigeons – combines with his celebration of adolescent male competitiveness (competitions in getting drunk, shoplifting, masturbating, which the hero always wins) to present what is, according to the criteria already given, a text which is 'male' to excess. And yet it is this very detachment which signals the literariness of the text. [...]

This literariness in turn signals the construction of the story of acquired masculine knowledge – or masculinity *through* knowledge – as a textual strategy, the writing of a story about the writing of a story; masculinity itself as a work of creative fiction; *homme*/made. The possibilities for word/play and punning make this text-within-a-text a series of secrets to which the reader is admitted, replicating the strategy of the text itself so that the story becomes entirely self-referencing, signposting its own construction. In a replication of the sexual relation between the narrator and his sister it allows the reader to participate in its knowledges, its areas of *connaissance*, with the result that, through the devices of language, we are able to gain access to an ironizing layer of meanings. □

(Lynda Broughton,
'Portrait of the Subject as a Young Man', 1991)[11]

McEwan's short stories were shocking on first publication and many have lost none of their force. From the perspective of his later works they are arguably apprentice pieces that have a limited range in terms of content and a pronounced sameness in terms of style. However, as innovative works of the time that anatomised taboo subjects they were in many ways groundbreaking, just as his second collection and his first novel were also to prove to be three years later.

CHAPTER TWO

Underworld: *In Between the Sheets* (1978)

McEwan's second collection of stories, which came out in the same year as his first novel, met with a similar reaction to his first. For Julian Moynahan, in the *New York Times Book Review*, the tales were derivative and sensationalist.[1] For Hermione Lee, by contrast, they were 'elegantly gruesome accounts' that she found 'grew in depth',[2] and for Caroline Blackwood McEwan showed himself to be an original writer even though the stories themselves might seem contrived.[3] Overall, reviews were favourable, finding merit in McEwan's style and control of his material while expressing distaste if not horror at his subject matter.

One of the most highly rated authors of short stories himself, V. S. Pritchett (1900–97), wrote an article in the *New York Review of Books* that is probably the most useful in trying to identify McEwan's strengths and weaknesses at this stage of his career:

> ■ Ian McEwan has been recognised as an arresting new talent in the youngest generation of English short-story writers. His subject matter is often squalid and sickening; his imagination has a painful preoccupation with the adolescent secrets of sexual aberration and fantasy. But in his accomplishment as a story writer he is an immediate master of styles and structures, his writing transfigures, and he can command variety in subject and feeling. His intellectual resources enable him – and the reader – to open windows in a claustrophobia which otherwise would have left us flinching and no more. Invention, irony, humour, a gift for satirical parody and curiosity give him the artist's initiative. We *do* recognise an underworld – for that is what it is – and it is natural that he has evoked an, albeit distant, connection with Samuel Beckett [1906–89] and Kafka. His limitation is that his range of felt experience is confined to his love of his disgusts.
>
> Two stories in his new collection, *In Between the Sheets*, suggest a new direction. I'll come to those later. The book opens with 'Pornography', which begins as a comical account of what goes on between two brothers in a Soho porn shop where customers are nervously trying to get a free furtive glance at the glossy porn. The elder brother is hysterically

trying to make a fortune out of his sexual peepshow; the younger is crudely dedicated to cunt. He is itching and smells of 'clap' and he is having it off with two nurses on alternate days. So far, obsessive observation of Soho grubbiness, cheap lodgings, filthy baths, sulky *macho* manners, nasty smells, bad food, cheap drink. Unhappily, Mr McEwan surrenders to a well-known fantasy from the world of schoolboy smut. When they discover the young man is deceiving and infecting them, the nurses enact the fantasy of the tart who castrates her man. We leave them at this sadistic feast after one of them has raped the young *macho*, screaming out the war cries of Women's Lib as she jumps him. The melodrama ruins a story whose strength lay in fact, not fantasy. One simply laughs off the schoolboy legend.

In 'Reflections of a Kept Ape' McEwan is more subtle. It is a droll tale. A pet monkey has been briefly seduced by a young woman who has written a bestseller, and in his eager, lonely, animal way he tells the story of a lust that has faded … . From [Miguel de] Cervantes [1547–1616] to Kafka, how many writers have tried the puzzled reflections of animals, though not their greedy sexuality; here we notice the change of prose style and especially the notes on the deceits of art. These will recur in McEwan's work [and reach their apogee in *Atonement*].

The ape reflects on the girl's frantic virginal typing of her difficult next book:

> Was art then nothing more than a wish to appear busy? Was it nothing more than a fear of silence, of boredom, which the merely reiterative rattle of the typewriter's keys was enough to allay? In short, having crafted one novel, would it suffice to write it again, type it out with care, page by page? (Gloomily I recycled nits from torso to mouth.) Deep in my heart I knew it would suffice and, knowing that, seemed to know less than I ever had known before. [p. 32]

I must say I object to the new cliché 'crafted'. But then comes a parody of George Sand-ish self-love when the ape knows she is tired of him [the reference here is to the French novelist George Sand, pseudonym of Amandine-Aurore Lucie Dupin, baronne Dudevant (1804–76)]: …

> My eyes stray to the front door and fix there. To leave, yes, regain my independence and dignity, to set out on the City Ring Road, my possessions clasped to my chest, the infinite stars towering above me and the songs of nightingales ringing in my ears. Sally Klee receding ever farther behind me, she caring nothing for me, no, nor I for her, to lope carefree towards the orange dawn and on into the next day and again into the following night, crossing rivers and penetrating woods, to search for and find a new love, a new post, a new function, a new life. [pp. 33–4]

The ape is an out-of-date Romantic. Ian McEwan is being very clever about the temptations of 'literature'. That 'orange dawn' will reappear in more solemn circumstances: the author is fighting hidden literary tendencies.

'Dead As They Come' is another familiar fable: its merits, as always with Ian McEwan, lie in the half-vulgar elegance in the detail. A rich man falls in love with a beautiful female dummy in a shop window. In a very funny scene he buys her, carries her home; he seduces her, the perfect passive beauty of daydream. Soon he is cuckolded by his chauffeur, who is well-drawn. But the point of the story is that it is an attack on the corrupting influence of connoisseur tastes: they turn one into a voyeur. The boss has really been deceived by a juvenile masturbator's taste for 'dead' works of art – for Vermeer, Blake, Richard Dadd, Paul Nash, Rothko. In his jealousy he spits on them, urinates on them, and destroys them. (There is a lot of urinating – why not pissing? – in McEwan's stories.) In 'In Between the Sheets' a divorced man, after a chilly scene with his ex-wife, is allowed to take his very young daughter and her child friend back to his house to stay the night. The little child friend is a dwarf-like horror and no sexual innocent. In 'To and Fro' the style changes again and the story becomes a prose poem. A man and his mistress lie in bed, half asleep, after making love. His mind wanders between what went on at the office and night thoughts:

> Sometimes I look at her and wonder who will die first ... face to face, wintering in the mess of down and patchwork, she places a hand over each of my ears, takes my head between her palms, regards me with thick, black eyes and pursed smile that does not show her teeth ... then I think, It's me, I shall die first, and you might live forever. [p. 100]

A little later:

> A voice breaks the stillness, a brilliant red flower dropped on the snow, one of her daughters calls out in a dream. A bear! ... the sound indistinct from its sense. Silence, and then again, A bear, softer this time, with a falling tone of disappointment ... now, a silence dramatic for its absence of the succinct voice ... now imperceptibly ... now, habitual silence, no expectations, the weight of stillness, the luminous afterimage of bears in fading orange. [p. 101]

An exercise for the artist's notebook: an experiment, but probably wasted? You notice that 'orange' again.

There are two encouraging breaks with 'mean' writing – 'mean' in the sense of James Joyce's *Dubliners* [Joyce said he wrote the stories in a spirit of scrupulous meanness] in two long pieces: 'Two Fragments: March 199–' and 'Psychopolis'. They enlarge his scene. The first is an evocation of a possible London in twenty years' time, half-destroyed by war or revolution. The narrative dodges the conventional melodramatic picture of catastrophe. It concentrates on the aftermath of decay. Government offices are still smouldering in a deteriorating wilderness; there is no transport, there is almost no lighting or heating, food has to be scrounged. People are reduced to living on what fish can be got out of the polluted Thames, and sit around bonfires in the streets or traipse on foot on pointless journeys across the city. Good. The skills of the machine age have gone. Such a fragmented life is simply and exactly suggested and far less sensationally than say, in *Nineteen Eighty-Four* (1949) [by George Orwell, 1903–50] – though politics are almost missing – and with far greater sense of physical and emotional dissolution. The lovers fall back on memories of things in the happier past: an inscrutable arty girl thinks that Art Deco may start people learning how to make things again. She is a contemporary bore.

> It was growing colder. We got between the sheets, me with my plans and clean feet, she with her fish. 'The point is,' I said referring to Marie's age [his child's age], 'that you cannot survive now without a plan.' I lay with my head on Diane's arm and she drew me towards her breast. 'I know someone,' she began, and I knew she was introducing a lover, 'who wants to start a radio station. He doesn't know anyone who could build a transmitter or repair an old one. And even if he did, he knows there are no radios to pick up his signal. He talks vaguely about repairing old ones, of finding a book that will tell him how to do it.' [p. 49–50]

They remember bits of things, like driving a car or taking children to the zoo, forgotten football matches. But cars are now rubbish and the zoo had become a closed ruin years before. The bits are good: catastrophe will be as it was in 1940 – bitty. One is struck by McEwan's gift of clarity. It moves easily from fragments of cold reality to fragments of fantasy, from the comic to the threatening. He is moving out of the sexual ennui into one more devastating.

'Psychopolis' takes his travelling mind to Los Angeles, and here we find him amusing himself with the collision of English and American boastings and opinions as they are thrown out. The finale is excellent. His impressionism is intelligent and he is still a fabulist who keeps clear of journalism. He is always the restless storyteller; every voice or incident moves forward as he follows the interplay of reality and fancy, the inner and the outer, the tender and violent, the banal and the grotesque. The voice (as it must be in the short story) is absolutely distinctive and the means are controlled. □

(V. S. Pritchett, *New York Review of Books*, 1980)[4]

McEwan corroborates much of what Pritchett says about 'Reflections of A Kept Ape' in his interview with Ian Hamilton, explaining: 'It's meant to be a funny story really. [...] It's a story I suppose about writerly alter-egos, the pressures writers generate for themselves. The fear of repeating oneself. And it's also about a rejected lover, an insistent, rejected lover peering over one's shoulder.'[5] In a later interview, with John Haffenden,

McEwan explains his intention behind two of the other stories in the collection:

■ [John Haffenden:] *In 'In Between the Sheets', the title story of your second collection, the reader is tempted to share the erotic fantasies of a father towards his daughter. You place the reader very close to his consciousness, especially when at night he overhears what he takes to be her erotic restlessness, to the point where one is convinced that incest will take place. But then she appears as just an unsettled child. The reader is agog with a sort of shared excitement, but the tact of the story returns both father and reader to decent normality.*

[Ian McEwan:] I'm glad you see it in terms of his *imagination* of her erotic behaviour, when he hears sounds and has such violent and confused ideas towards his daughter. I was uneasy about the way I had him pursuing his writing in a way that takes him away from any real relationship to a point when he is deeply fearful of women and their pleasure: that's reflected in the rather arid way he sets about his day's work, filing things, writing in a ledger, counting the number of words. Perhaps the connection is too simple. But then, I do think short stories demand simple and incisive sets of oppositions. You make a choice of where your complexity lies, and you must concentrate and pursue it.

'In Between the Sheets' ends with the image of 'a field of dazzling white snow which he, a small boy of eight, had not dare scar with footprints'. It is a marvellous metaphor for refusing to desecrate something pure.

Yes, I do think that last paragraph saves the story. I remember an incredibly heavy snow as a child when we were living in Kent, going out in my gumboots and being enchanted. The field was so pure I didn't want to walk on it.

You've said elsewhere that 'To and Fro' is one of your favourite stories, perhaps because it's rather personal. Could you say something about it, because many readers do find it a bit obscure?

It's fairly simple really. A man lying in bed beside his lover, imagining himself at work pursued by a colleague who seems to crowd in on his identity. Celebrating the sleeping lover, dreading the obtrusive colleague – these are the simple oppositions. □

(John Haffenden, *Novelists in Interview*, 1985)[6]

In 'To and Fro', the lover is asleep: supine, silent, supportive. Another story in the collection exaggerates this role of the sleeping, passive lover to its ultimate level, in a Pygmalion-like story where the feminized object of the self-absorbed male takes on (in his imagination) a rebellious life of 'her' own. Angela Roger considers this reification of the 'love object' in her discussion of 'Dead As They Come', exploring how the story shows a dysfunctional male sexuality exerting its control by first settling on an inanimate lover and then satisfying its uncontrollable jealousy by destroying the lover the man has literally 'bought':

■ The objectification of women is typified by the treatment meted out to the anthropomorphised female character, a shop-window mannequin, in 'Dead As They Come'. Although in that story the reader is always conscious that the businessman's actions are harmless because his 'victim' is inanimate, nevertheless the man is portrayed as believing that she has life, and it is therefore a powerful indicator of his destructive potential. The mannequin is a classic rape prototype: innocent, unresisting, vulnerable. The narrator names her Helen, possibly an indication of her seductive beauty, like that of Helen of Troy, and he longs to have her: 'I wished to possess her, own her, absorb her, eat her. I wanted her in my arms and in my bed, I longed that she should open her legs to me' (p. 62). Of course, the narrator, a successful businessman, can buy his mistress since he is rich and she is after all literally only a dummy. Although the idea is bizarre, the parallels between the parody and real life are clear: women may be treated as possessions, even bought, and the implications for other things that men can do with women become clear in the course of the story. As the narrator recounts the idyllic time he spends in her company we realise that for him Helen is an ideal partner: 'What passed that evening was quite certainly the most civilised few hours I have ever shared with a woman or, for that matter, with another person. [...] Helen and I lived in perfect harmony which nothing could disturb' (pp. 68, 70). He is a self-centred man who enjoys the sound of his own voice and for whom a silent companion is the ideal: 'With Helen I could converse ideally, I could *talk* to her [...] I talked, Helen listened' (pp. 69–70). As the hopelessly deluded narrator's fantasy develops, a dangerous possessiveness emerges – he imagines that his equally 'perfect' chauffeur has also started an affair with his Helen. Her silence, at first a sign of deference, is subsequently interpreted as scorn: 'I looked into her eyes and saw there quiet, naked contempt. It was all over, and I conceived in that frenzied instant two savage and related desires. To rape and destroy her.' He gives vent to his desire in a frenzied attack; he describes how he 'ripped the smock clean off her body', he was 'on her [...] in her [...] rammed deep inside' (p. 76) The fury of the attack on the dummy is a grotesque rendition of the perverse imagination of the rapist, who not only experiences intense pleasure from his domination over his victim, but can also convince himself that she too enjoyed her moment of death. □

(Angela Roger, 'Ian McEwan's Portrayal of Women', 1996)[7]

Broadening out her analysis, Roger goes on to observe:

■ Only five of the early stories (and there are eighteen of them in all) show women in a position of relative strength. In two of these the women exploit their power in the same way as most of McEwan's male characters do. In 'Disguises', for example, the woman, Mina, is a transvestite who psychologically and sexually abuses her young nephew. In 'Psychopolis', Terence's girlfriend orders him to urinate in his pants just before introducing him to her parents. This humiliation can be seen to have been adequately compensated for by the narrator's earlier bondage episode with another girlfriend, Mary. The two girlfriends of O'Byrne in 'Pornography' are less equivocally dominant as they castrate their faithless lover because he has infected them with venereal disease. Sissel, the young woman in 'First Love, Last Rites', lives equably with her lover, as does a more mature version of Sissel, who appears as Leech's wife in 'To and Fro'. The power of both of these last characters lies in their potential or real maternity. 'First Love, Last Rites' is basically an exploration of the narrator's obsession with pregnancy; and 'To and Fro' lyrically evokes the comfort and security of motherhood. It is this focus upon their capacity for motherhood which distinguishes the treatment of the strong women characters from the weak, a point developed progressively through *The Cement Garden, The Comfort of Strangers, or Shall We Die?, The Child in Time* and *Black Dogs.* □

(Angela Roger, 'Ian McEwan's Portrayal of Women', 1996)[8]

Christina Byrnes, in her analysis of the volume's opening story 'Pornography', is interested in the psychodynamic drives animating McEwan's characters. Her analysis draws out the implicit parallels between O'Byrne's relationship with his brother, the hospital workers' comparative ranks, and O'Byrne's pleasure in moving between the passive and active sides of his sexuality:

■ Like 'Homemade' [in *First Love, Last Rites*], 'Pornography' is about ambivalence and rivalry between two male characters, this time O'Byrne and his older brother Harold. 'Pornography' is the first story in the second collection and when it was first published in *The New Review* in February 1972 'a number of readers cancelled their subscriptions'.[9] It is arguably the 'dirtiest' of McEwan's stories in that it deals with the dissemination of venereal disease, frankly sadistic sex and punitive castration as well as pornography. Mercifully, the characters are all adult and equally culpable. It illustrates anal sadism – the perversion of sexual drive in the service of power and control. Unlike oral sadism, which seeks to rip, tear and dismember, anal sadism aims to enslave and subordinate. Pain and suffering are sometimes inflicted in the process because when humiliation does not suffice to exert control and realise power over the victim, torture and murder do. [...] O'Byrne cultivates sado-masochistic sexual relationships with two women simultaneously. The ease with which the role of sadist and masochist can be exchanged is vividly demonstrated here. Psychoanalysts agree that: 'masochistic and sadistic trends are always blended with each other. Although on the surface they seem contradictions, they are essentially rooted in the same basic need.'[10] When visiting Pauline, O'Byrne behaves in an arrogant, dismissive and callous fashion, hurting and humiliating her. With Lucy he adopts a supine, inferior role while she abuses and denigrates him. Lucy is ten years older than Pauline and a ward sister in the same hospital in which Pauline is a student nurse. Harold is ten years older than O'Byrne and also in a position of authority. O'Byrne has projected the roles of master and slave on to the two women. By deciding which woman to visit he ensures a choice of role for himself and therefore manages to remain in control of the satisfaction of his oscillating needs. □

(Christina Byrnes, *The Work of Ian McEwan*. 2002)[11]

Revealing how McEwan is as much interested in masochism as sadism, though the latter is more often commented upon by critics, O'Byrne's control is taken out of his hands by Lucy and Pauline. Other characters who (if only unconsciously) seek to lose control are the narrator of 'Dead As They Come', and both Mary and Terence in 'Psychopolis'. Kiernan Ryan, in an article from 1999, looks back on the careers of Martin Amis and Ian McEwan to consider the ways in which they recognize themselves to be complicit with late twentieth-century cultural trends, such as the media's interest in sex, violence and commodification. Ryan considers both writer and reader to be collusive in a market economy where the interest-agenda is set by the forces of supply and demand, which are ultimately underpinned by the principle of the 'best bang for a buck', which is to say that the most powerful market forces work at the level of the lowest common denominator. Yet, Ryan is also interested in the status of the literary artefact, the book, within this economy – with its creation, marketing and consumption. Underlying his analysis is a view that criticisms of Amis and McEwan are at root hypocritical in censuring the author for situations and narratives in which we are all complicit.

■ McEwan and Amis write in a fashion which presupposes our common implication in the same 'event horizon' (to hijack a grim euphemism from the nuclear phrase-book). This horizon is defined by the universal stranglehold of nuclear and market forces, which have turned Eros and Thanatos, love and death themselves, into commodities to be screened and narrated, watched and consumed. Violence has bled through into sexuality with a vengeance, as what once lurked in the shadows as pornography has crept into the cultural limelight; while violence, conversely, has been eroticised to a degree even [the Marquis] de Sade [1740–1814] might be dismayed by, acquiring an aesthetic aura which confrontation with the reality of its effects finds it ever harder to dispel. The scope for resistance or refusal, let alone transformation, seems to shrink geometrically as capitalist technology invades our very cells to programme our appetites and fantasies, to install the structures of addiction – to food, to sex, to drugs, to money, to violence, to voyeurism – which the market needs to survive. The pornographic and the cataclysmic waltz arm in arm through the novels of both these writers, who know that they are marketing flesh and fear to feed the habits in themselves and us, habits which are as corrosive as they are compulsive.

First Love, Last Rites commits us to the clammy embrace of three tales that turn on the sexual abuse of children. [...] The title tale of *In Between the Sheets* couples the incestuous and the paedophile motifs once more, as a divorced father recalls the night he barely resisted the fantasy of his own daughter's desire for him [...]. The volume opens with a story expressly billed as 'Pornography'. In this, two nurses take an exquisitely apt revenge on the seedy pornographer's apprentice who has been two-timing them, and who has generously shared his latest genital infection with them both. 'We'll leave you a pretty little stump to remember us by', they promise, as the sterilizer hisses beside the bed to which they have strapped him, for what he thought would be a less complete masochistic treat. And the concluding tale, 'Psychopolis', located in Los Angeles, kicks off with the teller chaining his girlfriend to the bed – at her own request – and keeping his word to ignore all her pleas for release: 'I was not at all excited. I thought to myself, if I keep her there, if I unlock the chain she will despise me for being weak. If I keep her there she might hate me, but at least I will have kept my promise ... I closed my eyes and concentrated on being blameless.' (p. 107) [...]

The adoption of a first-person narrative voice is hardly an innovation in itself. But Amis and McEwan exploit to an unusual degree the confessional possibilities built into the novel as a form since its inception. (I am thinking in particular of its well-documented debts to spiritual autobiography and the diary.) The first-person narrator creates an illusion of unmediated intimacy which the third-person perspective is obliged to forgo or insinuate by other means. All the surrogates, voice-overs and body-doubles hired by both novelists prove to be 'compulsive monologuists' (to filch a phrase from 'Psychopolis' [p. 113]). They are all itching to bend our ear and spill the beans. Each has something to hide which they are bent on divulging *to us*, their secret sharers and *hypocrite lecteurs* ['secret sharers' alludes to Joseph Conrad's short story 'The Secret Sharer' (1912) and *'hypocrite lecteurs'* ('hypocritical readers') to the last line of Part One of *The Waste Land* (1922) by T. S. Eliot (1885–1965). Eliot himself took the phrase from the 'Preface' to *Les Fleurs du Mal* (*The Flowers of Evil,* 1857) by Charles Baudelaire (1821–67)]. McEwan's child molesters and real or wishful murderers of wives and fathers are owning up to us; and that act of confession casts us in the corresponding role of the confidant expected to share their point of view or even shoulder their burden of shame. It is McEwan's cunning effacement of his presence, of all signs of authorial intent, that compels our identification with his estranged soliloquists. By allowing the confession of the child-killer in 'Butterflies' [in *First Love, Last Rites*] to proceed unchecked by commentary or judgement, McEwan implicates himself and us through our confinement to the vision of this isolated voice. To read such narratives demands, after all, a kind of acquiescence, which may pave the way for our own admission of affinity.

The books of both authors are full of furtive couplings, killings and concealments in which we are made to feel as embroiled as the novelist. In 'In Between the Sheets' the author is fingered as an accomplice by the fact that the narrator is himself a writer, who makes no bones about the voyeuristic, leech-like qualities he displays both as a man and as an author. His sexuality meets its match in his profession, which obliges him to raid his most intimate imaginings for material to transform into fictional products he can sell. The narrator's fastidious habit of entering his daily word-count in a ledger unearths, moreover, the buried economic implications of *giving an account* of something. It reminds us of the market force-field that underpins McEwan's act of writing, and our act of reading, the fetishized commodity between our hands. □

(Kiernan Ryan, 'Sex, Violence and Complicity: Martin Amis and Ian McEwan', 1999)[12]

Another way in which McEwan and Amis can be compared is explored by Richard Brown in his article on 'Postmodern Americas in the Fiction of Angela Carter, Martin Amis and Ian McEwan'. In this extract, Brown concentrates on 'Psychopolis', which McEwan began shortly after returning from Los Angeles in 1976.

■ The apparently fantastical world of Ian McEwan's first two collections of short stories also gives way to something more like geopolitical allegory in his work as it develops through the increasingly politically charged eighties, and some of the allegorical implications may be teased out by attempting to read the ways in which America is imagined in the works as a cultural complex or post-cultural sign. America, absent from the stories of *First Love, Last Rites* (1975), except in the reference to Americans as people 'who often indulge in fantastic tales' in 'Solid Geometry' (pp. 35–6), becomes important in *In Between the Sheets* (1978). The final story in the collection begins: 'Mary worked in a part-owned feminist bookstore in Venice' (p. 103), that Venice being part of Greater Los Angeles, the 'Psychopolis' of the story's title. Mary, with her paradoxical fetish for insisting that the narrator of the story chain her to the bed, is a symbol of one kind of feminism (her feminism recurs later in the story when she attempts a feminist critique of Christianity, pp. 122–3) but also represents the indescribable postmodern insanity of the city.

According to Edward Soja's *Postmodern Geographies* (1989), massively expansive, once gold-rushed Los Angeles enjoys a number of features which make it 'a *prototopos*, a paradigmatic place' or '*mesocosm*' (a place which is in some sense everywhere at the same time) for the postmodern, urban capitalist world.[13] For Soja to describe such a place empirically is literally impossible. Its wild accumulations of multinational capital are incommensurate with its acute housing crises which leave more people than anywhere else in America living in cardboard boxes. Its 'polynucleated decentralization' which has made it 'a hundred suburbs in search of a city' sorts ill with the centripetal economic forces that cause both recentralisation and a sense of the re-creation of the centre as another kind of periphery. The extreme multicultural diversity and drive towards personal individuation seem only to lead to new tonalities and the accelerating erosion of difference.

McEwan's story uses strikingly similar figures. Mary's paradoxical sex game, in which the English narrator bemusedly participates, is followed by a scene in which he dwells on the absurdity or paradox of a hire shop dealing in both 'items for party givers' and 'equipment for sick rooms' (p. 106). The hugeness, uncentredness, absurdity, and representativeness of this 'heterotopia' all feature as both background and foreground in the story. 'It's a city at the end of cities,' says Mary, and 'It's sixty miles across', the narrator is said to have 'agreed' (p. 105). His friend Terence Latterly says: 'It's OK for the British. You see everything here as a bizarre comedy of extremes, but that's because you're out of it. The truth is it's psychotic, totally psychotic' (p. 109). The narrator thinks mesocosmically: 'Everywhere on earth is the same. Los Angeles, California, the whole of the United States seemed to me then a very fine and frail crust on the limitless, subterranean world of my own boredom. I could be anywhere ...' (p. 112).

The climax of the story occurs in a final scene in which the characters meet together in an increasingly wild discussion of the corporal punishment of children, Christianity, the America of 'God, Guts and Guns' and so on. George's sceptical but pragmatic Christianity and his loud patriotism and Mary's attractive but ultimately limited and futile version of socialist feminism are both silenced by Terence's mad practical joke with George's gun. Throughout the story the nameless English first-person narrator has described in minute detail his flute-playing and, in particular, his practising of a Bach sonata, 'No. 1 in A Minor'. He plays without perfection or even ambition towards perfection, repeating the same familiar errors on his instrument and achieving only an imagined coherence 'remembered from gramophone records and superimposed over the present' (p. 113). At the close the coherence implied by such 'Classical' rationalistic music as a Bach sonata has itself come to seem misplaced. In the light of his experience of the 'vast, fragmented city without a centre, without citizens, a city that existed only in the mind' he begins to see Bach as 'inane in its rationality, paltry in its over-determination' (pp. 126–7). If Bach represents culture then this America is 'postcultural': an incommensurable; immense and grown beyond the powers of the imagination. Cultural Bach is set up in opposition to those postcultural representatives of Dionysian licence and irrationality, English representatives, of course, The Rolling Stones, from whose song 'Live With Me' the title of McEwan's story 'In Between the Sheets' and his collection are taken.[14] The fact that McEwan subsequently chose to write his second novel, *The Comfort of Strangers*, with another poignantly futile feminist heroine called Mary, but this time set in the thanatopic, capitalistic nightmare city of Venice, Italy, confirms the presence of this 'America' in the centre of Europe too. □

(Richard Brown, 'Postmodern Americas in the Fiction of Angela Carter, Martin Amis and Ian McEwan', 1994)[15]

'Psychopolis' ends with the narrator 'Overwhelmed by a nostalgia for a country I had not yet left' (p.134). This sense of longing for a past that has not been left behind, at least in one's thoughts, is a characteristic of much of McEwan's fiction. With the arguable exceptions of *The Innocent* and *Atonement,* which as historical novels contain their own sense of nostalgia, McEwan's writing has been concerned with the stages of life he has himself passed through and recently inhabited. More importantly, all of his books are about loss, of virginity, innocence, childhood, parents, love, or simply control. 'Psychopolis' itself resembles no fiction more than Christopher Isherwood's *Goodbye to Berlin* (1939), which Isherwood (1904–86) had intended as part of a cycle of tales to be called 'The Lost'. Like Isherwood, McEwan has a largely passive artist-narrator, recording not thinking, adrift in a seductive foreign city populated by larger than life characters who seem to be driven by passions and hopes that are unlikely to bring them happiness, but may bring them temporary satisfaction. McEwan said that writing 'Psychopolis' gave him the confidence to move on to longer fiction after the 'laboratory' of short-story writing. The result of this confidence was itself an extended short story, or novella, and it was one that again featured a first-person narrator whose seeming amorality would cement McEwan's reputation as a shocking if not sensationalist writer.

CHAPTER THREE

A Lovely Sleep: *The Cement Garden* (1978)

> *naturam expellas furca tamen usque recurret* (*'You can drive out nature with a pitchfork but it'll keep coming back'*, Horace, Epistles, 10:24)

McEwan's first novel was considered shocking, morbid and repellent, but also 'just about perfect'.[1] For Anne Tyler, by contrast, the problem with the novel is that the reader can't identify with or believe in such bitter and unpleasant children.[2] Yet, for many readers it is precisely the sober, unsentimental way in which the children are portrayed, warts and all, that makes the novel so refreshing, and indeed believable. For Blake Morrison *The Cement Garden* confirmed McEwan as one of the best British novelists of his generation.[3]

The title of McEwan's first novel contains allusions to some of its central concerns: culture's veneer over nature, the natural/unnatural taboo against incest, the modern city as concrete jungle. At one stage, the narrator Jack tries to conceal his life:

> Everything I looked at reminded me of myself. I opened wide the doors of the wardrobe and threw in all the debris from the floor. I pulled the sheets, blankets and pillows off my bed and put those in too. I ripped down pictures from the wall that I had once cut out of magazines. Under the bed I found plates and cups covered in green mould. I took every loose object and put it in the wardrobe till the room was bare. I even took down the light bulb and light shade. Then I took my clothes off, threw them in and closed the doors. (pp. 127–8)

And whatever is hidden away or covered over in the book refuses to stay 'buried'. Yet, McEwan's novel is not just a story about nature returning no matter how deeply it is hidden or forcefully expelled. It is concerned with questioning the ways in which the lines between the social and the personal, the natural and the cultural, the right and the wrong, are precariously drawn, and the senses in which the 'natural' world can be invoked in the artificiality of urban life. It is a narrative about social conventions, familial norms and the division between the human and the alien. It is also about fantasies, dreams and role-playing.

The Cement Garden is a book focused on childhood and it brings to mind many other novels concerned with children isolated from adults, most notably *The Lord of the Flies* (1954) by William Golding (1911–93). But, whereas Golding's children run wild, fighting each other, McEwan's grow closer together, and the reader is reminded how the adult world provides checks not on their natural aggression but on their natural sexuality. Any reference to 'nature' is problematic, however. McEwan does not suggest that if adults are removed, children revert to any kind of 'savage' state but that they will adapt, and adapt to, the role models that the removed adults provided for them. The book's primary burials/coverings are of the parents, but not their influence, which will prove to be a determining factor in the children's subsequent life together over the summer holidays as they develop their own sense of identity while negotiating the roles (sexual, parental, gendered) vacated by the parents' deaths.

Christopher Williams considers Jack's narration within the history of literary representations of the adolescent, and finds McEwan's depiction of the teenager to be somewhat different from previous ones:

> ■ *The Cement Garden* is devoid of reference to place-names, fictional or real (we are merely informed on one occasion that the mother had a distant relative in Ireland, p. 23), books (apart from a trashy science-fiction novel), songs (except 'Greensleeves'), films, TV programmes, brand-names, or any of the other familiar features of contemporary consumer society, thus enhancing the novel's qualities of timelessness and of mystery: as readers we perceive that the narrator is withholding information (where do the children live?), but we do not know why. Indeed, Jack never explicitly acknowledges our presence as readers [...]. When we read in *The Cement Garden* about the narrator's father – 'I am only including the little story of his death to explain how my sisters and I came to have such a large quantity of cement at our disposal' (p. 9) – it is not clear whether this is said for our benefit, or whether it is merely a kind of mental reminder to the narrator himself as he sets about structuring his tale. And while it is true that the flat, unemotional narrative generally avoids expressing any opinion about the extraordinary events that occur, value judgements occasionally seep through. How are we to interpret Jack's definition of the episode of his father's death as a 'little story'? Teenage bravado? An attempt to minimize an event too appalling to be faced? A case of understatement? Or is it the plain truth, the father's death representing at that moment no more than a minor incident in the life of this self-absorbed adolescent whose relationship with his father had never been close? Had the sentence been narrated retrospectively

through an adult consciousness, the choice of the adjective 'little' would necessarily have been perceived by us as a clear case of irony; seen through the eyes of our teenage narrator, we are aware that the choice may imply no irony whatsoever. [...]

McEwan's narrative is devoid of the humour, the exuberance, the explicit intention of taking an irreverential swipe at the literary tradition of the Romantic child. *The Cement Garden* also subverts this tradition, but in a quieter, more unobtrusive sort of way. The greyness of the prose, its almost total lack of imagery, and the absence of cultural and historical reference points all serve to heighten our perception of the drabness and emptiness of an existence seemingly outside time and society. □

(Christopher Williams, 'Ian McEwan's *The Cement Garden* and the Tradition of the Child/Adolescent as "I-Narrator"', 1996)[4]

Jack in fact appears emotionally underdeveloped from the start of the novel: his father's death is Oedipally related as 'insignificant' in the context of the story Jack tells, except for its temporal coincidence with his first ejaculation: 'a landmark in my own physical growth' (p. 9). Jack is preoccupied with his body, particularly its new adolescent productions: acne and semen. In his semi-mature condition, Jack appears to confuse, or conflate, all women, such that at one point he thinks a woman on the street is his dead mother, and then changes his mind to recognize her as his sister Julie, only to confront her and find it is a stranger. At his mother's death, Jack is seeking a replacement who will also be all women to him, as his mother was when he was a child. In Julie he therefore seeks mother, sister and lover. Until he consummates his heterosexual masculinity by sleeping with his sister, and so (mis)appropriates his father's vacated position as alpha male, Jack continues the act begun at the moment of his father's death, and warned against by his mother, by masturbating 'each morning and afternoon' (p. 74).

McEwan describes his intention for the dynamics between the children in this way:

■ I didn't want a situation in which, because the parents have died, the children just assumed roles which are identical to those of the parents. I had an idea that in the nuclear family the kind of forces that are being suppressed – the oedipal, incestuous forces – are also paradoxically the very forces which keep the family together. So if you remove the controls, you have a ripe anarchy in which the oedipal and the incestuous are the definitive emotions. From Jack's point of view Julie becomes something he aspires to sexually, even though she is his sister and also, in the circumstances, acting as mother to his younger brother and to some extent to Jack himself. I suppose I'm suggesting a situation in which the oedipal and incestuous are identical. □

(Ian Hamilton, 'Points of Departure', 1978)[5]

For Randall Stevenson, *The Cement Garden* is morbidly compelling but the claustrophobia of Jack's narrative results in a somewhat static situation in which the children show too few signs of development after their mother's death:

■ Helped by his brother and sisters, the novel's adolescent narrator, Jack, buries his mother's body gruesomely in cement in the cellar: he calmly remarks, however,

> ... nor could I think whether what we had done was an ordinary thing to do ... or something so strange that if it was ever found out it would be the headline of every newspaper in the country. (pp. 88–9)

... Jack seems unconcerned by moral or other conventions. His juxtaposition of nightmare and death with every domestic detail creates a narrative in which, rather in the manner of Kafka, unconscious or sexual forces are interfused with otherwise ordinary scenes or events. Jack's memories, dreams, visions of his mother, accounts of his sexual awakening or simply of daily domestic life commingle in a narrative often unusually compelling despite its morbid subject. Nevertheless, though there is some sense of progress in the revelation of Jack's psyche, McEwan's central situation remains disappointingly static, the family set in its various mutual attitudes as firmly, until the conclusion, as its mother in cement. □

(Randall Stevenson, *The British Novel Since the Thirties*, 1986)[6]

By contrast, John Carey sees far greater meaning in the children's response to orphanhood and suggests a continuity between the family before and after the parents' deaths. McEwan's bizarre story has logic to it in terms of adolescent emotion and family dynamics, and Carey suggests that the novel ought perhaps less to make the reader question the children's behaviour than the officious response society makes to personal crises, intent on enforcing its own taboos about sex and death rather than understanding the need for comfort and familiarity that is felt by the bereaved and the abandoned – ultimately implying that McEwan's children cope with their orphanhood far better than the social services might.[7]

Carey's reading is to a degree echoed in that of Carmen Callil and Colm Tóibín who understand the novel in terms of urban alienation, political inertia and social dysfunction. For them, *The Cement Garden* leaves the reader feeling that the children have coped better with their loss than the authorities might:

■ This novel was published in the year before Margaret Thatcher took power in Britain, and its tone and content seem to imply that there was a very great need for her. The house where the four children [...] are being brought up by their parents is in sight of new tower blocks, and the motorway which caused the houses around them to be knocked down has never been built. Neither parent has any siblings so there are no relatives; the father dies first, and then the mother after a long illness. The children, three of whom are in their teens, decide to bury her in the cellar and tell no one. This is presented as perfectly normal by Jack, who narrates the story. They loved their mother, but they want the giddy freedom which running the household will offer them.

There is not a false note in the whole book; McEwan makes you feel that this is, perhaps, what you would do too under similar circumstances. In any case, the siblings are locked into their own dramas. Tom, the youngest, wants to dress like a girl and is allowed to do so, then he wants to be a baby and this too is arranged. Jack is obsessed with his own adolescent body. Sue keeps a diary. Julie gets a boyfriend. They settle down into an uneasy and fragile harmony, broken only by Derek the boyfriend and the gradual rise of the smell from the cellar. Their world has been so perfectly created that you feel miserable at the prospect of it being broken up. □

(Carmen Callil and Colm Tóibín, *The Modern Library*, 1999)[8]

The suggestion that the children's behaviour is natural to them can be supported by the book in many ways. For example, the second of the novel's two parts begins with Jack recounting that his parents had attended the funeral of 'one of their last remaining relatives' a few years earlier (p. 69). Jack does not know who exactly died, and concludes that 'the death meant very little to our parents. Certainly it meant nothing to us children.' This last comment in fact refers less to the death than to the fact that the children will be left in the house alone for a day. Jack remarks that his mother and father tell them what to do and that they are quite happy staying alone and being 'in charge of Tom'. Most importantly, their father has to tell them what to do if someone comes to the door, underlining the fact of their isolation, which is confirmed by Jack's startling comment that 'no one had ever knocked at the front door'.

Below, McEwan speaks of *The Cement Garden* as though it were a novel about a house that descends into a kind of hibernation. This echoes Jack's own comment that in the long day after his mother's death 'the house seemed to have fallen asleep' (p. 71). It is a sleep that lasts until the end of the novel when Julie's boyfriend Derek and then the authorities arrive to break up Jack's somniloquy, the family, and the concrete in the cellar, at which point Julie remarks, in the last words of the novel: 'wasn't that a lovely sleep' (p. 138). Indeed, the children's experience of the hot summer is characterized by slipping into slumber: Julie sunbathes drowsily outside, Sue curls up to write in her diary, and Tom reverts to the cot. Meanwhile Jack describes his life in these terms: 'I woke in the late morning, masturbated and dozed off again. I had dreams, not exactly nightmares, but bad dreams that I struggled to wake out of … .

Some afternoons I fell asleep in the armchair even though I had only been awake a couple of hours' (p. 85). In interview with John Haffenden, McEwan explains how this aspect of the novel was in fact the genesis of the story:

■ [*John Haffenden*:] *Can you tell me how you set about writing* The Cement Garden?

[*Ian McEwan*:] It has a definite genesis in one paragraph of my notes, at the doodling stage, where I suddenly had a whole novel unfold about a family living 'like burrowing animals ... after mother dies the house seems to fall asleep'. Then I saw the four children: 'the initial spread of power ... the girls steal youngest to babyfy ... gives narrator more space'. I remember writing that paragraph and then lying on the bed and falling into a deep sleep for an hour in the afternoon. When I came back to work I made a false start, and later I realised that the beginning really belonged with the father. I also wondered for a time whether I shouldn't have each of the children recounting the novel. And then for a long time I thought it would turn out that the second sister would be the true narrator, since she was keeping a notebook. I kept thinking the narrator was going to go completely crazy: 'His imbalance becoming an issue and the household cannot contain him.' I thought for a while that Jack would just go under [quotations are from Ian McEwan's notebook drafts].

I think that one character in The Cement Garden *who really authenticates the fantasy, as it were, is the outsider, Derek, who envies the world of the children: he wants both to enter their world and to break it.*

Yes, I sympathize with Derek, because I was a sort of only child, and when I went to stay with friends who had brothers and sisters I would fantasize that my own parents had dematerialized to enable me to join a large family [this also becomes the fantasy of Jeremy in *Black Dogs*]. *The Cement Garden* has a source in my childhood wish to have sisters. □

(John Haffenden, *Novelists in Interview*, 1985)[9]

Angela Roger, in her discussion of the portrayal of women in McEwan's fiction, considers the relationship between Jack and Julie in several ways: as a power struggle, as sexual attraction, and also as a means of keeping the family together.

■ The relationship between Jack and Julie in *The Cement Garden* moves inexorably from normal sibling affection to incest. In between, the pair engage in a power struggle which Julie easily wins. Julie is nevertheless portrayed as a subject of affection and admiration for her brother, Jack. Physical descriptions of Julie permeate the narrative, emphasising not only her meticulous attention to her appearance, which is in stark contrast to her brother's, but also the impact of her physical presence on him. Several passages of such physical description portend the incestuous outcome in that they contain overt sexual allusions. For example, a description of Julie from Jack's point of view employs allusions to the representation of women as coy temptresses, objects of desire: '[Julie] half-smiled, half-pouted [...] her lips softly pursed' (pp. 23–4). There is also a sexual element in Jack's tickling attack on Julie which is suggestive of rape (p. 30). A more overt example of sexual innuendo is clear in Jack's rubbing sun-tan lotion onto his sister's back, especially since we have witnessed the boy spending a great deal of his time masturbating. He kneels 'between her open legs' and 'squirt[s] pale, creamy fluid' into his hand. While he does so, he is described as stealing a glance at his sister's breasts (pp. 43–4).

McEwan recognizes that the sexual admiration between brother and sister portrayed in *The Cement Garden*, with its conclusion in incest, just as in 'Homemade', has its origins in his own desire to have sisters. [...]

Narrated as it is by Jack, whose growing sexual attraction to his sister is a prominent theme in the novel, Julie's sensuality is apparent throughout the narrative, both when she is alone and when she is in company with her younger brothers and sister. She is frequently described languishing in the sun and she often touches and cuddles her siblings; she is also endowed with motherly qualities such as efficiency and authority, qualities distinctly lacking otherwise in the household. Her ability to comfort her siblings, however, seems never far removed from her enjoyment of the power she can exert over them. The children's mother's death leaves them orphaned and Julie assumes control of the household to become the undisguised, though not undisputed, mother substitute, looking after her brothers and sister. It is presented as no surprise to Jack that Julie should do so, but it is a source of constant aggravation to him, since he has vague notions that from the perspective of the male narrator, a woman's role should be subservient to his, a view which is never expressed by the reconstructed male narrators of later novels. For example, as the children prepare the concrete to bury their mother's body, Jack comments: 'Obscurely, I felt entitled to do the shovelling and mixing, but Julie had the shovel and had already made up a pile of sand' (p. 61). He is even shown to assume the role of his dead father, vetting Julie's relationship with her boyfriend: 'I had a confused notion that as Julie's brother I had a right to ask questions about her boyfriend' (p. 81).

The tension between male and female is also worked out involving the older brother and sister. On the death of the father, the culture of the family becomes overwhelmingly female-oriented, a dominance enhanced by the rise to power of Julie when Mother dies. The youngest child is depicted as succumbing completely to the feminine influence, first dressing as a girl before reverting to babyhood; even Jack admits, and submits, to a certain amount of feminising. When his sisters comfort each other on their mother's death, Jack 'wished [he] could abandon [him]self like them' (p. 54). When Julie ties a ribbon around his neck, he lets her, so that he can feel included as a girl but also because it gives him a chance to be physically close to his sister.

Jack and Julie achieve their most harmonious moment in the incestuous scene which closes the novel. The brother–sister incest fulfils two functions: it emphasises the closeness of the siblings, preceded as it is with their exploration of the differences and similarities of their bodies; and attempts to keep the family together. □

(Angela Roger, 'Ian McEwan's Portrayal of Women', 1996)[10]

As indicated by McEwan earlier, the novel is easily subjected to a reading in terms of the Oedipus complex. Jack opens his narrative by pointedly asserting that he did not kill his father, as though he would have liked to. He sleeps with Julie when she becomes the family's surrogate mother. Their real mother is buried in the house's basement, which seems to serve as a metaphor for the repression of Jack's desires. There is also a pervasive concern with the father's position of dominance in the family. The household's running jokes are about Julie's sporting ambitions, Jack's pimples, Sue's looks, Tom's bedwetting, and mother's poor mathematics (p. 15). Father is not a subject of mockery, and when Jack tries to ridicule him he feels 'guilt' where he wishes to feel 'elation' (p. 16). Only in making the unnatural cement garden does Jack feel at ease with his father.

David Sampson, using the theories of the French post/structuralist critic Roland Barthes (1915–80), divides readers between the close and the perverse. Close readers attempt to 'master' the text, to interpret it and fix it with their own meanings. Perverse readers, by contrast, have little use for power or logic, but play with language, unconcerned with the close reader's emphasis on what is permitted and what is forbidden in reading the text. Close reading is male, truth-seeking and aggressive, wanting praise; perverse reading is self-conscious, anarchic and anti-authoritarian, wanting love. Using this model of readers, Sampson argues that *The Cement Garden* evades the logic of this binary, presenting both Jack and Julie as simultaneously normal (close) and perverse readers:

■ God in *The Cement Garden* dies before the expulsion from Eden can be properly effected. And after her mother's death Julie, the eldest child, becomes both surrogate-father and surrogate-mother and so is the obscure object of Jack's desire and rivalry. When Jack recommends his science-fiction novel to her, he is then both a close and a perverse reader; he wishes to be both praised and loved for his recommendation. Julie, in turn, responds in two ways, with close reading and playful assault. She exploits the punitive power of the normal reader by closely analysing the book's cover:

> Julie spent some time staring at the cover, and I stood behind her chair and looked at it too. The monster, which resembled an octopus, was attacking a spaceship. In the distance Commander Hunt's ship was

racing to the rescue. I had not examined the cover closely before, and now it looked ridiculous. I felt ashamed of it, as if I had painted it myself. (p. 83)

After judging the book by its cover (the judgements of close reading are always arbitrary), Julie then sits on it, humiliating Jack who has seen in the book a reflection of himself (he continually pretends to be Commander Hunt). Immediately afterwards Julie plays at killing Jack (Commander Hunt becomes the monster and Julie becomes Commander Hunt):

> Julie whipped round and filled my belly with her bullets. I collapsed on the floor at her feet, a butter wrapper inches from my nose. Julie took a handful of my hair and pulled my head back. She swapped her gun for a knife and as she pressed it against my throat she said, 'Any more trouble and I'll stick it in here.' Then she knelt down and pressed her fist near my groin. 'Or here', she whispered dramatically, and we both laughed. (pp. 85–6)

In keeping with the evasive logic of the novel, Julie represents two contradictory kinds of feminism, concrete feminism and deconstructive feminism. Concrete feminists emulate close readers. In their scrutiny of texts they attempt to discover what close readers have overlooked. They aim to establish an oppositional but equally authoritarian discourse which is matriarchal rather than patriarchal; they want to sit on close readers. Concrete feminism makes its appearance in *The Cement Garden* as transvestism, a philosophy that Julie explains to Jack:

> 'Girls can wear jeans and cut their hair short and wear shirts and boots because it's okay to be a boy, for girls it's like promotion. But for a boy to look like a girl is degrading, according to you, because secretly you believe that being a girl is degrading [...] If I wore your trousers to school tomorrow and you wore my skirt, we'd soon see who had the worse time. Everyone would point at you and laugh.' Here Julie pointed across the table, her fingers inches from my nose.
>
> 'Look at him! He looks just like ... ugh! ... a *girl!*'
>
> 'And look at her', Sue was pointing at Julie, 'she looks rather ... *clever* in those trousers.' My two sisters laughed so hard they collapsed in each other's arms. (pp. 47–8)

In protest at the social injustice the sisters dress their younger brother, Tom, as a girl. Yet Julie is not a committed concrete feminist; she treats imitation as a game. The two kinds of feminism are characterised by different gestures. Concrete feminism is accusatory (it points the finger; it uses symbols of phallic power). Deconstructive feminism is disruptive; it does not establish difference as a different kind of unity but plays with '*différance.*' [The French philosopher Jacques Derrida's (1930–2004) term for the way in which meaning operates is *différance*, a portmanteau word which contains the senses of 'differ' and 'defer'. If words are defined by their difference from other words, their meanings can only be pursued in detours through more words whose meanings are similarly postponed in an endless deferral.] Like concrete feminism, it seeks to castrate men; it makes use of phallic symbols (the gun, the knife) – *but in play.* It aims not to destroy (exclude) men but to assert difference while at the same time undermining the grounds of its choice. It mocks difference (laughs) by deferring it (collapses), demonstrating solidarity ('in each other's arms') by disrupting antinomies (man/woman: superior/inferior). Deconstructive feminists attempt to break the codes by which men maintain their hegemony (as Cathy does in McEwan's play, *The Imitation Game*) but not in order to replace them with their own alternative codes. At the same time they concede that they can never break out of language (Cathy ends the play in prison; *The Cement Garden* is written in the past tense as a confession). They argue that our only choice is between an alternative, currently unimaginable prison-house of language and the dialectic of pleasure and repression in the torture-chamber of our present discourse (Hobson's choice). There is no freedom without imprisonment, no pleasure without pain. □

(David Sampson, 'McEwan/Barthes', 1984)[11]

In many ways, *The Cement Garden* presents the preoccupation with fantasy at the heart of an ordinary family. The characters imagine their lives through the lenses of comic books, dreams, sexual fantasies, dressing up, playing doctors and nurses, and the world of science fiction, with its staples of heroes and aliens. McEwan suggests the desire for different fictions at different ages, from Tom (who is 5/6), Sue (12/13), Jack (14/15) and Julie (16/17). After the deaths of their parents, the outside world is represented to these children by Derek, himself only a young man of 23. Derek's main hangout is a snooker hall, a dark, male, adolescent world where he can rule the roost. McEwan says that what is desired by Derek, an only child envious of the children's new family unit (Jack and Julie as parents, Sue and Tom as children), is 'both to enter the world and to break it'.[12] To understand what it is that Derek is trying to break – given that this is already a 'broken' home in the sense that the parents have departed – it is necessary to consider the new relationships forged by the children over the long hot summer of their independence. Jack Slay sees this as a family built on Julie's strength, thus casting her as a new single parent, and the other children's eventual willingness to become her children – the culmination of which is the consummation of Jack's Oedipal desire:

■ Though Jack is the most unnerved and unnerving of the children, his siblings are far from the usual adolescents. Julie, for example, is the anomaly in her family: she is daring and independent, confident and beautiful. Early in the novel Jack describes her as having the 'deep look of some rare wild animal' (p. 11); later he mentions that she is 'one of a handful of daring girls at school who wore starched white petticoats beneath their skirts to fill out and make them swirl when they turned on their heel. She wore stockings and black knickers, strictly forbidden' (p. 20). Julie's feral nature is obviously an attraction for Jack; whereas he must strain to create a sense of anarchy, Julie's rebellion is innate and true. Likewise, her self-confidence is instinctive. Jack says that she 'had the quiet strength and detachment and lived in the separate world of those who are, and secretly know they are, exceptionally beautiful' (pp. 23–4). Julie, in many ways, stands alone in her family, and because of this position she naturally falls into the role of authority when her parents die.

This role of motherhood is forced upon Julie, but she willingly, and naturally, accepts the part. She alone is privy to the seriousness of Mother's illness; aware of the state of her health, Mother places her eldest daughter in charge, knowing that she is the most responsible, the most capable of holding the family together. Julie is comforted in her new position; however, for a while, Jack resents her new power, saying that he 'suspected she was exploiting the position, that she enjoyed ordering me about' (p. 42). Only reluctantly does he eventually accept Julie's authority, realizing that she is indeed the new stabilizing force in their family.

While Julie becomes a matriarchal figure for all her siblings, it is Tom who forces her to assume completely the role of mother; he makes it quite clear that without her maternal pampering he could not survive in this new world. As Michael Adams says, McEwan uses these newly forged maternal relationships to 'satirize the male tendency to make women into mothers to get attention from them [...] His point seems to be that the family roles people assume are simply that: roles.'[13] Julie deduces early that all Tom wants or needs is attention. One evening when Tom is acting 'particularly demanding', Julie forces him into a bath, his pyjamas, and bed before five o'clock; Tom becomes 'utterly subdued', as Julie reveals that 'that's what he wanted' (p. 72). Likewise, it is Julie who recognizes and promotes Tom's regression into infancy. Out of necessity, Julie becomes an instant mother; out of love, she manages to hold the family together just a bit longer.

Sue is the most introverted of the family. In describing her, Jack frequently portrays her as an alien: in the sex game she is the 'specimen from outer space' (p. 11). Later he says that she 'really did look like a girl from another planet' (p. 25). In her role as the 'alien', Sue often separates herself from the other members of the family. She is the only one who cries at Father's death; likewise, she is the sole sibling who truly seems anguished over Mother's death, several times crying out her grief behind closed doors. Sue alone spends time beside the tomb. She keeps her mother's memory alive by writing letters to her, telling her of the days' events. Sue also consciously isolates herself, choosing to lock herself in her room with her books and writing tablets. Her response is normal grief; she struggles to accept the loss of her mother and to survive in her new life. In many ways Sue is not the 'alien' but the most conventional, the most normal, of the four children.

Tom, the youngest of the four children, is Mother's child from the beginning; he continually whines for her attention, constantly attempts to stay near her, throwing tantrums when he is forced to leave her side. He is the quintessential victim: 'Tom was just the kind to be picked on. He was small for a six-year-old, and frail. He was pale, a little jug-eared, had an idiotic grin and black hair which grew in a thick, lopsided fringe. Worse, he was clever in a niggling argumentative way – the perfect playground victim' (p. 45). Subsequently, when he is beaten up at school, Tom decides that it would be easier to be a girl because 'you don't get hit when you're a girl' (p. 47). Julie and Sue are only too happy to comply with Tom's wishes, dressing him in skirt, wig, and ribbons. Jack, of course, is shocked and outraged at this transvestism.

Along with Tom's transformation and Jack's consequent repugnance, a subtle feminism begins to appear in McEwan's work, a theme he continues to explore with greater intensity in later fiction. Jack sees Tom's desire as something 'idiotic' and 'humiliating', and he thinks that his sisters support Tom only 'so [they] can have a laugh' (p. 47). To Jack, this gender transformation is unnatural ... .

Far more disturbing is Tom's slow but sure regression into infancy. With his mother gone, Tom demands the protection and attention of Julie. When Julie does baby him, Tom's 'eyes grew larger and further apart, his mouth slackened and he seemed to sink inside himself' (p. 111). He literally surrenders to an infantile state. At first he simply needs the assurance of a mother figure; soon, however, he slips further into an infantile state, sucking his thumb, wearing a bib, sleeping in his old baby bed, speaking in a new baby voice, wailing and crying for attention, even smearing food over his face. Like Julie's bossiness, Sue's isolation, and Jack's alienation, Tom's regression is a defence mechanism. Through it he achieves a life of little effort and no responsibility; it is the easiest way for him to escape this new and confusing life. Like his cross-dressing, his infantile behaviour provides a safe haven.

Jack, too, experiences fleeting desires to regress to a less troublesome age. Near the end of the novel Jack dreams that he is again an infant, wailing for his parents to carry him. In his present state he has discovered that his authority-free life is not the adventure he had once envisioned; he realizes that he wants and *needs* parents. □

(Jack Slay, *Ian McEwan*, 1996)[14]

McEwan's next novel is also concerned with regression (and aggression), but this time it is that of adults rather than children.

McEwan has said: 'When I came to early adolescence, I was like [my mother], too tongue-tied to face down [my father's] iron certainties. I was at boarding school anyway, and in my mid-teens began to spend my holidays abroad with friends. After that, I drifted away, and saved my darker thoughts for my fiction, where fathers – especially the one in *The Cement Garden* – were not kindly presented.'[15]

At this stage of his career McEwan was seeking, as a male writer with no sisters, to come to terms with feminism. He says, 'I read *The Female Eunuch* [1970, by Germaine Greer (born 1939)] in 1971 and thought it was a revelation. The feminism of the 1970s spoke directly to a knot of problems at the heart of our family's life. I developed a romantic notion that if the spirit of women was liberated, the world would be healed. My female characters became the repository of all the goodness that men fell short of.'[16] Yet his next novel was one in which he tried to explore the sexual dynamics of heterosexual relationships in ways that provoked angry responses from feminists, protests of a kind that formed a more common reaction to the fiction of his near-contemporary, Martin Amis.

CHAPTER FOUR

The Desire to be a Victim: *The Comfort of Strangers* (1981)

> 'You write very well about the desire to be a victim. Being a victim, according to you, is not simply something which happens to someone, it is also something that someone, the victim, dreams.' – Ian McEwan to Milan Kundera[1]

The Comfort of Strangers, despite its mixed reviews, was shortlisted for the Booker Prize. It was variously considered 'diseased', a 'disappointment', 'arbitrary and implausible', and 'hateful'.[2] Yet, in several ways, McEwan's second novel seems to follow on from his first. The central couple of lovers, Colin and Mary, are so close they could almost be brother and sister: 'They often said they found it difficult to remember that the other was a separate person' (p. 17). They sleep in the afternoon, communicate without talking, and do not even have the energy or motivation to tidy their hotel room. They revert to a childlike state, reliant on their hotel maid: 'they came to depend on her and grew lazy with their possessions. They became incapable of looking after one another ... . One late morning, they returned to their room to find it as they had left it, simply uninhabitable, and they had no choice but to go out again and wait until it had been dealt with' (p. 12). Where Jack and Julie in *The Cement Garden* are adolescents who prematurely become adults in the familiar family home, Colin and Mary are holidaying adults (she divorced with children) who revert to an earlier childlike stage of life in the unfamiliar temporary home of a hotel in what appears to be Venice. In both books there is an almost solipsistic feel to people, a family and a couple, into whose midst strangers come in search of sex and power. In each novel, too great an intimacy (Colin and Mary 'knew each other much as they knew themselves, and their intimacy ... was a matter of perpetual concern' p. 13) creates its own problems for the protagonists, and they come under threat from others who will expose the vulnerabilities and dangers of their closeness.

Mary has reached a stage in which 'she sleepwalked from moment to moment, and whole months slipped by without memory, without bearing the faintest imprint of her conscious will' (p. 18). This is a very different setting for a similar state of being to that ascribed to Jack in *The Cement Garden*. Yet Mary does not tell her own story, as Jack did his. An important shift in the second novel is from a first- to a third-person narrator. The McEwan voice, introduced in his short stories, hovers inscrutably over the narrative. This voice is detached, but teasing. For example, the first chapter ends with sentences that seem written to overlay the ordinariness of events with ominous threat, concluding with an intimation of the darkness that awaits them on the streets outside after they lock themselves out of their hotel room: ' "Ready?" Colin called. She went inside, closing the french window behind her. She took the key from the bedside table, locked the door, and followed Colin down the unlit staircase' (p. 18).

While many of McEwan's novels seem to begin with a death that changes lives (*The Cement Garden, Amsterdam, Enduring Love*), *The Comfort of Strangers* leads up to a murder. And yet, as the last page of chapter 1 illustrates, the narrator's knowledge of Colin's imminent death is flaunted before the reader. Such prolepses, bringing the future into alignment with the present of the narrative, mean that Colin's inevitable death is as present at the start of the narrative as it is at the end. Nearly all of McEwan's novels begin with a crucial disruption, laden with multiple significances. As Joe says in *Enduring Love*: 'A beginning is an artifice, and what recommends one over another is how much sense it makes of what follows' (pp. 17–18). In *The Comfort of Strangers* that key opening is signalled in less direct ways, but the impression is as of a stone dropped in water, marking the moment from which events spread out: 'Colin and Mary had never left the hotel so late, and Mary was to attribute much of what followed to this fact' (p. 18).

McEwan's second novel expands on his first by including two main settings: the hotel room and Robert and Caroline's apartment. Where *The Cement Garden* featured one central place, the house, *The Comfort of Strangers* moves from Colin and Mary's safe existence at the hotel to their danger at Robert and Caroline's flat. The contrast between hotel and apartment is similar to the contrast between the two halves of *The Cement Garden*. Where Jack and his siblings had to change from dependence to independence, from being children at home with their parents to children alone without them, Colin and Mary alternate between a childlike relationship early in *The Comfort of Strangers* to an increasingly adult and intense relationship as they learn more about the couple who 'befriend' them. This is a transition from a loving friendship in which both partners take the other's existence as an extension of their own to a progressively charged sexual relationship in which they objectify and fantasize about each other's body. The book also introduces a theme of surveillance. Robert has been photographing the couple, but especially

Colin, since they arrived in the city. His meeting with them is no coincidence but an outcome of his observation of their movements. In this way the book moves between different kinds of optical desire, paralleling the visual consumption of others with the way that tourists consume the beauty of a city such as Venice.

For Malcolm Bradbury, McEwan's second novel is a fable about sexual feelings and gender roles:

■ In *The Comfort of Strangers* (1981), McEwan signalled a change, at least of the underlying perspective. The story is set in an imaginary, waterborne European city which is clearly Venice, a literary home to the elusive and sinister. It is an impressionist, nightmare fable of labyrinthine and dangerous relationships, shading from first normality toward an ever more ominously promised fulfilment of 'a violence that is in the air', and is born from a fundamental dislocation of sexual and gender roles and feelings which have 'distorted all relations, all truth'. □

(Malcolm Bradbury, *The Modern British Novel, 1878–2001*, 2001)[3]

Given the novel's sense of a progression towards an inevitable conclusion, it is interesting that McEwan composed the novel with little sense of how it would develop. He has said in interview: '*The Comfort of Strangers* got written in the most lugubrious way possible, because I would finish one chapter and have no idea what to do with the next. I felt that I would never finish, because the novel was giving me so much personal pain. I had a rough idea of what to do in the first half, but no ideas in advance for the second.'[4] In the extract below, he explains the origins of the novel at greater length:

■ [*Ian McEwan*:] Penny Allen and I spent a week in Venice in 1978, at the height of the tourist season, and something of our visit found its way into the book. I can't really describe the book as setting out with any clear intention. After being to [*sic*] Venice I came back and wrote some notes about it, which I lost, and then I found them a good one-and-a-half years later; it seemed to me that I had already been describing characters who were not quite like either myself or Penny, and already it seemed to be describing the city in terms of a state of mind, and vice versa. So the novel took off from the notes. Those notes contain the phrase 'self-fulfilling accusation', as well as the first sentence, so I must have been thinking about a novel even then.

I found it terribly difficult to write, and it is a book I find very hard to understand or talk about. It seemed to be saying something either true or so true that it was banal. It was an elaboration of an argument in *The Imitation Game*. This again brings up the question of form, since it wasn't enough to talk about men and women in social terms, I had to address myself to the nature of the unconscious, and how the unconscious is shaped. It wasn't enough to be rational, since there might be desires – masochism in women, sadism in men – which act out the oppression of women or patriarchal societies but which have actually become related to sources of pleasure. Now this is a very difficult argument to make.

I recently attended a *Marxism Today* conference about eroticism and the left, and I made an *extempore* speech – very clumsily – about eroticism not being totally amenable to rationalism, that it wasn't just a matter of talking out a programme of the feminist left. The conference was a broad coalition of socialists and feminists, and I got on to incredibly dangerous ground when I suggested that many women probably have masochistic fantasies and that many men probably have sadistic fantasies, which are acted out in private but never spoken about in any kind of public debate. And then I said that it would be far better in a relationship to embrace this than to deny it, and that true freedom would be for such women to recognise their masochism and to understand how it had become related to sexual pleasure. The same was no less true for male masochists. I was talking here of sexual fantasy. The whole room exploded, and I came away feeling terribly bruised because I had been very inarticulate, as one is when speaking against such hostility. But I was attacked for providing a 'rapist's charter' and for poaching on forbidden territory – women's experience.

[*John Haffenden*:] *That goes a long way to explain the characters of Robert and Caroline in* The Comfort of Strangers*. Robert obtrusively recounts his intimate childhood experiences to Colin and Mary, who are strangers to him. What he tells them amounts to a threat, and yet the young couple retreat to their hotel and curiously do not speak about their extraordinary encounter. But they do respond to it unconsciously, in their behaviour towards one another. You mention their 'conspiracy of silence' and – in chapter 7 – the way they start to 'invent themselves anew' and to make up sexual fantasies.*

I felt they had become mesmerized by Robert and Caroline in ways they could not speak about. Robert and Caroline were for me simply a sort of comic drawing of a relationship of domination, and when this decently liberal and slightly tired couple, Colin and Mary, come in contact with that relationship they find it has a sway over their unconscious life, and they begin to act out – or rather speak to each other – these incredible masochistic and sadistic fantasies while they are making love. By example, as it were, their very carefully constructed rational view – he being a mild feminist, she a rather stronger one, and their sort of balance – becomes undone, because they haven't ever addressed the matter at a deeper level of themselves; they've always seen it as a social matter.

What I was trying to say at the conference was that there is a certain sort of silliness attached to talking about eroticism if you are just talking about it in terms of domestic relationships. There is something intractable about the sexual imagination, and what you desire is not very amenable to programmes of change. You might well have grown up deciding that you accept certain intellectual points of view, and you might also change the way you behave as a man or as a woman, but there are also other things – vulnerabilities, desires – within you that might well have been irreversibly shaped in childhood. People of our generation, who grew up in the 1950s, grew up in the time of the fathers, and I made the point that there are many women for whom the figure of the father lies very deeply and powerfully within their sexuality. I got into incredibly hot water, but I still think I was right. I came away thinking that the left was actually bristling with taboos, almost as many taboos as there would have been at a synod of clergy in the late nineteenth century. Everyone was so used to a kind of likemindedness, that it was stirring for them to see me as an enemy in their midst.

In The Comfort of Strangers, *Colin and Mary take unconscious refuge in indulgent self-involvement, what you call a 'rhetorical mode, a means of proceeding', and it's as if they can agree on the politics of sex because they avoid discussing the social confrontation which drove them into collusion.*

Yes, the one thing they don't talk about is Robert and Caroline, and they interiorize it instead. In order to collude they mustn't talk about Robert and Caroline, and so they become Robert and Caroline.

I think of it as an old-fashioned novel about the head and the heart; two creatures of the head meet two creatures of the heart, and the head goes a bit haywire as a consequence. Robert is a sort of cartoon figure of extreme patriarchal domination, and he cannot tolerate the existence of Colin, who represents a threat to him. Colin becomes useful grist to Robert's ultimate fantasies of cruelty, wherein Robert can exercise his full sadism and Caroline can identify with it.

One of the interesting scenes on the way is where Mary goes swimming. Colin thinks she is drowning and he exhaustingly swims out to rescue her. When he reaches her he finds that she is in fact quite safe and happy, but his care for her is never communicated ...

There is also another current involved there, as it were, in the sense that if you are so wrong about something you have to question whether your desires aren't involved in your judgement, and maybe Colin wants Mary to be drowned and sees her in that way. But for me the dominant feature of that scene is the notion of swimming out too far, which is what they are about to do.

Christopher Ricks wrote a very interesting review of the novel (London Review of Books, *41:2, 21 January–3 February 1982), in which he talks about the incorrigibility of certain manifestations of evil, that they just cannot be explained. Yet it is the case that Robert enters very full evidence about the aetiology of his perversion. He explains the source of his sadism in a way which is not otherwise questioned in the novel, and I found that because of that unquestioned ratiocination apropos of Robert*

I was much more taken up by the subtle and exploratory treatment of Colin and Mary.

I think of Robert more as a cipher than as a character. People either buy Robert or they don't. He is part of the premise of the novel rather than an entirely convincing character.

But you still chose not to leave him as an unaccountable figure; you wanted to show how much he understands his sadism.

Yes, the violence that Robert does to Colin, which is a violence that is in the air – people do murder each other, wars do break out – has a lot to do with people's perceptions of their own exercise of power, and the pleasure they find in exercising power. What is interesting is the extent to which people will collude in their own subjection, which is true not only of Caroline in relation to Robert but also of Colin. There is something about Colin's behaviour which suggests from the beginning that he is a victim; he goes along with Robert and is easily manipulated, which suggests an unconscious contractual agreement. I think such an agreement can exist between oppressor and victim. □

(John Haffenden, *Novelists in Interview*, 1985)[5]

As Kiernan Ryan points out, the only history the reader learns about in any depth is Robert's. He has been brought up to both fear his father and consider himself the heir to his father's power in an otherwise all-female household. The book implies that Robert's sadism is an inheritance from his upbringing and its atmosphere of male violence and female subservience. Robert believes that this is what it is to be a man or a woman, and his influence on Colin and Mary is to trigger desires within them that their minds do not want to admit:

■ In chapter 2 Mary stops at the window of a department store to examine with distaste a bedroom tableau illustrating the tenacity of patriarchal roles and assumptions. The postures of the male and female dummies and the gendered distribution of household props typify everything from which Mary and Colin recoil. Turning in anger from this shrine of sexual clichés and the rigid effigies at its centre, 'their arms and legs raised uselessly, like insects surprised by poison' (p. 22), Mary is delighted to come across the fly-posted manifestos of a militant feminist group. She pauses to read them, noting with approval that these Italian women are more radical than their English counterparts, and applauding their demand that convicted rapists be castrated.

Within moments they encounter a man who will put the credibility of such sentiments to the test. Robert may be the incarnation of all that Mary and Colin repudiate, but when he materializes from the shadows to appropriate them, we are left in no doubt that there is nothing accidental about their meeting. It later transpires that Robert had targeted Colin and stalked the couple from the start. But somehow, at a depth of awareness they prefer not to plumb, Colin and Mary have been expecting him too. In chapter 1 we are told: 'They used expensive, duty-free colognes and powders on their bodies, they chose their clothes meticulously and without consulting the other, as though somewhere among the thousands they were soon to join, there waited someone who cared deeply how they appeared' (p. 11). And when Robert does finally crystallize before the couple, they seem to have conjured him up like some malign genie:

> She pointed at a doorway several yards ahead and, as if summoned, a squat figure stepped out of the dark into a pool of streetlight and stood blocking their path.
>
> 'Now look what you've done.' Colin joked and Mary laughed. (pp. 25–6)

Robert and Caroline are not so much a threat from without as the enemy within; they are less the monstrous antithesis of our hero and heroine than their secret sharers, their untethered alter egos.

At first glance, however, the contrast seems total. When Mary lingers over another feminist proclamation on their way to his bar, Robert explains apologetically:

> 'These are women who cannot find a man. They want to destroy everything that is good between men and women.' He added matter-of-factly, 'They are too ugly.' Mary watched him as she might a face on television.
>
> 'There,' said Colin, 'meet the opposition.' (p. 28)

They could hardly have been waylaid by a grosser caricature of macho posturing than this hirsute medallion man with his transparent black shirt split to the waist. But Robert's early biography is an object lesson in how to mangle a gentle child who adores his mother into a sadistic misogynist and closet homosexual who cripples his wife for life.

Robert, of course, views his rearing as the cultivation of a real man like his father and grandfather: ' "They were men, and they were proud of their sex. Women understood them too." Robert emptied his glass and added, "There was no confusion" ' (p. 75) whereas nowadays, he maintains, men hate themselves and women do not respect them, because

> 'whatever they might say they believe, women love aggression and strength and power in men [...] And even though they hate themselves for it, women long to be ruled by men. It's deep in their minds. They lie to themselves. They talk of freedom, and dream of captivity.' (p. 76)

His own wife is a limping testimony to the truth of his contention. She can imagine nothing more exalted than suffering utter agony and even death at the hands of the man she loves. As Caroline expounds to an incredulous Mary her creed of blissful subjection, an ocean of altered attitudes and ideals seems to divide the couples. Both women and both men appear to belong not simply to different generations and cultures, but to different galaxies.

Which is why Colin and Mary are so startled to discover, on their return from visiting Robert and Caroline, that their desire for each other has been rejuvenated and infused with a new kind of excitement. □

(Kiernan Ryan, *Ian McEwan*, 1994)[6]

Ryan concludes that the novel leaves the reader poised between the implications of its two epigraphs, the one by the American lesbian critic and poet Adrienne Rich (born 1929) – 'how we dwelt in two worlds / the daughters and the mothers / in the kingdom of the sons' (from 'Sibling Mysteries') – and the other by the Italian poet and novelist Cesare Pavese (1905–50), who committed suicide in a hotel room and whose most famous volume of poetry is the posthumous *Death Will Stare at Me Out of Your Eye (La morte e avrà i tuoi occhi,* 1951): 'Travelling is a brutality. It forces you to trust strangers and to lose sight of all that familiar comfort of home and friends ...'.

Developing the point about desire for the other with which the extract from Ryan ends, Judith Seaboyer reads *The Comfort of Strangers* as 'an exploration of the violent psychic dreams through which we imagine ourselves into existence as gendered subjects'.[7] In the following extract she considers this exploration in the light of the city setting of the novel. To an extent, because 'Venice' is unnamed it becomes any city – a symbolic landscape for the book's concerns. But it is also a specific city of conspicuous beauty consumed by tourists such as Colin and Mary; it is free from traffic and other signs of modern living, suggesting an older world, or a deeper one in the case of desire:

■ The actors in McEwan's psychodrama play out prescribed roles precisely because the script that structures their behaviour is invisible to them; psychic space proves as unmappable as the city of Venice, which I suggest is the perfect mirroring backdrop, at once a museum and a historical map for western culture. [...] McEwan's Venice serves as a metaphorical map against which to read and interpret not only Western history and culture but also our modernist and postmodernist understanding of the psyche, and at the same time it is a figure for ancient narratives of the labyrinth, that impenetrable space which resists mapping or topographical survey. For reasons that include its decaying beauty and watery, labyrinthine topography, Venice in all its seductive otherness has long been read as a figure for death and for the feminine body, hallucinatory object of and liminal obstacle to the hero's desire. [...] McEwan's Venice, material enough for all that it is an unnamed fantasy city, is alternately a clearly articulated space, all sunlit, glittering surface as it opens out from the Piazza San Marco onto the Lagoon and the Adriatic, and an illegible labyrinth, confusing and sinister as it collapses back into a womblike enclosure of narrow streets and canals [...] a figure for the end of everything as it slowly loses the battle against time, pollution and rising water levels and returns to the [...] Lagoon from which it was created. From this perspective, too, the Venetian stage is an ideal site for McEwan's story of Colin and Mary, English tourists in Venice, and Robert and Caroline, who live there: the dark, pure perversity of Robert and Caroline's relationship is the overt expression of that which, repressed, structures the somewhat dishonest, somewhat dull, occasionally passionate, largely comfortable normalcy of Colin and Mary's [...]

For all its labyrinthine confusion, this city is in many ways a clearly articulated space, its medieval construction rendered still more legible through Renaissance town planning ... [Colin and Mary] persistently leave behind the easily read tourist areas of San Marco and Dorsoduro for the labyrinthine alleys of Castello and Cannaregio, but 'the fine old churches, the altar-pieces, the stone bridges over the canals' (p. 10) remain alienated illegible fragments rather than taking on shape as individual parishes that have, over the centuries, coalesced into a complex but unified whole. By day they distractedly experience the city as a series of jumbled images projected in rapid succession against the screen of the eye as they are swept along on a tide of tourists. At night, after the crush subsides, instead of actively plotting a course on a map or choosing a path according to the logic of the city's configuration, they are led, passively, by their senses. They dip into what is for them an unmappable, invisible city after the manner of the flâneur [idle stroller], responding randomly to the tantalizing curve of a street, the smell of frying fish, the comforting sight of a distant stranger.

That this failure to map urban spaces proves deadly suggests by extension the careful attention that must be paid to the negotiation of cultural space, and also of McEwan's mirroring *textual* space. On the occasions Mary and Colin do resort to maps they find them to be either badly printed, incomplete, or a series of disconnected fragments, and they find, like McEwan's readers, that it is easy 'to get lost [*walking*] from one page to another' (p. 20). Colin and Mary move impulsively, their failure to read or to remember almost willful; we may of course choose to do the same, but for all the labyrinthine complexity of McEwan's text, it is possible to move back and forth within it, literally or by means of memory, recognizing and misrecognizing, remembering and misremembering, noting a repeated phrase or image, interpreting now this piece of the puzzle and now that, until pattern and meaning are gradually revealed. It is possible to make links between his images, words, and silences, and also to move beyond the bounds of the text itself, since if culture and the role of the 'dominant fiction' are to be understood and interpreted, it will be necessary to extrapolate an allegorical 'mental map of city space [...]

to that mental map of the social and global totality we all carry around in our heads in variously garbled forms'.[8]

McEwan plays on a Venetian sense of enclosure and claustrophobia by introducing only four characters. Three of them are alien to Venice. Mary and Colin move through a museum-like space in which one may look at a culture through its artifacts, skimming across the surface without the need to go deeper. Caroline is Canadian, and has been imprisoned within the house since her arrival with Robert several years earlier. Although Robert grew up in London, he inherited his grandfather's Venetian palazzo and functions within a milieu of local people as the other three do not. Of the four, only he has the key, the controlling power that comes from a knowledge of the city that enables him to co-opt it as a stage for the drama by means of which he will transform psychic reality into real event – although by the end of the text it is apparent that Caroline has been directing from the wings. □

(Judith Seaboyer, 'Sadism Demands a Story', 1999)[9]

At the centre of this performance is the chosen victim: Colin. The reason for Robert's selection of him can perhaps be seen in the close description of Colin at the start of chapter 5 (p. 58), when Mary and Colin awake at Robert's house. Here, Colin is the object of desire: childlike and beautiful, prone and passive – his delicate features and manner are both an affront and a temptation to Robert. On waking, Colin asks Mary, 'Where are we then?' (p. 59) but she has no more idea than he, having responded the previous night to Robert's guidance with 'the slow automation of a sleep-walker' (p. 56).

McEwan suggests that Colin and Mary as enlightened liberals are unable to assert themselves and their beliefs in the face of Robert's will. Colin's femininity and his desire to feel as women do (Colin 'said that he had long envied women's orgasms, and that there were times when he felt an aching emptiness, close to desire, between his scrotum and his anus', p. 79) mark him in the role of 'victim' for Robert, who sees him as a reminder of his former self as a boy and wishes to punish him for the 'weakness' he perceives in him, which is confirmed for him when Colin does not respond when Robert hits him. It is also fundamental to recall, in any reading of the novel, that Mary and Colin return to the apartment of their own accord. They walk towards their own abuse, not because they have made a promise to Caroline, but for reasons they never themselves voice, yet which Caroline and Robert seem to appreciate. Mary and Colin are expected to return to the scene, for reasons that are implicit in Angela Roger's discussion of their relationship:

■ Colin and Mary are represented as habitually rather than romantically attached to each other. Mary is portrayed as a mature, liberated middle-class woman, fairly content and undemanding of her partner. She has a history of feminist involvement, having once been a member of an all-woman theatre group. Their love is not a great passion; rather, as Mary explains to Caroline, it is a deep friendship which they share: 'I trust him. He's my closest friend' (p. 66). Indeed, her love for him is represented as more maternal and protective than sexual: 'Colin touched Mary's breasts, she turned and kissed first his lips and then, in a tender, motherly way, his nose' (p. 17). She adopts a protective posture even in sleep: 'their most characteristic embrace in sleep was for Mary to put her arms round Colin's neck, and Colin's arms round Mary's waist, and for their legs to cross' (p. 86). Mary's motherliness is also emphasized in the portrait of Mary and Colin together. As Mary is beginning to grasp the threat which Robert poses for Colin she is described as: 'hugg[ing] him hard' and 'cradl[ing] his head against her breasts' (p. 95). Colin for his part 'nursed at her breasts', which evokes for us a picture of the infantilised David with his girlfriend, Ruth, in 'Jack Flea's Birthday Celebration' [McEwan's first play for television, 1976], though here it is set in the context of a more mature relationship. By contrast to Mary, Caroline is dominated by her brutal husband, Robert, the embodiment of the traditional patriarch. The relationship between Robert and Caroline is based upon overt sado-masochism presented here as a natural development of physical love. McEwan portrays Caroline as a woman who has been fully inculcated into a patriarchal system, helping her mother to look after her father, and bolstering up Robert in the face of his embarrassment on their first meeting. She is defined, and is portrayed as defining herself, in terms of men. For example, Robert will speak about her only in terms of his own father: 'Robert said it was impossible to explain [how he had met his wife] without first describing his sisters and his mother, and these in turn could be explained only in terms of his father' (p. 30). Caroline, too, is presented as seeing herself in terms of men. In her discussion with Mary about a women-only theatre-group, for example, she articulates the view that whatever women may be acting out together, there must be a man waiting in the wings: 'A play with only women? I don't understand how that could work. I mean what could *happen*?' (p. 71). Mary tries to explain by analogy to their own situation, as part of a potential plot for a play: 'two women who have only just met sitting on a balcony talking'. To show the depth of her self-defeat, Caroline immediately counters, 'But they're probably waiting for a man [...] when he arrives [s]omething will happen' (p. 71). Caroline's version of the scenario proves more accurate of course, since all of the characters in the novel are being manipulated by Robert according to his own fantasies and behind Robert is the author who portrays the male/female relationship in specifically male terms.

McEwan explores Robert's view of womanhood in Freudian terms. He depicts Robert offering a description of his maltreatment in childhood at the hands of his sisters, of his authoritarian father, of the close relationship he had with Robert's mother, but Robert's own failure to father children, which McEwan suggests is a contributing cause of his need to dominate, is described by Caroline. Caroline becomes the victim of her husband's oppression, a typical battered wife, terrorized into submission and even into collusion in committing further atrocities with her husband. She is depicted as totally submissive to her husband, suffering the pain and humiliation of violence with supposed equanimity. The first glimpse Mary has of Caroline is of a ghostly presence: 'a small, pale face watching her from the shadows, a disembodied face [...] a perfectly oval face' (p. 63). The haunting image is sustained in Caroline's subsequent behaviour when she is depicted as though she does not have an independent existence; indeed, she is represented as so submissive that she is prepared to contemplate her own annihilation. At the point where she and Mary compare notes on the meaning of 'being in love', Caroline offers her own (or, rather, her husband's) definition: 'By "in love" I mean that you'd do anything for the other person, and [...] you'd let them do anything to you. [...] If you are in love with someone, you would even be prepared to let them kill you, if necessary' (p. 66). Significantly, Caroline qualifies this definition to make it gender-specific to women when Mary queries whether such a desire to kill the person one loves could also reside in a woman. [...]

It is clear why, in *The Comfort of Strangers*, Mary survives relatively unscathed and Caroline does not. Like Julie in *The Cement Garden*, Mary defines her own terms of engagement with men in her relationships. Mary could not have been the victim in *The Comfort of Strangers* because she has established her own identity as a woman, albeit a fairly undynamic one. Caroline, on the other hand, accepts and ultimately embraces Robert's construction of relationships which is premised on sadomasochism; incredibly, Mary is depicted at the end of the novel theorizing about what has happened: 'men's ancient dream of hurting, and women's of being hurt' (p. 134). If McEwan had shown Mary to possess the fortitude and strength of a mother-figure such as Julie in *The Child in Time*, her protective and nurturing attributes might have been allowed to save Colin. But Mary's maternal qualities are kept at a distance: her children have been left with her estranged husband and although she and Colin talk about being good parents McEwan does not provide any evidence of it. On the contrary, he details that they have not even sent their postcards or bought the children presents. The theory which Mary arrives at at the end of the novel does not explain Colin's treatment. To understand why Colin is destroyed in Robert's enactment of extreme domination, we must examine him from the perspective of Robert – he is not a 'real man', by which is meant one who subscribes to the patriarchal construction of relationships, and therefore he is equally prone to victimization. Furthermore, the argument that Caroline in particular and women in general collude in their subjugation also applies to Colin. He allows himself to be manipulated by Robert and significantly keeps the secret of the first punch to himself for a long time. The novel closes unsatisfactorily, allowing Robert to get away with his crimes, and it could be argued that McEwan himself is complicit in subscribing to the patriarchal power structures which the novel seeks to criticise. □

(Angela Roger, 'Ian McEwan's Portrayal of Women', 1996)[10]

McEwan's book is occupied throughout with the principled passivity that 'allows' aggression, male violence and patriarchy to be perpetuated. In terms of desire, Robert is not that far from Mary and Colin, the book suggests. The influence of his father and grandfather has brought out his will to power (in a domestic society otherwise comprising women), while his influence on Colin and Mary is to bring to the surface their aggression: Mary's fantasy is to cut off Colin's limbs and make him her slave, Colin's is to devise a machine to 'fuck' Mary brutally and inexorably (p. 86). McEwan adds debates over patriarchy and feminism to this mix, but the gender divide is not simplistically adhered to, as male aggression is not directed solely towards women, but towards beauty, towards that which is desired. In this case, it is Colin who is the object of Robert and Caroline's desire: a drive to possess that can only find fulfilment in the annihilation of the Other. McEwan is dealing here with the idea that human desire may be fundamentally underwritten by a master/slave dialectic, in which the roles are not fixed but contested, and individuals can move between the position of sadist and masochist, subject and object, dominator and dominated.[11]

The novel seemed to many critics to take McEwan to the end of a set of concerns he had embarked upon with his first short stories. His next novel would not appear for six years, by which time he had swapped the perspective of the child and the childlike for that of the adult and the parent obsessed with the care of the child and the loss of childhood.

CHAPTER FIVE

True Maturity: *The Child in Time* (1987)

Shall there be womanly times or shall we die?
    Are there men unafraid of gentleness?
Can we have strength without aggression,
Without disgust,
Strength to bring feeling to the intellect?
Shall we change or shall we die?
(*or Shall We Die?*)[1]

Or Shall We Die? was performed at London's Royal Festival Hall, with a score by Michael Berkeley, in 1983. It was Berkeley who also introduced McEwan to Michael Tippett's (1905–98) oratorio *A Child of Our Time* (1938), which influenced not only McEwan's writing of *or Shall We Die?*, but also the title of his next novel. *The Child in Time* was met with general critical approval but also with a certain surprise that McEwan had broadened out from the somewhat claustrophobic concerns of the short stories and of his first two novels.[2] McEwan describes its genesis in *A Move Abroad* (1989):

■ In the summer of 1983, two months after *The Ploughman's Lunch* had been released, I found myself tilting my chair and daydreaming about a novel I might write. I began to make notes. I was about to become a father, and my thoughts were narrowed and intensified. I was haunted by the memory, or perhaps the memory of a dream, of a footpath that emerges onto a bend in a country road. It is luxuriant high summer, and there is a fine drizzle. There is a pub just along the road. A figure who is me and not me is walking towards it, certain that he is about to witness something of overwhelming importance. Writing *The Child in Time*, which took me to the end of 1986, was about the discovery of what that man saw. Other elements – a man pulled from the wreckage of a lorry, a birth, a lost child, a man who attempts to return to his childhood, an authoritarian childcare handbook, the elusive and protean nature of time – all these seemed to rotate about this central scene, and would somehow

> explain it, or contribute to it. In other words, I had a detail, a country road on a certain day, an echo whose apparent urgency was its only justification, and this seemed the proper starting point for a novel. □
>
> (Ian McEwan, *A Move Abroad*, 1989)[3]

McEwan's third novel, initially set in the 'last decent summer' of the 1990s (probably 1996, judging by internal clues such as the Olympic Games earlier in the year), is interested in the intersection between the personal and the public. This manifests itself most explicitly in the novel's concern with both the private childcare of parents and the interest professionals and the government take in the rearing of children. McEwan explains that he was partly inspired by reading Christina Hardyment's book *Dream Babies: Three Centuries of Good Advice on Childcare* (1983), 'a sort of history of childcare manuals' in which McEwan believed Hardyment was suggesting that childcare manuals accurately indicate 'the spirit of an age': 'You have the intense regulation of the Victorian notion of breaking a child's will, followed by a rather sentimental child-centred Edwardian view, followed by the rather grisly pseudo-scientific notion of childcare that predominated in the 1920s and '30s, with a lot of input from behaviourists, and then in 1948 ... Spock.'[4]

McEwan thought that in the 1980s it was probably time for another childcare guide to come to prominence, and the extracts that preface each of the chapters of *The Child in Time* are snippets intended at one time for a parodic 1980s manual that McEwan considered writing. In practice he restricted the manual to these extracts, which are supposedly taken from 'The Authorised Childcare Handbook' eventually written by Charles Darke, the novel's publisher-turned-politician.

One of the most striking aspects of *The Child in Time* is the fact that McEwan sets it ten years on from his time of writing, as though attempting to indicate the direction British society might be taking. For Malcolm Bradbury, probably thinking of *Black Dogs* and *Enduring Love*, McEwan's first novel set in the future in some ways anticipates McEwan's own thematic concerns in the 1990s.

> ■ [*The Child in Time*] is set in a future English world, a degraded Thatcherite Britain, where there is licensed begging, private ambulance services, an armed police force (not a bad set of prophecies); and this plot too depends on a striking 'time-slip'. But this is McEwan's most social novel to date; here what had essentially been private concerns, personal fantasies and psychic disorders become public and political ones. Childhood, always central in McEwan's fiction, is the main theme, but now no longer seen as an angle on a hard adult world from a child's perplexed and ambiguous point of view, but as an element in the ambiguous world of contemporary family life. The story involves the abduction of

a child from a supermarket, a grim road accident and the regression of an adult to his own failed and tattered boyhood. Stephen Lewis, a writer of children's books who has lost both wife and daughter, is the protagonist. The theme of the novel – the nature of childhood, the welfare of children – is seriously considered and carefully worked; the reintegration of the child within the adult, and the regeneration of male, female and child through love. This was a book that laid down many of the themes of McEwan's fiction of the Nineties, where questions of malign powers and restoration of hope would be posed. □

(Malcolm Bradbury, *The Modern British Novel, 1878–2001*, 2001)[5]

For other critics, such as D. J. Taylor, the expansion into a wider political world was the weakest part of the novel because it revealed McEwan's limitations by unconvincingly portraying a dystopian society in a derivative and piecemeal fashion:

■ Set in a drab, authoritarian future – a conscious projection of the straight leftist view of third-term Thatcherism – it has three main components: the attempt of Stephen Lewis, a successful writer of children's books, to find his lost infant daughter and repair the relationship with his estranged wife; his membership of a government commission on childcare; and his dealings with a former government minister, once his publisher, who is regressing to a state of childhood. In a tangle of quotations from 'The Authorised Childcare Handbook' McEwan's intentions are not hard to disinter. Charles, the publisher turned politician, is a peacock parody of the rising Tory MP [...]. The commission supplies an opportunity to send up the traditionalist point of view in education [...]. Elsewhere there are reports of 'riots in a northern suburb', of nuclear submarines nosing out into the cold North Sea. There is nothing wrong with that in itself – hats off to McEwan for mixing it with the politicians – but as fiction it doesn't work. The style, in describing the commission's proceedings, is formal and fatigued: the political debate is sheer caricature, and while it may be that McEwan is sending up the more arid aspects of committee land and the low level of national political engagement, this does not make for an alluring prose style.

By contrast, the novel's informal scenes – particularly those describing Stephen's relationship with his wife, his musings over his lost child, his reflections on his own fugitive past – strike a consistently relaxed yet forceful note. Similarly, the portions of the book devoted to Stephen's conversations with Charles's physicist wife offer a sustained meditation on the individual and time. As an examination of the way in which families function, the novel is masterly. As an examination of the way in which people formally react to political contingency it strikes me as fundamentally flawed. Despite its continual felicities of style and observation,

The Child in Time has still not solved the question of how far 'politics' can go without irritating the reader or undermining the writer's sense of himself. □

(D. J. Taylor, *A Vain Conceit*, 1988)[6]

Like Taylor, Allan Massie situates the success of the novel in the central depiction of Stephen; a view that echoes the opinion of several critics that McEwan's expansion into social politics revealed that he was best focusing on the family.

■ *The Child in Time*, though a far less confident piece of craftsmanship than his first two [novels], being confused in theme and uneven in the writing, nevertheless revealed a humanity and capacity to feel, and to arouse feeling, which had been absent from his earlier work … . It belongs to the tradition of the 'Condition of England Novel'.[7] It offers McEwan's view of Thatcher's England, a country teeming with licensed beggars, in which control is exercised in the name of freedom, and where poverty and squalor are to be found everywhere in the midst of affluence. The picture owes as much to the conventions of science fiction, especially in the cinema, as it does to observation or imagination, but it is powerful enough, even at second-hand.

One theme is the disintegration of a politician whose public life, as his wife puts it, has been 'all frenetic compensation for what he took to be an excess of vulnerability'. This is handled dramatically enough, though the effect is weakened when McEwan slides into the whimsy of his early short stories. Most remarkable, and certainly most satisfactory, is the treatment of his central character, a young novelist who has lost his daughter, abducted from a supermarket, two years earlier. [...] The character's fear, self-disgust and despair are convincingly done, and in two scenes, one with the hero's former wife, the other with his father, McEwan for the first time treats adult emotion with sympathy and understanding. □

(Allan Massie, *The Novel Today 1970–89*, 1990)[8]

Critical of *The Child in Time* for entirely different reasons from those adduced by Massie, Adam Mars-Jones positions the novel as a masculinist narrative masquerading as a feminist one. Stephen's vision is seen a way of placing himself as the cause of his own birth. Mars-Jones thinks 'the fantasy that underlies the whole book is uncomfortably naked' in Stephen's vision. 'It becomes rather too evident that the desires of a man so taken up with the processes and privileges of reproduction actually move towards doing without women, or certainly minimising their part in the creation of life.'[9] He goes on to position the book as an example of 'symbolic ownership':

■ The nearest, by contrast, that the book comes to acknowledging that fathers can be manipulative, even destructive, is in its portrayal of

Charles Darke, whose paternity is of course purely symbolic. Darke publishes Stephen's novel *Lemonade* and makes him famous, but exacts the price that it is marketed (not at all Stephen's intention) as a children's book. Darke promotes him in a way that is also a demotion, both making and unmaking him as a man. There is a similar pattern to Stephen's involvement in an Official Commission on Childcare – he is only appointed to it through Charles Darke's influence, but Darke also writes the unofficial document which pre-empts the Committee's work and makes its conclusions irrelevant. Darke gives, and Darke takes away.

But Darke is not a real father, and his sponsorship of Stephen is a manipulative perversion of the real thing. The conclusion of the novel's Darke-strand is that men who do not produce children are condemned to become them. Charles Darke produces a guide to childcare that is oppressively authoritarian, but himself longs to return to an infantile irresponsibility. In the novel, he gets to realise this fantasy, in a way that leads to his death. He becomes a failed and futureless child.

Each chapter of *The Child in Time* is headed by a passage from *The Authorised Childcare Handbook*, the volume written by Charles Darke. Darke functions in the book as a whole as a decoy, making Stephen's version of masculinity seem natural by the contrast with his highly unstable overcompensations, but the extracts from his book play an even more useful distracting role. They enable McEwan to conjure up a world in which the family is at threat from within.

However much the world has changed around Ian McEwan in the years since he started writing, it seems fair to say that he has changed more. In his early stories the only rule about sex seemed to be that it should *not* take place, with marital commitment and reproductive intent, within a fertile cleft – and the further removed it was from the situation the more it seemed to interest him. It would be hard to extrapolate this state of affairs backwards from *The Child in Time*, now that desire has been so completely mortgaged to the creation of new life. To read McEwan's novels in order, from the fixated adolescents of *The Cement Garden* through the drily passionate couple, childless and solipsistic, of *The Comfort of Strangers*, to the exemplary carers of *The Child in Time*, is to trace a drastic retraction of libido. (His new novel *The Innocent* seems to acknowledge that this progression has reached a dead end by starting again with virginity and romantic love.)

But it would be as much a mistake to exaggerate the distance this author has travelled as to ignore it. Just as McEwan's early stories contained an element of artificial perversity, so *The Child in Time* conceals within it, for all its emphasis on universal experiences of love and loss, a fierce private agenda. There is a strong paradoxical thread leading from the apparent, but perhaps misleading, coldness of his early work and the apparent, but perhaps also misleading, warmth of the maturity announced by *The Child in Time*.

Charles Darke's wife delivers the verdict on her husband that his case '"was just an extreme form of a general problem"', men's inability to carry over the virtues of their immaturity into adulthood. Stephen agrees with this argument, and Thelma Darke then briefly turns it against him, saying his indulgence of his emotions since Kate's disappearance has been a form of wilful blindness, and moreover a refusal of knowledge.

This fleeting indictment has a certain amount of authority, since by gender and profession Thelma unites the novel's two strongest images of mutability profounder than the established order: femininity and the new physics. But it is the last of Stephen's ordeals before the novel gives him his reward. It will be everything he dreamed of.

The procedures of *The Child in Time* are intensely 'feminine', as men tend to use that word, indirect and dissembling, making each fresh inroad seem like a retreat. But now the book moves up a number of gears, from deferent advances to submissive annexation. McEwan mounts an extraordinarily daring raid on the citadel of fertility. In the last, closely written scene of the book, Stephen attends the birth of a child he did not even know Julie was expecting. (The couple have hardly communicated since Stephen's visit to the country during which the child was conceived, the same visit that gave him his vision of his parents).

The Child in Time is a narrative of pain and loss, but it is also a suppressed drama of symbolic ownership. The irony of its construction is that the disappearance of Kate makes the claims of her parents artificially equal. Only in the absence of the child does it become possible for the father's claims to be heard so favourably. The missing daughter becomes common property, and Stephen's feelings can dominate the novel.

Consequently, when Stephen finds Julie close to term, her pregnancy – suddenly looming, without preparation – seems more than anything an objective correlative to the development Stephen has undergone during the novel. But he receives more gifts from the fiction he inhabits than that. He and Julie make love, and their love-making flows into, if it doesn't actually trigger, the birth. □

(Adam Mars-Jones, *Venus Envy*, 1990)[10]

Perhaps surprisingly, the gender politics of the novel have thus been scrutinised by critics as much as those of *The Comfort of Strangers*. There should, however, be a sense of progression within the book after the early responses that Stephen and Julie have to Kate's disappearance: 'He was angry with Julie, disgusted by what he took to be a feminine self-destructiveness, a wilful defeatism. [...] He suspected – and it turned out later he was correct – that she took his efforts to be a typically masculine evasion, an attempt to mask feelings behind displays of competence and organisation and physical effort' (p. 24). Progression is also there throughout the novel inasmuch as Stephen follows the four stages of loss outlined in John Bowlby's influential study of attachment and loss: numbing; searching for the lost figure; disorganization; and reorientation to reality.[11]

It is also evident that McEwan addresses, and perhaps anticipates, Mars-Jones's kind of criticisms within the book: 'Against the faith men had in the institutions they and not women had shaped, women upheld some principle of selfhood in which being surpassed doing. Long ago men had noted something unruly in this. Women simply enclosed the space which men longed to penetrate. The men's hostility was aroused' (p. 55). In interview, McEwan has glossed this viewpoint: 'I think, men's insistence on power, in relationships or in society, is based on fear; fear maybe of being engulfed, fear that might have its roots in childhood dependency on a woman.'[12]

The Child in Time partly attempts to confront the stereotypes of gender by refusing to identify the sex of two people: the Prime Minister and the baby born at the narrative's conclusion. The baby's sex is not revealed to the reader, or yet to the characters, exemplifying the novel's themes of unexpected, uncontrollable life-factors and the ways in which gender is socially constructed. The complexities of life and its unpredictability are at all points in the novel represented by the theme of time, which takes everyone out of an unalterable past, through a known stable moment of the present into an uncertain, contingent future.

Yet, it is the book's concern with the meaning of childhood that has attracted most attention. In McEwan's first novel, children had to become their own parents; in his second, a couple reverted to a vulnerable childhood state; and in his third, the novel most concerned with the responsibilities of adult life, the direct relationship between children and parents is oddly absent. The presence of children is removed at the start of the novel and only reintroduced on its closing page. Thus, *The Child in Time* is far more concerned with the child within the adult than with children in themselves. When Stephen recalls Kate he fondly remembers 'her lessons in celebrating the specific', and asks himself: 'Wasn't that Nietzsche's idea of true maturity, to attain the seriousness of a child at play?' (pp. 105–6). By contrast, Stephen as an adult has lost the child within himself: 'He was partly somewhere else, never quite paying attention, never wholly serious' (p. 105). Yet, to return to childhood, like Charles Darke, would be a kind of death; thus the novel suggests that the mature individual has to balance the child and the adult, like the ego balancing the demands of the superego and the id. McEwan has elaborated on how the theme of childhood related to his interest in time:

■ there are many notions played with in *The Child in Time* that I'm not sure I really hold with, but that were attractive and convenient in an exploration, an investigation of childhood and how it sits within us all our lives, and how in some respects, when we contemplate our whole existence, it seems to be in a perpetual present. That's a very subjective sense of time and childhood, of course, but I was rather intrigued by the way that certain quantum-mechanical versions of time seem to completely undo the standard clock-time sense of it, and I thought that I could forge – with a little bit of creaking and groaning from the subject itself – a connection between the mathematically-based notion of time and all sorts of other versions of it: not only the permanent sense of the whole past living inside your head, but also the way time accelerates in a crisis. Remember, too, that the novel more or less unfolds within the gestation period of a pregnancy. The child is conceived in chapter three and the novel then is framed by that sense of impending arrival. □

(Margaret Reynolds and Jonathan Noakes (eds), *Ian McEwan: the Essential Guide*, 2002)[13]

So, the novel pointedly begins with the loss of one child and ends with the arrival of another. Its nine chapters echo the nine months of gestation, the foetus's gradual development in some way corresponding to Stephen's own slow growth to maturation, described by Ellen Pifer:

■ Stephen's journey toward true maturity, the process by which he wakes up to existence and discovers how to participate more fully in it, begins with the loss of his child. Kate's disappearance shatters the complacent routine of his life as it shatters his marriage. As many similarly discover when catastrophe strikes, the conventional wisdom by which we tend to live, automatically and half consciously, proves inadequate or useless in times of crisis. Hurled into stark confrontation with themselves, each other, and their environment, Stephen and Julie must summon more courage, insight and awareness than were ever demanded of them before [...].

In *The Child in Time* the stages of Stephen's interior journey are marked by a series of literal journeys, each of which ends in a telling insight or epiphany. In nearly every case the revelation involves an experience of time that radically diverges from the conventional version. Represented in the novel by the clocks of quotidian life (Stephen's parents meet in a department store over a broken clock) is the linear, mechanical version of time measured in minutes and hours. Within that framework, signalled by the sudden expansion or 'slowing of time', Stephen discovers a dimension of 'meaningful time' intimately linked with the child's image. When, for example, he makes his initial visit to Thelma and Charles at their cottage in Suffolk, he humours his friend by climbing to the tree house Charles has constructed high up in a beech tree. Though appalled by the 'absurdity' of his middle-aged friend's appearance and behaviour, Stephen has a sudden insight when faced with making his way up the dangerous, seemingly 'endless, vertiginous branching' of the tall tree. Aware that he is 'risking his life', he has to summon all his powers of concentration to keep from crashing to the ground. At this crucial moment he realizes that he cannot afford to be half conscious, half in the moment and half outside it: 'It occurred to me fleetingly that he was engrossed, fully in the moment. Quite simply, if he allowed another thought to distract him, he would fall out of the tree' (p. 110).

Here a life-or-death situation thrusts Stephen into that mode of existing *in* time – of 'fill[ing] the present and be[ing] filled by it' – that he had earlier identified with the child, for whom 'the moment [is] everything' (p. 105). Earlier that day, on his way to the Darkes' cottage, Stephen has had another near brush with death. Speeding along the highway, he barely manages to avoid crashing into a huge pink truck that has jack-knifed in front of him. By fully concentrating on the moment, Stephen saves himself from disaster; instead of becoming distracted by fear or trying to analyze the situation, he exercises a form of 'magical thinking'. Relaxing *into* the moment, he 'imagine[s] himself into the [six-foot] gap' between a 'road sign and the front bumper' of 'the upended lorry' – and miraculously drives through it. As though expanded by Stephen's vital participation in the moment, time appears to slow down; and 'in this slowing of time, there was a sense of a fresh beginning' (p. 94). Afterward, Stephen's sense of rebirth is validated by his rescue of the truck driver stuck in the overturned cab, his head 'protrud[ing] from a vertical gash in the steel' (p. 96). As Stephen pulls the man's body from the 'dark chamber' of the crushed cab, his rescue graphically simulates the delivery of a newborn child into the world (pp. 97–8). Here and throughout, the novel signals the principal stages of Stephen's recovery, his renewed participation in existence, with images of birth and rebirth. The image of the child, particularly the newborn, serves once again as a sign of hope: the embodiment of humankind at its most potent, poised on the threshold of a fresh beginning.

Such intense participation in the moment, or the fullness of time, is utterly lacking in Darke's studied and static reconstruction of boyhood, with its regulation-style short pants, slingshot, and sticky sweets. Graphically hinting at the sterility of Charles's regression is the image that concludes Stephen's visit to his friend's tree house. Summoned to dinner by Thelma at the end of the day, Charles exits the tree house through a hole he has cut in its platform. As Stephen waits for his friend to descend below him, he observes Darke's middle-aged 'head show[ing] above the level of the platform' just before it disappears, in a kind of reverse birth, through 'the hole' (p. 114). This image suggests the most extreme and unnatural form of regression: an attempt to return to the womb. In a sense, that is exactly what Darke does. In his desire to regress, he forces his wife to serve as his mother and nurse. The image of Darke's head disappearing down the hole offers a dramatic contrast to the truck driver Joe's head emerging from the gash in the truck cab from which Stephen delivers him. The awakening that attends Joe's brush with death prompts him, moreover, to stop running away from his adult responsibilities. Realizing how much he loves his wife and children, he promptly composes a good-bye letter to his girlfriend (p. 100). □

(Ellen Pifer, *Demon or Doll: Images of the Child in Contemporary Writing and Culture*, 2000)[14]

McEwan has said that his third novel had its origins in a number of ideas and enthusiasms: 'One of them was a recurrent dream, the sort of dream that you only remember that you've had before when it comes again – finally I remembered it and wrote it down. [...] This dream was of myself on a drizzly day walking along a country footpath and coming to a bend in the road and pausing there, with a very powerful premonition that if I walked off to my left I would come to a place ... a pub or a meeting place of some sort, and I would find out something very important about my origins.'[15] This dream is transposed in the novel into the seemingly impossible event of Stephen's vision across time, an incident that can be explained from the perspectives of art, religion, or science (like the three endings of *Enduring Love*). McEwan had been interested in science since childhood and in the years before the publication of *The Child in Time* continued to read books on Newtonian physics, quantum mechanics and relativity theory. Science's connection to Stephen's vision in *The Child in Time* is discussed by Jack Slay:

■ Time, in fact, is the key to discovering the child that dwells within each adult. As Roberta Smoodin writes, this lost childhood remains in the mature adult 'not only in memory but in a kind of time that spirals in upon itself, seems to be recapturable in some plausible intermingling of Einstein and Proust, quantum physics and magic realism.'[16] This magical, whimsical aspect of time is delightfully obvious through Stephen's course of recovery, during which he experiences periods of time that seem to slow, to elongate, or to warp completely out of context.

For example, in journeying to visit Charles and Thelma, Stephen narrowly escapes a serious automobile accident. When a lorry overturns in front of his car and forces him to veer dangerously between the wrecked vehicle and a road sign, Stephen experiences a 'slowing of time' (p. 93), one in which time itself seems to stall momentarily, allowing him to record events with unnatural clarity. Dodging the lorry but coming so close to the road sign that it shears away his door handle and side mirror, Stephen is at first elated by the near miss and then stunned by the fact that the entire incident had 'lasted no longer than five seconds' (p. 95). Later, after being rescued by Stephen, the lorry driver also expresses having experienced a similar slowing of time. Asking, ' "How long was I in there? Two hours? Three?" ' he finds it incredible when Stephen replies, ' "Ten minutes. Or less" ' (p. 100). Time, inexplicably, is apparently malleable, a concept that Stephen has difficulty in understanding; nonetheless, it is an idea – like the mysterious child within himself – that he accepts as an ordinary aspect of an extraordinary world.

An even more astonishing distortion of time occurs when Stephen encounters a flaw in time. In an episode of magical realism, Stephen steps into the past and meets his parents. Walking through the countryside, in a place he has never before been, Stephen experiences an overwhelming sense of familiarity, an eerie sense of *déjà vu*. Coming across an old tavern, he senses that 'the day he now inhabited was not the day he had woken into [...] He was in another time' (pp. 57–8). Seeing a young couple through the tavern window, he experiences 'not recognition so much as its shadow, not its familiar sound but a brief resonance ...' (p. 58). When the young woman looks out and stares intently at Stephen, he suddenly, inexplicably, realizes that she is his mother.

Stephen is baffled by this incident, uncertain about how to accept seeing his parents in a time before he existed. Not until his mother relives the event, through the 'timelessness of memory' (p. 166), does Stephen begin to understand the repercussions of his experience with time.[17] Claire tells her son of the courtship between her and his father,[18] and the dilemma that they faced when she became pregnant. It was at the small tavern – where Stephen experienced the contortion of time – that Douglas had indirectly suggested an abortion. Before answering her husband-to-be, before considering the implications of marriage or abortion, Claire looked out the tavern window and experienced her own distortion of time:

> 'I can see it now as clearly as I can see you. There was a face at the window, the face of a child, sort of floating there, it was staring into the pub. It had a kind of pleading look, and it was so white, white as an aspirin, it was looking right at me. Thinking about it over the years, I realize it was probably the landlord's boy, or some other kid off one of the local farms. But as far as I was concerned then, I was convinced, I just *knew* that I was looking at my own child. If you like, I was looking at you.' (p. 175)

From that point in time, she says, the baby was not 'an abstraction [...]. It was ... a complete self, begging for its existence, and it was inside her, unfolding intricately, living off the pulse of her own blood' (p. 175). Thus, Stephen himself becomes a child in time, magically appearing 44 years later as the face his mother sees just weeks after his conception. In a sense, then, Stephen confirms his own existence. However, the full significance of his experience is not revealed until the end of the novel; when he has his interlude with the past, Stephen is just hours away from creating his own child in time.

Stephen continually ponders his seemingly preternatural experiences with time as well as the mysterious nature of time itself. Thelma, a theoretical physicist, offers scientific explanations, speaking to him as she would a classroom full of scientists, revealing that 'there's a whole supermarket of theories these days' (p. 117). For example, she lectures, one possibility ' "has the world dividing every infinitesimal fraction of a second into an infinite number of possible versions, constantly branching and proliferating, with consciousness neatly picking its way through to create the illusion of a stable reality" ' (p. 117). Another theory states that ' "time is variable. We know it from Einstein, who is still our bedrock here. In relativity theory, time is dependent on the speed of the observer" ' (pp. 117–18). Yet another theory suggests that time is a separate entity in and of itself: ' "In the big-bang theory, time is thought to have been created at the same moment as matter, it's inseparable from it" ' (p. 118). The only certainty about time, Thelma says, is its uncertainty ' "... whatever time is, the common-sense, everyday version of it as linear, regular, absolute, marching from left to right, from the past through the present to the future, is either nonsense or a tiny fraction of the truth" ' (p. 117). *The Child in Time* exemplifies how time is not a certainty, not a reality in the world. Rather, as in Stephen's experience, it is a magical essence of life, an inexplicable entity that allows Kate to grow and exist within her father, that allows the ephemeral childhood of each person to continue existing throughout life, that enables Stephen to encounter his mother's decision to let him live. Time, then, is as ambiguous and as difficult as life itself. □

(Jack Slay, *Ian McEwan*, 1996)[19]

The conversation between Stephen and Thelma discussed by Slay also touches upon literary considerations of time, most notably T. S. Eliot's lines from *Four Quartets* (1943): 'Time present and time past / Are both perhaps present in time future, / And time future contained in time past' (it is worth remembering that when he wrote 'Lemonade', which was mistakenly read by a publisher's editor of not adult but children's fiction, Stephen was aiming to be a novelist in the style of the great modernists such as James Joyce or the German author Thomas Mann, 1875–1955). It is thus clear that in *The Child in Time* as much as in *Enduring Love* McEwan is interested in exploring the differences and similarities between the explanations and convictions of science and art.

Dominic Head considers McEwan's novel to be the most striking recent example in fiction of the influence of the new physics:

■ McEwan here employs a post-Einsteinian conception of the plasticity of time and space to allow his protagonist to intervene in the past and secure his own future. Such a fluid perception of time suits McEwan's purpose admirably in a novel about the child within us all, and the need to foster strong personal, and inter-generational bonds as a necessary component of the healthy body politic. But there is an intriguing impulse to push beyond this essentially metaphorical connection between the social theme and the scientific speculation. ... McEwan [via Thelma] insists on the possibility of a literal explanation for the fantastic experience. Partly, this is a strategy to distance this political novel from the less tangible operations of magic realism; at the same time, McEwan's novel serves to undermine scientific pretensions to the discovery of absolute truth. If the discussion of 'a higher order of theory' (p. 118) in the field of physics stands, ultimately, as a metaphor for McEwan's social theme, so too does McEwan remind us that all science must have recourse to metaphor, in seeking to explain phenomena for which there are no pre-existing terms. The new science, in *The Child in Time*, might be said simply to reinforce the novel's unique capacity to unite past, present, and future in the depiction of personal time. □

(Dominic Head, *Modern British Fiction*, 2002)[20]

To an extent in contrast to Head, Ben Knights sees *The Child in Time* as a green parable that 'addresses itself to a world seen to have gone disastrously wrong'.[21] The roots of that disaster lie in patriarchy for Knights, and he feels that McEwan's novel is asking society to link public policy and feeling back together. Knights also wonders with Mars-Jones if, in a book where the private and public worlds still seem to be drawn along gender lines, there is a 'strong suggestion of womb-envy' in McEwan's hankering after 'an androgynous harmony to which men might gain at least symbolic access'.[22]

■ The new social world with its gridlocked cities, decayed public services, its armed police and its licensed beggar scheme, is the product of public policy knowingly espoused. Yet the sense of apocalyptic catastrophe which broods over this novel has to do with more than the accelerating destruction of the social and biological environment. This is also a world perched on the brink of nuclear war, a disaster which, again in a chilling flashback, we understand almost happened during the Olympic Games crisis earlier in the year (p. 34 and following pages). Such items are not just part of the stage-set for the plot, a kind of painted backdrop for the story. The vulnerability of human life, and the fragility of the collective arrangements for the maintenance of that life lie at the core of McEwan's novel.[23] The social, ecological, and political environment is at the heart of the story. It is in this sense that I am arguing that *The Child in Time* may be read as a 'green parable.' But if it is a green parable, it is one in which masculinity, fathering, and gender relations figure prominently.

The thread that connects the elements of *The Child in Time* concerns public policy and political power. From the very beginning of the novel it is made clear that the social realm has been given its contemporary shape by acts of public policy, the breakdown of public transport providing a metonymy for some of the results. (The remaining trains have an important narrative function in the novel in bridging separated worlds: journeys towards death and towards new life.) The whole novel is a critique of mainstream masculinity and patriarchal power, and it is fundamental to that critique that the public policy articulated and sustained by such power violates both the natural and the social worlds. The devastation of both environment and nurturing matrix is a masculine accomplishment. Early in the novel Stephen (here the voice of the narrative) reflects the 'art of bad government was to sever the line between public policy and intimate feeling' (pp. 8–9), and the whole novel appears to be a symbolic attempt to redress that severance by realigning the mutual interaction of the public and the private domains. □

(Ben Knights, *Writing Masculinities*, 1999)[24]

Finally, taking up the 'important narrative function' of trains that Knights alludes to, Paul Edwards offers a reading of the third chapter of the novel in the context of British literary responses to modernity, especially those of the poet Philip Larkin (1922–85) and the poet and critic Donald Davie (1922–95). In his reading, Edwards also touches on Stephen's passivity in the early stages of the narrative, where his agency is minimal, epitomised by his half-hearted engagement with the childcare sub-committee. This is as much a comment on the sociopolitical malaise as on Stephen's lethargy, a wider state of affairs that engenders the Larkinesque misanthropy Edwards mentions: 'The audiences, however, brought him to bouts of delirious misanthropy. ... The faces tilted into the studio lights were those of adults, parents, workers, but the wide open expressions were those of children watching a teatime party conjurer' (p. 124). McEwan presents an infantilized culture, brought back to childlike obedience by television hosts as much as by the Prime Minister, the 'nation's parent'.

■ [Chapter 3] begins with a train journey. Railways are themselves, the novel slyly reminds us at one point, the stuff of politics: 'The Prime Minister ... was known to despise railways' (p. 186). In terms of the opposition between Thatcherite politics and the values of childhood, this has a significance that is playfully indicated in the narrative when Stephen makes his way down to Sussex after the pregnant Julie's urgent summons. Arriving too late for the final train (he has no car, again in opposition to the 'great car economy' – Baroness Thatcher's phrase – that is shown as choking the city in the novel), he persuades a train driver to give him a lift in the cab of the engine. The line, with its cathedral-like tunnels, will shortly be closed and replaced by a motorway. We already know that Stephen still nourishes a boyhood ambition to ride in a railway engine cab (p. 191). The journey thus becomes emblematic of the fortuitous (how else can it occur?) integration of the boy within the man, and thus forms a contrast with Charles Darke's willed and artificial second childhood. Within Chapter Three itself a brief passage of recollection has already made the association between childhood and trains, as well as linking both to a sense of wonder that subtly prepares for the ghostly experience at the pub. As a child, standing on the footbridge over the railway, Stephen has asked his father why the lines grew together as they got further away. His father had explained that this was because

> the trains got smaller and smaller as they moved away, and that to accommodate them the rails did the same. Otherwise there would be derailments. Shortly after that an express shook the bridge as it shot beneath their feet. Stephen marvelled then at the intricate relation of things, the deep symmetry which conspired to narrow the rail's gauge precisely in keeping with the train's diminishment; no matter how fast it rushed, the rails were always ready. (p. 51)

His father's explanation is a fiction, of course, a story to be told to a child, but it is a fiction which expresses truth and reveals it to the child. It thus forms a miniature apologia for the form of the novel itself.

But railway trains and train journeys also have a particular place in the English poetic tradition, where they serve to define a certain sense of the nation, from Edward Thomas's 'Adlestrop' and Auden's 'Night Mail' to Philip Larkin's 'The Whitsun Weddings' and 'Here' [poems suggestive of Englishness by Edward Thomas (1878–1917), W. H. Auden (1907–73) and Philip Larkin].[25] The Larkin poems are both central exhibits in Donald Davie's discussion of the 'lowered sights' of post-war British poetry in *Thomas Hardy and British Poetry* [1973]. Both of these poems also seem to me to lie behind Chapter Three of *The Child in Time*. Davie makes what is now a common point about the English landscape that appears in Larkin's poems; that its heterogeneous confusion of the industrial, sub-urban, post-industrial and pre-industrial reflects for the first time in English poetry both the bare fact of that landscape and the manner in which we take its degradation for granted. McEwan's description of the landscape is clearly in the tradition that Larkin initiated. Mildly infected with a Larkinesque misanthropy, Stephen shuts himself away from the other 'customers' in a first-class compartment:

> They ran along the rear gardens of Victorian terraces whose back additions offered glimpses through open doors into kitchens, past Edwardian and pre-war semis, and then they were threading through suburbs, southwards then eastwards, past encampments of minute, new houses with dirty, well-thumbed scraps of country in between. The train slowed over a tangle of junctions and shuddered to a halt. In the abrupt, expectant silence exuded by railway lines he realised how impatient he was to arrive. They had stopped by a new housing estate of raw undersized semi-detached houses, starter homes for first time buyers. The front gardens were still rutted earth; out the back, fluttering white nappies proclaimed from diagrammatic, metal trees a surrender to a new life. Two infants, hand in hand, staggered beneath the washing and waved at the train.
>
> Shortly before his stop it began to rain. (p. 50)

The passage (and I have quoted only a part of it) is a beautiful set of variations on 'The Whitsun Weddings': 'We ran Behind the backs of houses ... the next town, new and nondescript, Approached with acres of dismantled cars ... now fields were building plots ... And as the tightened brakes took hold, there swelled A sense of falling, like an arrow-shower Sent out of sight, somewhere becoming rain.' Larkin's poem is not simply about landscape, of course. It is about weddings, and the mixed values and emotions that marriages (and by implication, parenthood) imply. Its conclusion, like many of the better moments in Larkin's poetry, represents a triumph over the small-minded misanthropy shown in the descriptions of the wedding parties themselves. And that triumph (in absolute terms not much more than an acceptance of the reality of other people's emotional lives, whose field will be the continuation of the species) is expressed largely in terms of transformed pastoral. The syntactic complementarity in 'Now fields were building plots' (carrying its ghostly equivalent: now building plots were fields) is realised in the famous and still startling lines:

> I thought of London spread out in the sun
> Its postal districts packed like squares of wheat ...

Davie's comment deserves quoting:

> ... The collision between the organicism of wheat and the rigidity of 'postal districts' is calculated. It is the human pathos of the many weddings he has seen from the train which spills over to sanctify for the poet, the postal districts of London, the train's destination; the human value suffuses the abstractly schematised with the grace of organic fertility.[26]

The same might be said of the image of the rain, which, as well as evoking the dreariness of a wet day indoors with bored children, plays its part in the natural cycle which culminates in the grown wheat. Like Larkin, McEwan assimilates the natural to the human in the passage quoted above, in his image of the metal trees bearing white nappies. This assimilation is a process that, in its accurate replication of the condition of post-war England (the reduction of a sense of the landscape as something other than merely human) Davie protests against, understandably, I think. Davie does not really address the question of how far it is actually possible to avoid some form of anthropomorphism in any representation of nature, and is presumably aware that the matter is one of degree: Larkin in some poems, and the English in their land, have tamed and humanised nature too much. McEwan's metal trees, representing (proclaiming, indeed) a surrender to the exigencies of the fertility of the species, are themselves a sardonic emblem of what Davie is objecting to. The 'natural' image, and nature itself, become 'abstractly schematized' to fit the schematization of our human lives; and we and nature both suffer the diminishment on that account.

Davie recognises that this is a result of a historical process, while objecting that to think of people as merely the victims of such a process (rather than its perpetrators) adds to the diminishment. But Davie was writing his discussion as long ago as 1973,[27] and McEwan's novel is suffused with a sense that the processes Davie describes have progressed almost beyond what could have been imagined at that time. The countryside of his alternative present, through which Stephen walks after leaving the train, is dotted with hypermarkets, car parks and motorways. 'Real, open country' is a concrete track traversing symmetrical conifer plantations. The closest thing to an animal (a counterpart to the metal trees), a 'grey beast languidly lifting its blunt, heavy head with a steady purr', is a nodding donkey engine pumping at a small oil-well (p. 51). From a perspective derived from Davie's discussion, what might be most depressing about this is Stephen's apparent acquiescence in the substitution of this landscape for the less schematised land that preceded it. Stephen feels 'light-hearted' now he is in open country. I take it that it is the double diminishment that Davie is concerned about. Human, not solely environmental, diminishment distresses him. This, also, is McEwan's subject, it seems to me. Stephen is in danger of losing a more nourishing sense of wonder than what a tidied and industrialised environment can provide: the 'flashing parallax as one row [of the geometrically arrayed conifers] cede to the next, a pleasing effect ...'. We can connect this with Stephen's rather indifferent and at times cynical acquiescence in the political fraud of the child-care commission on which he serves. Despite his beliefs, he is capable of simply shrugging his shoulders at the whole business, so impoverished are his political expectations in this England. □

(Paul Edwards, 'Time Romanticism, Modernism and Modernity in Ian McEwan's *The Child in Time*', 1995)[28]

In his next two books, McEwan is more concerned with expectations of Europe, and, in *The Innocent,* with England's diminished post-imperial role in the world. The fall of the Berlin Wall in 1989 further alerted McEwan to the wider European context of contemporary Britain and also the importance of particular key events in political history, already touched on in his film script for *The Ploughman's Lunch,* which impinge on and mirror the private lives of individuals.

CHAPTER SIX

No Different From You: *The Innocent* (1990)

The Innocent (1990) is in some ways an uncomplicated spy novel, a thriller written in straightforward prose. However, it also met with almost universal praise from critics who felt that McEwan had taken the staple ingredients of the Cold War thriller and fashioned them into a psychological *tour de force*.[1] As well as a critical trumph, it was McEwan's most commercially successful novel to date. The narrative setting is postwar Berlin at the time of a British–American attempt to tunnel into the Soviet sector in 1955–56. A stereotypical Cold War enterprise, the aim of 'Operation Gold' was to infiltrate communist communication systems. In this novel, as well as focusing on the actual Berlin Tunnel built by MI6 and the CIA, McEwan also breaks the fictional frame of the narrative by introducing the real figure of George Blake, the double agent who betrayed 'Operation Gold' before it even started. The book is concerned with the postwar world (also that of McEwan's childhood) which had bifurcated into mutual suspicion between East and West. It is also a story about the end of empire, and England's eclipse by the USA as a major world power, together with the rise of global American cultural dominance. Set in the watershed years of the mid-1950s, *The Innocent* is in part about the loss of Britain's international role and the dawn of its new position as a naive, old-fashioned figure in the world order. This is epitomized in the central character, the innocent Leonard Marnham: 'He had spent the war with his granny in a Welsh village over which no enemy aircraft had ever flown. He had never touched a gun, or heard one go off outside a rifle range; despite this, and the fact that it had been the Russians who had liberated the city, he made his way through [Berlin ...] with a certain proprietorial swagger, as though his feet beat out the rhythms of a speech by Mr. Churchill' (p. 5).

McEwan's novel has a number of preoccupations: covers and concealment, tunneling and burrowing, doubles and duplicity, ignorance and revelation. It is also of course about deception, ignorance, aggression and the loss of innocence: themes taken up by Michael Wood in his review of the novel:

■ The world of espionage is the perfect place for a writer interested in the difference between knowingness and knowledge, and *The Innocent* is set in Berlin in 1955 and 1956, with a brief epilogue in 1987. The Voice of America plays 'Rock around the Clock' and then 'Heartbreak Hotel'. This is Berlin before the Wall, torn by memories, littered with ruins, and even more littered with spies, 'between five and ten thousand', if a report quoted in the novel is to be believed. George Blake, sentenced in 1961 to 42 years in prison for spying, makes a few brief appearances and plays an interesting part in the plot. Intelligence, we learn, is a matter of levels of clearance. One set of persons believes they are building a warehouse. Those whose clearance takes them to the next level know that the warehouse is a radar station. Those at the next level know that the radar station is cover for a tunnel which will permit the British and Americans to tap the Russians' telephone cables. And those at the level after that? It's easy to see how espionage runs over into theology, and one American agent here bases a whole theory of human culture on secrecy. 'Secrecy made us possible', he says, meaning that the first human who knew something that others didn't know was the first individual.

Secrecy, of course, can be a cover for ignorance as well as knowledge, the very notion of the secret is a form of bluff. Much intelligence work must be done along these lines. And innocence might then get entangled in secrecy in quite complicated ways – not knowing, for instance, what it thinks it knows, an innocence in spite of itself. [...]

There are other innocents [than Leonard] in the novel – notably the Americans, who remain naïve even when they are up to complicated things, and are both dangerous and decent for that reason. Their minds, as Maria says of one of them, are 'too simple and too busy'. Is the 'special relationship' between America and Britain a relationship between innocence and knowingness, or between brands of innocence? Between brands of innocence which are also brands of knowingness, perhaps. Little knowledge either way. And in a disturbing sense the Germans too, are innocent – this is the subtlest, most glancing implication in the book. Leonard, who was 14 when the war ended, enters a bar on his first night in Berlin and hears a group of men talking. His poor German and his historical superstitions are enough to make him believe the men are unrepentantly discussing genocide, and he is quite wrong: the conversation is innocent. Later, when an 'innocent' character has been caught up in unimaginable butchery, he thinks, 'I am no different from you, ... I am not evil', and we half-believe him. Or rather, we believe he is different from us only because the Gothic has got him, but hasn't (yet) got us. He is not a German, but the terms of his defence apply more closely to the Germans than to anyone else in the novel. □

(Michael Wood, 'Well Done, Ian McEwan', 1990)[2]

Leonard's 'innocence' is not an innate quality but one based on ignorance. He lacks knowledge and experience of the world and so emerges as an innocent abroad, but not necessarily a benign one. For example, Leonard is irritated and enthralled by two Americans he observes exiting a hut:

> Both men were well over six feet. They wore crew cuts, and grey T-shirts which were untucked from their loose khaki trousers. They seemed immune to the cold. They had an orange rugby ball which they lobbed back and forth as they walked away from each other. They kept on walking until the ball was arcing through an improbable distance, spinning smoothly about its longer axis. It was not a two-handed rugger throw-in, but a single-handed pitch, a sinuous, whip-like movement over the shoulder. Leonard had never seen an American football game, never even heard one described. This routine, with the catches snapping high, right up on the collar bone, seemed over-demonstrative, too self-loving, to represent any serious form of game practice. This was a blatant exercise of physical prowess. These were grown men showing off. Their only audience, an Englishman in a freezing German car, watched with disgusted fascination. (pp. 15–16)

Leonard finds the display 'jubilant' and 'beautiful' but unseemly. His response mimics the broader relation between the two countries, with England's traditional insularity epitomized by Leonard's home background (pp. 122–3) in contrast to the physical ease and expressive freedom of the Americans in Berlin.

Richard Brown also considers the novel in terms of the relationship between Britain and the USA, suggesting it metonymically describes the postwar world through its use of emblematic figures such as Leonard, Glass and Otto:

> ■ Because of the setting almost everything is specifically marked by national identity. Leonard Marnham, McEwan's innocent, is defined from the start by his Englishness, a quality which was 'not quite the comfort it had been to a preceding generation' (p. 8). In this he is contrasted with Bob Glass, one of the 'Americans' who 'don't know a thing ... won't learn' (p. 1) and 'seemed utterly at ease being themselves' (p. 8). Even the defeated Germans seem to have more self-confidence and swagger in their national identities than Leonard. [...]
>
> One of the most disturbing sequences in the novel concerns Leonard's dismembering of Otto's body and his journey around Berlin carrying the remains in two suitcases, eventually hiding them in the secret tunnel: a task that McEwan describes slowly and meticulously over some four chapters of the book. In the penultimate scene [...] Leonard makes his escape, and he and Maria part, but the resolution is not that of romance. Leonard flies off, leaving Maria in the care of Bob Glass who

had fixed his escape. In the ironic final chapter Leonard returns to Berlin thirty years later with a letter from Maria in which he reads that she emigrated to America and became Maria Glass, leaving Leonard with his self-constraining English shyness and gentlemanliness but also the ineradicable suspicion that in the real 'special relationship' he was just the dupe or even the guilt-bearing scapegoat for another romance.

Behind the love and murder story and the evocation of the world of secret intelligence operations there is in *The Innocent* something approaching an allegory of the postwar condition of Britain. Common stereotypes of national character clearly condition the portrayal of Otto, Bob, and Leonard but if anything it is Leonard's Englishness (which seems so proper and innocent but gets him into near rape and murder) that is most to blame. Maria writes: 'It was wrong of you to retreat with your anger and silence. So English! So male! If you felt betrayed you should have stood your ground and fought for what was yours' (p. 242). Such a conclusion no longer opposes an image of British or European culture or rationality against American postmodern crisis but rather suggests that nothing needs liberating from inhibiting postwar cultural assumptions more than the British Leonard. □

(Richard Brown, 'Postmodern Americas in the Fiction of Angela Carter, Martin Amis and Ian McEwan', 1994)[3]

McEwan's protagonist, if that can be the right word in a military world where few individuals are not pawns, is a post-office telephone technician in his mid-twenties. Leonard Marnham has come to Berlin to help tap Russian phone lines. He falls in love with and loses his virginity to a 30-year-old German woman, Maria Eckdorf. The early parts of McEwan's novel are concerned with Leonard's peripheral role in the 'Operation Gold' project, his relationship with Glass, his American superior, and his wide-eyed love for the experienced Maria. Leonard is an innocent who becomes involved in various plots and events that are out of his control. For reasons of national security and private affection, he is spurred on to act in ways he would not normally choose. His imagination is largely peopled with clichéd figures from the movies or popular war fiction: various conceptions of how a man should behave, largely linked to notions of aggression against both other men and (sexually) women. In this the book is concerned with levels of understanding and awareness, but it is also interested in how an innocent such as Leonard can become a murderer.

Mark Ledbetter places Leonard in a different light by considering the metaphors and images McEwan uses when describing the dismemberment of Otto in Maria's apartment:

■ The silenced voice in McEwan's *The Innocent* is community; in particular, the international community. The body-politic postures a rhetoric of secrecy whose code words are patriotism, nationalism and the common good [...] which serve to sever and to distance political community from political community because we fear one another's difference. Like Otto's body, the international body-politic has been skilfully dismembered by the sharp knives of espionage and diplomacy.[4]

A close look at the novel's dismemberment scene reveals that the text's language points beyond its living-room setting and the lives of two individuals. Perhaps this observation is a result of our everyday reference to the global community as the world body. And yet this seemingly simple connection between human body and world body is the critical point, our moment of connection to the horror that is perpetrated by international body-politics.

Otto's rigor mortis makes him 'like a plank' (p. 173), a reference to the stiff intransigence of international relations. Leonard and Maria put his body 'stretched out diagonally on the table' (p. 173) in a way that reminds one of a map. With knife and saw, he divides the body-map, the body-politic, in post-Second World War, Cold War fashion. 'The lower leg was suddenly an item' (p. 176). Are we dismembering a body or isolating Poland? Bosnia? Iraq? Since the novel was written, we could as easily talk about the post-Soviet Union and the many states it has now become.

The text begins to retell its story of body dismemberment in a way to suggest that Otto's body is not really human; the text, like Leonard, is unwilling to face the horror of its own making. Narrative has a desire for a moral coherency and often resists 'turning on itself' for the sake of posturing an ethic other than the one found in the surface reading of the master plot. Yet good narrative, I am convinced, will not sacrifice moral responsibility for moral coherency. The greater desire of narrative is to reflect human experience in all its vagary and ambiguity. At which point, we find narrative's scar, and we discover narrative's ethic.

As the dismemberment continues, the transition from human body to body-politic merely exchanges one violation for another, a single victim becomes global victims. 'They were not killing anyone here. Otto was dead. Solingen. They were dismantling him. Solingen. Nobody was missing. Solingen, Solingen. Otto is disarmed. Solingen, Solingen'[5] (p. 178). Political prisoners, the military machines, they are all here in the body-politic, and each is a violence that contributes to broken community.

The tragic dimension of political games is that we come to enjoy them. If Otto becomes the political map of Europe, the silenced international community, then Leonard becomes the voice of a powerful body-politic, who willingly severs the communal body in order to control it, creating pieces small enough to pack away. 'Between the arms he drank the gin. It was easy, it was sensible [...] The blood was everywhere, and he accepted it' (p. 178). I am most frightened by this moment, the party atmosphere of drink, saluting and numbing, and in particular the casualness with which he accepts the spilling of blood. The most violent moment of all, perhaps the text's most profound scar, is in the most brief moment of reflection when Leonard thinks, 'It was a job' (p. 178).

At this narrative moment, the violence to body and to body-politic is its most sanitised and its most evil by denying any connection at all to the human.

> What was on the table now was no one at all. It was the field of operations, it was a city far below that Leonard had been ordered to destroy. Solingen. The gin again, the sticky Beefeater, then the big one, the thighs, the big push, and that would be it, a hot bath, a debriefing. (p. 178)

The military language is cold and dehumanising, but of course, this is the goal of body-politic's rhetoric of secrecy, to deny 'knowing'. [...]

Unable to dispose of the body, [Leonard] returns to his apartment for rest. The text's point is quite clear. The violent body-politic exists only in relation to the voices it must silence: Western colonial states, Eastern Europe, the Middle East, the list is endless. In the never-ending attempt to silence, through a pernicious rhetoric of secrecy, the silenced become even more resistant to their oppressors and therefore are brought even more acutely and damningly to our attention. They cannot be disposed of.

In his apartment, Leonard opens the suitcases, thinking that 'he was not too late' (p. 194). Removing the parts of the body, 'putting Otto back together' (p. 195), he returns the head to its proper place and Otto sits up and is holding a knife in his hand. 'Leonard knelt in front of him and tipped back his head to offer up his throat' (p. 195). Leonard, as the manipulative body-politic, offers himself for slaughter, a divestment of power, a willingness to become like the other, broken and disjointed. And then he awakes from his dream. [...]

The fallacy of Leonard's dream is that he puts Otto back together. [...] The Leonards of the world, that is the powerful body-politics, have for a long time been putting together the pieces of the body-politics they have severed, a reflective practice that requires a people to see themselves in an other before the puzzle is complete.

The strength of Leonard's dream is that he relinquishes the knife to the victim; the powerful becomes powerless. At this point, political self-determination begins. This act of telling one's own political narrative is not without violence, for it too will deny an other in order to claim political autonomy. Yet this new body-politic will bear the scars of dismemberment, a reality that historical time may distort but, unlike the dream, remains a physically indelible mark of self-effacing memory, another moment between truth and erasure that makes community possible.

The Innocent ends with Leonard going to Iowa to reclaim his relationship with Maria, and we are back where we started. If the language of body metaphor is to represent our most profound way of knowing the world and each other, which is the one persistent claim I make, narratives, like us, must return to the individual body/ies as its 'place for knowing'. Possibilities for community, global and otherwise, begin in the hearts and minds, in the desires of personal bodies. This point is made quite clear by Leonard's desire to bring Maria back to Berlin, the scene of the crime, and the place from which they would 'climb the wooden platform and take a good long look at the Wall together, before it was all torn down' (p. 245). □

(Mark Ledbetter. 'The Games Body-Politics Plays: a Rhetoric of Secrecy in Ian McEwan's "The Innocent" ', 1996)[6]

The novel thus ends still in Berlin, in a final chapter that jumps over thirty years in time to June 1987 when Leonard, appropriately given the novel's themes, is the owner of a small company that makes hearing-aid components. He has come to exorcise the past and stands at the site of the aborted tunnel, just yards from the Berlin Wall. Here he reads Maria's letter, suggesting a reconciliation and reunion between them after all this time. The novel ends ambivalently but hopefully, with Leonard imagining them able to walk out together in order to take one last look at the wall before it is finally torn down and dismembered.

Struck by the fact that Leonard chooses the tunnel as the place to return to at the narrative's conclusion, Tamás Bényei discusses the significance of the image of 'the tunnel' in *The Innocent*, seeing it as 'the place between'. In his discussion he draws attention to Leonard's feelings about commuting between his dual selves, both of them 'secret': 'He was not certain whether this time spent travelling between his two secret worlds was when he was truly himself, when he was able to hold the two in balance and know them to be separate from himself; or whether this was the one time he was nothing-at-all' (p. 77). Travelling between the two secret selves, the one official, the other private, makes him appear like a connecting tunnel, and can remind the reader that the primary two people from these worlds that Leonard thus connects are Glass and Maria.

■ Leonard needs to read the letter by the tunnel because the tunnel is the place where the time between his two times in Berlin might be understood; the ruins and the mouth of the shaft constitute a proper place of reading because they are like what is being read: like 'his time and her time, like so much unbuilt-on land' (p. 244). This phrase, which encapsulates the strategy of the entire novel, that of spatialising intended time, defines the central love story as one deprived of a future of which it could have been the ground.

'This place meant far more to him than Adalbertstrasse. He had already decided not to bother with Platanenallee. It was here in this ruin that he felt the full weight of time' (p. 237). Why this place – apart from the obvious archaeological metaphor suggested by the scene?

A tunnel is not built. It is excavated, it is earth shifted and removed, a cavity, a void carved into something solid [...]. A tunnel is not a place, but a place between two proper places – which recalls Leonard's self-definition [...] as 'a void travelling between two points' (p. 77). It is a place for going through and not for inhabiting, a place that cannot become a home: 'tunnels were stealth and safety; boys and trains crept through them, lost to sight and care, and then emerged unscathed' (p. 72). This sentence defines the ambiguous narrative significance of the tunnel. It is a place that is both safe and dangerous, its safety and danger deriving from the same source: it is an entry into the dark, humid interior of the earth, and therefore a momentary return into primeval, maternal safety, but also a site of existential danger: loss of sight, loss of light, implying the possibility of entombment, of remaining permanently buried. As a narrative space, it tropes the rite of passage, the moment of crossing [...] that seems to structure the narrative: it is the dangerous place that one has to go through; the Berlin tunnel is illicitly crossing a section boundary, and in fact all tunnels are places which are border-crossings at the same time: places (moments) of crossing from one nameable, lighted place to the other. □

(Tamás Bényei, *Acts of Attention: Figure and Narrative in Postwar British Novels*, 1999)[7]

Bényei sees crossing the tunnel as 'a moment of initiation', a time of transition figured in a movement through space. Of Leonard's many moments of initiation, the principal one focused on by critics is Otto's murder and its aftermath. In interview, McEwan has spoken of the genesis of the novel and discussed directly his own intentions in comparing Otto's dismemberment with that of Berlin:

■ [Ian McEwan:] I'm interested in how a violent impulse grows inside us. In *The Innocent* a rather ordinary man is caught up in a difficult situation and becomes extremely violent. The protagonist's mind is full of images of the Second World War. I wanted to show the brutality man can aspire to by comparing the dismemberment of a corpse to the dismemberment of a city: the bomb-devastated Berlin of the post-war.

[Rosa González-Casademont:] *Why did you choose this particular setting, and what was the point of departure of the novel?*

I went to the Soviet Union in 1987 with a small delegation of anti-nuclear people called European Nuclear Disarmament. Perestroika was then just a few months old. We were there because we wanted to take advantage of these new developments to persuade the Soviet authorities to stop persecuting members of their own anti-nuclear groups. This all seems ancient history now. We were there to make contact with these groups, the Russians who dared to speak about Russian weapons. The Soviet government only spoke about American weapons. We wanted to talk about both and we were trying to bring these two groups together.

So we met policy makers in the institutes, in particular the Institute of American and Canadian Affairs and we were treated, I think, to a most extraordinary trailer to what was going to happen in Europe in the next two or three years. These people, foreign policy intellectuals who wrote out the policy options for the Kremlin, were talking of the most extraordinary things, one of which was that Eastern Europe would have to go its own way and that the Soviet Union would begin unilaterally to withdraw troops from East Germany. When we asked, in our excitement, where we could read these ideas, we were told nothing was written down because if Mr Gorbachev went and someone else came along, they would lose their jobs. It wasn't until President Gorbachev addressed the UN – I think it was the end of 1988 – that the true force of these changes became apparent.

I left Moscow full of thoughts that the Cold War was coming to an end. It so happened that three weeks later I found myself in Berlin, which I hadn't visited in a long time. I did many of the things that tourists used to do: I went to Potsdamer Platz and stood on a wooden platform and looked over what was once a busy thoroughfare and was now just raked sand full of mines and automatic guns, and I began to think that soon this too might disappear. By soon I thought some 5 to 10 years – that seemed pretty soon to me. So, I began to plan a novel about the Cold War, not the end of the Cold War but the height, or the depths of the Cold War, in 1955. I was looking for a story, a true story, and for a long time I thought it was going to be about an escape from the East. Then I read about a tunnel dug by the Americans and the British in collaboration, a very daring project, a tunnel that ran 400 metres into the Russian sector in order to tap telephone lines, that connected with Moscow.

Two things attracted me about this tunnel: one was that the Russians knew about it even before the Americans had started to dig it and yet didn't do anything about it because they didn't want to endanger the position of the spy who had told them. I thought what a curious, useless thing spying is, what an oddly circular, self-contained, self-referential system it is. I began to read more, and I began to see that you had to look very hard for a country that had ever changed its foreign policy on the basis of information acquired through spying. Spying is simply move and countermove within this closed system. In some ways it is analogous to forms of literary modernism.

The year 1955 threw up some interesting things too for an Englishman. By that time it was quite clear to at least half, and I'd say the better half, the more intelligent half, of the British population, that the British Empire's days were now over – this was one year before the Suez crisis, which was a watershed in British self-perception. The baton of empire was being self-consciously handed over to the USA. The consoling myth for many Britons was that we were Greece to their Rome, that we were the older mature Empire, the Americans were the brasher, more powerful empire, that what we lacked in economic and military power we made up for in a certain kind of wisdom. 1955 was perhaps the first flowering of the Pax Americana. As Empires go, I'd say the American empire was less vicious in some respects because its power and its influence extended not, in the first instance at least, through the sword but through other means: pop music, movies, fast food – the word 'teenager' was invented in 1953. so the young man who is at the centre of *The Innocent*, Leonard Marnham, goes abroad for the first time in his life and is rather unconfident, rather in the way his country is so recently unconfident. In a previous generation an Englishman abroad, the Englishman of Evelyn Waugh's *The Loved One* [1948], would've felt he belonged to a superior race. Evelyn Waugh's hero could afford to look down his nose at the Americans; their habits appear extravagant but fundamentally empty and vulgar. For Leonard Marnham, on the other hand, the Americans offer a world he'd rather like to enter. Much of the novel is concerned with Leonard overcoming his distaste for rock and roll and coming to like freezing cold Coca Cola, and accepting that grown men might drink chocolate milk, accepting the paradox that this very powerful nation seems also to have a culture of the nursery: the food, the drink, the music, all seem somewhat very childish at first to a serious Englishman. But Leonard is won over to it. □

(Rosa González-Casademont, 'The Pleasure of Prose Writing vs Pornographic violence', 1992)[8]

Alongside the many commentators who have focused on Leonard's transition from innocence to experience through violence, Jack Slay discusses a further aspect of 'Leonard's initiation' (p. 77) into the wider world: his relationship with Maria (which also degenerates into violence). Interestingly, this sexual romance is likened to being 'in a tunnel' (p. 58), to 'excavations' and 'burrow[ing] down' (p. 78), to suggest the intimacy and claustrophobia of love but also the explorations and actions of sex: ' "Tell me why you like it half-way," he whispered, and she pleaded, "But I like it deep, really deep" ' (p. 79).

■ With *The Innocent* the focal relationship is between Leonard Marnham, a 25-year-old British naïf, and Maria Louise Eckdorf, a 30-year-old, worldly-wise German. Both are emblematic of their respective countries and cultures. Leonard, an innocent on multiple levels, is constantly amazed by the simplest occurrences of life (a waiter's prompt response, an American's boisterousness, Maria's interest in him). Not surprisingly, he is also a virgin, something that vaguely embarrasses him but that delights Maria. She thrills to this discovery and her eventual conquest. It *frees* her, she says, of the requisite social restraints and expectations: 'She would not have to adopt a conventional role and be judged in it, and she would not be measured against other women. Her fear of being physically abused had receded. She would not be obliged to do anything she did not want. She was free, they both were free, to invent their own terms. They could be partners in invention. [...] [S]he had him first, she would have him all to herself' (p. 57). She is willing and anxious to guide Leonard into the world of experience, the world of love.

Maria proves to be a thorough instructor, and Leonard is an appreciative and eager pupil: 'He learned to love the smells: sweat like mown grass, and the moistness of her arousal with its two elements, sharp but rounded, tangy and blunt: fruit and cheese, the very tastes of desire itself. This synaesthesia was a kind of delirium' (p. 78). Soon Leonard is 'able to define himself in strictest terms as an initiate, a truly mature adult at last' (p. 60). Just as important, Leonard, through Maria's loving and capable hands, also begins to mature as a person, politically and culturally. For example, he begins to see the Germans around him as 'no longer ex-Nazis, they were Maria's compatriots' (p. 68). Their love, then, is also a symbolic political union, a reuniting of forces torn asunder by the upheavals of the twentieth century. Glass toasts their engagement, saying, 'Leonard and Maria belong to countries that ten years ago were at war. By engaging to be married, they are bringing their own peace, in their own way, to their nations. Their marriage, and all others like it, bind countries tighter than any treaty can' (p. 134). In *The Innocent*, then, McEwan presents politics as love, individual union as the derivation for transcultural pacification and acceptance.[9]

Quite expectedly for readers of McEwan, this perfect and willing courtship soon takes a sour veer. The freedom from innocence opens for Leonard the untapped, darker side of the id, and, once again, a relationship is fouled by the horror of male sexuality. When Leonard sees Maria for the first time after having met her, he is struck by her seeming vulnerability: 'It was the sort of face, the sort of manner, onto which men were likely to project their own requirements. One could read womanly power into her silent abstraction, or find a childlike dependence in her quiet attentiveness' (p. 47). Eventually, this initial impression mutates into a fantasy of dominance and submission, a rape fantasy. Soon these thoughts of forcing himself on Maria 'grew inseparable from his desire' (p. 83). Obviously, McEwan intends Leonard to represent the moral anarchy that entices stronger nations to force their world views on weaker countries; once again *The Innocent* becomes political allegory. Though Leonard realizes that it is horribly against his nature, against *human* nature, these thoughts consume him, tainting every move he makes with Maria. Ultimately, they echo the sadistic desires of Robert in *The Comfort of Strangers*: '[Leonard] wanted his power recognized and Maria to suffer from it, just a bit, in the most pleasurable way' (p. 85). With this desire, McEwan returns to the theory that anchors his second novel: the idea which 'explained how the imagination, the sexual imagination, men's dream of hurting, and women's of being hurt, embodied and declared a powerful single organizing principle, which distorted all relations, all truth'.[10]

Leonard soon acts upon his desires; but this time the woman refuses to submit, refuses to succumb to the notions and archetypes of the patriarchy. Maria refuses to enable him; she grows stiff, cold, emotionless, all desire and trust abandoning her and, in turn, their relationship. This dissolution, quite naturally, suggests the overt complexities of world politics: there are no easy, all-encompassing solutions. As in individual relationships, politics is a question of equality and moral assiduousness.

Unknowable to Leonard is that Maria has witnessed atrocities during the Russian invasion of Berlin. Just 10 years previous, she had watched a Berliner, a woman who had been shot in both legs, raped by a Russian soldier. Leonard's assault awakens the old memories; just as devastating, it destroys the total trust that she has so willingly placed in him. His actions are all the more heinous, all the more a violation. Leonard quickly realizes his mistake: 'As more time passed, the more unbelievable his attack on Maria seemed, and the less forgivable. There had been some logic, some crazed, step-by-step reasoning that he could no longer recall' (p. 94). He recognizes the attack as childish, as brutish, as *stupid*. McEwan notes that this instant is the true initiation for Leonard, the real moment of manhood:

> There's a curious myth – which literary fiction promotes – that you lose your innocence when you first have sexual experience ... . In fact, I think it's the beginning of innocence. It's the beginning, not the end, of the process of learning; it's the emotions that are so difficult to learn how to deal with. So it isn't first sex that transforms Leonard, it's having to explain himself to Maria for the first time.[11]

In this moment of abuse and denial, of masculine dominance and feminine denial, McEwan makes amends for the theory espoused in *The Comfort of Strangers*. Indeed, men may harbour secret desires to dominate, even hurt, but women *are* empowered. There is power and respect, then, in the refusal, the denial. This is certainly a much more natural view of relationships and sexuality, and, therefore, along with Stephen and Julie in *The Child in Time* and the Tremaines in *Black Dogs*, one of McEwan's most successful presentations.

In his clumsy attempt to mend the nearly irreparable divide in their relationship and trust, Leonard reminds Maria that he is 'the young innocent she had sweetly coaxed and brought on' (p. 108). Both are well aware, however, that this is no longer true, that Leonard has progressed beyond innocence and naïveté. Eventually the two do reunite, and only at this point, when Leonard quells his libidinous anarchies and realizes Maria as an equal partner, is he 'truly grown-up at last' (p. 117). □

(Jack Slay, *Ian McEwan*, 1996)[12]

The themes touched upon in the readings above are neatly summarized in Kiernan Ryan's discussion of the novel, which links *The Innocent* to the preoccupations of McEwan's earlier fiction and explains how the spy genre lends itself to McEwan's particular kinds of exploration into human experience.

■ In the early fiction the body had to be hidden – encased in concrete, swallowed by a river, or made invisible by the magic of solid geometry. But it was always forcing its way back from exile, smuggling its way back from exile, smuggling itself in through smell or touch or sight. It left traces of itself in countless bodily secretions and emissions, in snot and sweat and sperm and spittle and blood. These glimpses of the moist internal texture of being betray the scandalous *secret de tous connu* [secret known to all], in whose preservation we all learn to conspire. What must be buried over and over again is our brute physicality, which explodes all pretence of transcendence by insisting that nothing but cultural illusions and accidents of evolution divide us from the most squalid life-forms. The title story of *First Love, Last Rites* glanced memorably at this knowledge in the image of the pregnant rat, whose ripped corpse divulged its biological kinship with its executioners. But in *The Innocent* the anaesthetic of displacement is withheld. We are obliged to gaze unblinking with McEwan at the visceral truth of human nature, whose mystery starts and ends right here in the obscenity Leonard Marnham lays bare.

As Leonard starts to saw through Otto's torso, we know as he knows that we are about to trespass into forbidden territory: 'He was in the cavity that contained all that he did not want to see' (pp. 180–1). When the half-severed trunk slips from his grasp, however, disgorging its contents onto the carpet, he has no choice but to see:

> Before he made his run for the bathroom he had an impression of liverish reds, glistening irregular tubing of a boiled egg bluish white, and something purple and black, all of it shining and livid at the outrage of violated privacy, of secrets exposed. Despite the open windows, the room filled with the close stench of musty air, which itself was a medium for other smells: of sweet earth, sulphurous crap, and Sauerkraut. The insult was, Leonard had time to think as he stepped hurriedly round the up-ended halves of the torso that were still joined, that all this stuff was also in himself. (p. 182)

This is what the unfathomable complexity of human history and culture is spun out of and what it boils down to: the ultimate, crude secret on which the survival of our grander mysteries depends. The dead, dissected body is the point where signifying halts and hermeneutics ends, where the final ground of meaning is unmasked and metaphysical delusions implode. Hence the simultaneous horror and liberating gusto with which *The Innocent* assaults and defiles the human form.

A novel of espionage affords an apt medium in which to pursue this remorseless unfolding. There are many reasons why McEwan revisits the world of surveillance that first hooked him in *The Imitation Game*,

> but not the least important is the space it grants him to monitor his own procedures as a writer. Tunnelling down beneath the surface and burrowing across borders into forbidden territory to hijack and crack coded messages is a perfect image for what McEwan's fiction is up to. His imagination finds the universe mapped by Deighton [born 1929] and Le Carré [born 1931] so congenial because it gives both writer and reader the voyeuristic kick of invading privacy unseen and watching with impunity 'the slow unveiling of a secret' (p. 18). Like the spying game itself, *The Innocent* involves learning to unpack one layer of diversion after another to expose the ulterior motive. To quote Leonard's American boss, Bob Glass, whose mind is anything but as transparent as his surname suggests: 'everybody thinks his clearance is the highest there is, everyone thinks he has the final story. You only hear of a higher level at the moment you're being told about it' (p. 14). *The Innocent* lures us on from one level to the next by promising a terminal initiation, a final story, which will not turn out to be a stalking-horse for something else. But no sooner has it fulfilled its promise in Leonard's anatomy lesson than it breaks it by contesting that scene's sovereignty in the closing chapter. □
>
> (Kiernan Ryan, *Ian McEwan*, 1994)[13]

For Ryan, McEwan's fourth novel similarly works by taking the reader through a series of levels of understanding. It starts as a spy thriller, then reveals itself to be 'a wry historical novel about the twilight of British supremacy, the triumph of American cultural imperialism and the ice age of the Cold War', before emerging as also a *Bildungsroman* (a novel of development and maturation) 'in which a young man barters his guiltless heart for bittersweet carnal knowledge and a gruesome schooling in the craft of the abbatoir'.[14]

McEwan's fifth novel was also to be about an individual's acquisition of unwanted knowledge, partly set in Berlin. Merritt Moseley writes: '*The Innocent* showed us Cold War Berlin at its strangest and most unnatural; in *Black Dogs* some of the characters visit a Germany where the wall is coming down, where decades-old political divisions are becoming meaningless'.[15] Yet, *Black Dogs* is a novel about a division that cannot be torn down, no matter how much its narrator tries to reconcile opposed views. The division between materialist and spiritual viewpoints in McEwan's next novel remains as intractable as the division between good and evil.

CHAPTER SEVEN

Ça Suffit: *Black Dogs* (1992)

Reviews of *Black Dogs* drew comparisons between McEwan and some of the most influential twentieth-century British novelists, such as E. M. Forster (1879–1970) and William Golding;[1] but overall critics were once more divided. Some declared it his finest achievement to date, while others condemned it as contrived and melodramatic. Considered by some to be an excellent novel of ideas and also McEwan's most humane work, for others it was an unhappy mixture of polemic and farce.[2]

The novel purports to be a memoir by its narrator, Jeremy, an orphan drawn to and fascinated by the families, and particularly the parents, of others. A preface provides the reader with Jeremy's background, but in several ways, the principal couple in the novel are the parents of Jeremy's wife, Jenny. June and Bernard Tremaine are presented as two people who met as communist sympathizers but whose experiences and temperaments took them in diametrically opposed directions. June is a spiritual being, an intuitive believer and a natural communicator, while Bernard is a logical rationalist and unswerving materialist. She searches for the hidden truth of the universe while he believes there is none that science cannot ultimately reveal. In his discussion of the novel, Merritt Moseley considers the relationship Jeremy has with his in-laws.

■ This novel has at its heart (its private heart, anyway) an odd triangle. The narrator, Jeremy, describes himself as irresistibly drawn to other people's parents because earlier he lost his own. In this case it is his wife's parents, June and Bernard Tremaine. He is writing about June, who lies dying; with Bernard he visits Berlin to see the wall come down.

June and Bernard are an odd couple. They were once Marxists; however, June was transformed into a mystic by an experience on her honeymoon in France in 1946. Bernard is still a rationalist (amateur entomologist), an atheist, and a politician, now a socialist. Jeremy, an agnostic, relays the epistemological concerns of the novel, which he describes this way: 'Rationalist and mystic, commissar and yogi, joiner and abstainer, scientist and intuitionist, Bernard and June are the extremities, the twin poles along whose slippery axis my own unbelief slithers and never comes to rest.'

And in fact it never does come to rest. If Bernard and June are thesis and antithesis, there is no synthesis. Jeremy moves toward a disclosure of what happened to June on her honeymoon; it turns out to have been an encounter with enormous, monstrous black dogs that are rumoured (somewhat implausibly) to have been trained by the Nazis to rape women. She escapes this fate, but the dogs also escape, back into the hills.

They function as a symbol of the omnipresence of evil, as do skinheads encountered by Bernard and Jeremy in Germany and a man who mistreats his children. The novel, then, broods over evil and its irruptions, in a way that is closer to *First Love, Last Rites*, perhaps, than it first appears. □

(Merritt Moseley, 'Ian McEwan', 1998)[3]

The narrative of the novel does not proceed chronologically but leads up to an incident in 1946, when June had an encounter with two snarling, predatory dogs, which brought her to her belief in God. A précis will be helpful to foreground the novel's unusual structure.

Part One, set in Wiltshire in 1987, introduces the reader to the main characters, and in particular to Jeremy's fascination with June and Bernard, the former of whom he interviews in the hospice where she is dying from leukaemia. Part Two is set two years later, in Berlin in 1989, when Jeremy travels to Germany to witness the collapse of the wall for himself. He goes with Bernard, whose humanism, we are told, caused him to leave the Communist Party after the invasion of Hungary in 1956. They become involved in a fracas as Nazi sympathisers set upon a Turkish immigrant near Checkpoint Charlie to the pleasure of nearby respectable German citizens. It seems that while the destruction of the wall is meant to mark the end of racial hatred and the triumph of reason and humanity, it has merely signalled the end of one period of oppression under the Cold War to be replaced by another under democracy.

The third part of the novel takes place in Poland in 1981 and France in 1989. The earlier scene recounts Jeremy's meeting with his future wife Jenny when he was invited to travel behind the Iron Curtain as part of a cultural delegation. He was then a director of a provincial theatre company. Jenny, the only woman in the party, was a representative from an institution based in Paris. Together they visit the concentration camp at Majdanek and react to the horrific sights there by returning to their hotel and making love. They stay ensconced in the hotel for three days and become a couple, marrying ten months later. The catalyst for their relationship has been the intense emotion that made them race into the life-affirming security of sex and love from the sorrow and the pity they felt at the death-camp in Poland. The second half of the chapter focuses on two events that happen to Jeremy eight years later. First, he visits June and Bernard's deserted French country cottage and narrowly escapes being stung by a scorpion because he has a feeling that June's 'presence' in the room is warning him. He then intervenes in a family quarrel in a restaurant and violently attacks a man whom he has seen beating his son. This second incident taps into a number of concerns in the novel: notably Jeremy's sense of responsibility and protection for his niece Sally, an abused child herself, and also the notion that any individual has the capacity for extreme hatred and violence, whether from good motives or bad ones. The final part returns to the French scenes of Part Three, but shifts back to 1946. It centres on June's confrontation with the two black dogs. Out walking on their honeymoon, June becomes separated from Bernard and finds herself alone on a path with two distant shapes moving ahead of her. She becomes aware that these are two feral dogs and that she is to be their prey. June formulates some words of prayer and then prepares to defend herself with a small penknife. She fights off the dogs and they retreat before Bernard reappears, unimpressed by her story. Later, back at the village, they are told that the abandoned dogs had belonged to the Gestapo and were trained not only to attack, but to rape.

This history leaves Jeremy unable to reconcile June's and Bernard's views of the world and of the nature of evil: 'In this memoir I have included certain incidents from my own life – in Berlin, Majdanek, Les Salces and St. Maurice de Navacelles – that are open equally to Bernard and to June's kind of interpretation' (p. 19). As Michel Delville notes, this apparently leaves the novel without a consistent value system, except that its perspective may embrace the dualism expressed by the Tremaines as a couple, rather than either of their individual points of view.

■ Jeremy's 'unbelief' reflects his helplessness towards the disappearance of moral and intellectual standards by which to judge not only his personal experience as an orphan and a father, but also the ideological upheavals which have taken place in Europe since the end of WWII and culminated in the fall of communism, one of the central motifs of the novel; indeed, his inability to reconcile June and Bernard's divergent beliefs – which are also represented by McEwan as a feminine opposed to a masculine approach to reality at large – is symptomatic of his failure to come to terms with the contradictions of twentieth-century history. As he puts it in McEwan's fictional preface:

> To believe in everything, to make no choices, amounts to much the same thing, to my mind, as believing in nothing at all. I am uncertain whether our civilization at the turn of the millennium is cursed by too

much or too little belief, whether people like Bernard and June cause the trouble, or people like me. (p. 20)

Jeremy's self-confessed intellectual and moral stagnation proves useless in his endeavours to 'make retroactive sense of the past' and fully comprehend the different instances of domestic and public violence *Black Dogs* sets out to discuss.

The novel's epigraph ('In these times I don't, in a manner of speaking, know what I want; perhaps I don't want what I know and want what I don't know'), a quotation from Marsilio Ficino's *Letters*, offers an ironical counterpoint to Jeremy's intellectual stagnation. However, Ficino (1433–1499) – the leader of the Florence Platonic Academy, who sought to establish an essential harmony between Platonism and Christianity – also stands as a reminder of other attempts in European history to bring together contradictory belief systems. In this respect, Ficino's synthesis, inspired by a daring syncretism which bears the stamp of Renaissance conciliatoriness, appears as the exact antithesis of Jeremy's intellectual void. By contrasting Ficino's dialectical mind with Jeremy's inability to transcend opposites, McEwan nonetheless suggests that the possibility to recover a solid basis for moral and political judgement may lie in an awareness of the necessary dualism of any political or metaphysical system – one which eventually turns Jeremy into 'a passionate expert, if not in the answers, then in the right kind of questions'. □

(Michel Delville, 'Marsilio Ficino and Political Syncretism in Ian McEwan's *Black Dogs*', 1996)[4]

In her review of the novel, Wendy Lesser also pays attention to McEwan's presentation of the book's narrator, but she concentrates on the way in which Jeremy represents his own past, his adolescent pretensions, and his prose style. Jeremy admits that he has spent his life searching for his childhood innocence before the death of his parents. This has clearly led him to seek parental figures, those with authority but compassion, solutions but sympathy. As he makes notes from what June tells him, and reflects upon his conversations with Bernard, he becomes the intermediary between this alienated couple with their warring beliefs; however, as he learns more of their background and the circumstances of their marriage, Jeremy also increasingly becomes an image of the novelist, of the observing outsider trying to make sense of the lives and opinions of others. As Lesser suggests, this is a development from his attempt in the Preface to make sense of his own life.

■ 'Ever since I lost mine in a road accident when I was 8,' Jeremy tells us in the first sentence of the preface, 'I have had my eyes on other people's parents.' Despite the parent-borrowing that began in adolescence, he remained an orphan, essentially familyless, until he met his wife,

Jenny, and became part of her family: not only the family they created together ('the simplest way of restoring a lost parent was to become one yourself'), but also the family she was born into, the estranged but still married Bernard and June.

Jeremy is not the only one in the novel to reach beyond his birthright. *Black Dogs* is filled with things and people and ideas crossing their national boundaries, taking over territory that does not officially belong to them. On the largest scale this notion pervades the background plot of the Second World War, in the Nazi invasions of France and Poland. Less chillingly, the idea of broken boundaries emerges in the contemporary reference to the Berlin Wall coming down – an event that Jeremy and Bernard excitedly rush to witness. And on the level of detail it appears over and over in the metaphors throughout the book – for instance in Jeremy's assertion that his older sister 'Jean had spread her beautiful limbs – to adapt Kafka's formulation – across my map of the world and obliterated the territory marked "sex", so that I was obliged to voyage elsewhere' (p. 15), or in his musing comment about whether it was always raining when he visited June in the Wiltshire nursing home: 'Perhaps there was only one such day, and it has blown itself across the others.'

He may have his shortcomings as a meteorologist, but Jeremy is in general a persuasive guide. Just as he had effectively conveyed the essence of nursing-home-induced passivity, so does he elsewhere seize on the one or two or three determining details that define a place, a time, a person. Reporting on the moment the Berlin Wall came down, he says: 'We stood in the living room in our dressing gowns with mugs of tea, staring at the set, it did not seem right to sit. East Berliners in nylon anoraks and bleached-out jean jackets, pushing buggies or holding their children's hands, were filing past Checkpoint Charlie, unchecked.' Elsewhere, in a few sentences, he gives us the 1960s in an upper-middle-class London household (the home of two of the parents the adolescent Jeremy has borrowed):

> Toby was at my place [...] while I was at his, comfortable on the chesterfield in front of an open fire, a glass of his father's single malt warming in my hand, under my shoeless feet the lovely Bokhara that Toby had claimed was a symbol of cultural rape, listening to Tom Langley's account of a deadly poisonous spider and the death throes of a certain third secretary on the first landing of the British embassy in Caracas, while across the hall, through open doors, we heard Brenda at one of Scott Joplin's lilting, syncopated rags, which at that time were being rediscovered and had not yet been played to death. (p. 14)

There is something lilting and syncopated in Jeremy's prose as well – the off-rhyme of 'staring at the set [...] right to sit'; the little joke in 'Checkpoint Charlie, unchecked'; the ironic counterpoint of the third secretary's 'death throes' and the Scott Joplin 'played to death'.

If such precision can be enormously pleasing, it can also risk seeming finicky or precious at times, but this too Jeremy takes account of. In the paragraph that immediately follows the Scott Joplin set piece, he admits that:

> In describing this period of my life I have unconsciously mimicked not only, here and there, the superior sounding attitudes of my adolescent self, but also the rather formal, distancing, labyrinthine tone in which I used to speak, clumsily derived from my scant reading of Proust, which was supposed to announce me to the world as an intellectual. (p. 14)

Admits it, and thereby gets away with it.

If Proust [1871–1922] is evident in the sentences of *Black Dogs*, Graham Greene [1904–91] is the shadowy eminence who colours the plot, visible not only in the central choices made by the two older characters [...], but also in the very notion of a crucial moment of choice. 'Turning points are the inventions of storytellers and dramatists,' Jeremy interrupts the plot to tell us, 'a necessary mechanism when a life is reduced to, traduced by a plot, when a morality must be distilled from a sequence of actions, when an audience must be sent home with something unforgettable to mark a character's growth.'

Jeremy, as usual, mocks the tactic and then continues to use it. □

(Wendy Lesser, *New Republic*, 1992)[5]

Lesser is here alluding to the way Jeremy organizes his 'divagation' around the incident in 1946 described in the last chapter of the novel: June's encounter with the black dogs. Christina Byrnes has considered the symbolism of this encounter, and in the following extract identifies some of the literary and classical precedents for McEwan's choice of an emblem for evil.

■ The symbolism of the black dogs is carefully explained in the book itself. Bernard tells Jeremy:

> I was the one who told her about Churchill's black dog. You remember? The name he gave to the depressions he used to get from time to time. I think he pinched the expression from Samuel Johnson. So June's idea was that if one dog was a personal depression, two dogs were a kind of cultural depression, civilisation's worst moods. Not bad really. (p. 104)

McEwan describes a walking holiday in France, when he ran into a pair of black dogs:

> They were so big and so enormous, so out of place in the terrain, that we left the path and armed ourselves with rocks and circled round them. When they had gone, I started thinking how quickly one transforms such things into a symbol.[6]

[McEwan's interviewer], Billen offers some examples of mythical dogs:

> The black dog slumbering at the foot of Dūrer's 'Melancholia', Horace's reference to black dogs or Johnson and the black dog of his depression, or even Churchill's. The mythic qualities of these animals predate the myths.[7]

The black dogs are a powerful symbol from the universal unconscious. Black usually denotes death, the shadow or the evil side of the psyche and dogs or other dangerous animals stand for man's animal nature, his instincts and uncivilised impulses. In addition to the dogs mentioned by McEwan and Billen there is a long history of the use of this symbol. Dogs are associated with Artemis who is an anima figure, generally hostile to men, who sometimes sets her dogs on them. Dogs devour the unburied remains of defeated Greek Heroes. Cerberus, the three-headed black dog, is a guardian of Hades. Satan is often referred to as 'the Hound of Hell'. Jezebel was eaten by dogs and Hecuba was turned into a dog – Cynossema (dog's monument) on the Hellespont is believed to be her tomb. Most pertinent is the Egyptian god Set, who has the body of a man and the head of a dog. Set murdered and dismembered his twin brother Osiris by cutting him up into fourteen pieces and buried each piece in a different place in order to prevent his resurrection. All these dogs bite, tear, dismember and are the objects of terror and the instruments of death and damnation. □

(Christina Byrnes, *The Work of Ian McEwan*, 2002)[8]

June understands the dogs to be embodiments of evil, of a pervasive, ever-present force that can arise anywhere at any time. The events of the book, from the attack at the Berlin Wall, through the history of the concentration camp, to Jeremy's experience at the restaurant, can all be considered in this way. Against this, Bernard would argue rationally that all these examples of 'evil' are historically specific incidents of violence that better social and political systems could eradicate. Ultimately, Jeremy, and one therefore suspects McEwan, leans less towards Bernard's understanding of the universe than June's view that the world is not entirely in 'our' hands to control, that there are forces at work that the conscious human mind will never have in its possession. Though an inquiry into the nature of evil, the book ends optimistically with the belief that love is a sufficient redemptive power, and can in some sense overcome the tragedies of violence.

This last aspect is taken up by Marc Delrez in a sustained critique of the values and contradictions evident beneath the surface of McEwan's work:

■ The point seems to be that human love is in short supply and should be apportioned accordingly, between selected recipients; otherwise, there is no possible understanding of Jeremy's statement of 'belief in the possibility of love transforming and redeeming a life' (p. 20). *Whose* life is very much the moot point here, of course, for it goes without saying that love, taken as the highest human value, yields a world view that consistently elides issues of sociopolitical concern. Jeremy's particular brand of love ranges only just far enough to include his wife Jenny, his children (though they remain strangely absent from the novel), and, in the best of worlds, his niece Sally (whose history of violence and alcoholism, however, turns her into a borderline case). Actually, the fate held in store for Sally provides a tell-tale illustration of the hypocrisies built into Jeremy's system of value; and it is significant that she will come to focalize the guilt brought into play by successive breaches of solidarity. Legitimate though it may have been, his early abandonment of her for the sake of a career condemns Sally to a spiral of violence that continues into several disastrous marriages, which only replicate the disaster of her battered childhood. The expanding violence and suffering at work in Sally's life encourage Jeremy to universalise these principles and to consider all evil in the world as an extrapolation of her private pain; not only does he feel that 'her unhappy life was [his] responsibility' (p. 68), then, but he also sees in Sally an accessible close-at-hand lever on the rest of history. This is why Jeremy is prone to envelop with meaning his one decisive action in the novel, his taking to task a violent father for beating his child, thus acting out some kind of vicarious revenge for the wrongs suffered by Sally. The universal import of the incident is thoroughly underlined, since the boy's misery is likened to 'the condition of the world' (p. 128), while Jeremy gets 'a brief ennobling sense of [himself] as one of those obscure French citizens who blossom from nowhere at a transforming moment in their nation's history to improvise the words that history will engrave in stone' (p. 130). He manages to reconcile this with a smug feeling that the whole drama 'seemed to be enacted for [him] alone' (p. 124); this proves true enough since Jeremy has to be restrained in his murderous impulses in order that he develops a convenient insight into the conundrum of violence, which will exempt him in the future from further steeping himself in the blood of history. In the meantime, of course, the real Sally must fend for herself, for 'the strain on family life' (p. 68) imposed by her presence has been found too great for her to be allowed to stay.

Sally is thus used (and abused) as a universal scapegoat, apt to be sacrificed for the greater good of family life. By the same token, Jeremy's love affair with Jenny seems to be rooted in a private-individualist ethos that implies utter disregard for the body politic. In this respect it is probably no coincidence that Jeremy comes across as a nervous, easily intimidated young man who only finds himself and propositions Jenny after a joint visit to one of Poland's concentration camps – in apparent flight from what he perceives as an intolerable 'disease of the imagination and a living peril' (p. 110). Also, their first move as a couple is to turn their backs on barbed wire and to withdraw to the closet afforded by the local hotel, where they spend three days of unbroken love-making. The symbolic configuration of space here suggests a separation between the public and the private (or between history and a forgetful present) as well as a shift of focus towards the latter – a shift that devalues the notion of a political project and promotes a view of ethics as entirely bound up with the ideal of self-fulfilment in love. Throughout McEwan's work, this move is presented as a matter of philosophical necessity, perhaps of survival, in a postmodern age in which the old systems of value have ceased to command any credence; on the other hand, it can be argued that a novel such as *Black Dogs* fails to act upon its best insights because, as I suggest, it also includes a resigned awareness of its own forced complicity with evil.

The point is that the retreat from the political that forms a leitmotif in McEwan's work is burdened with a mesmerizing sense of guilt, which is the price to pay for this commodity called innocence. In other words, the escape into the sheltered domain of personal self-fulfilment is preceded and forestalled by an awareness of its impossibility, since this kind of post-Holocaust innocence is always already overshadowed by guilt anyway. This is perfectly clear in *Black Dogs*, where Jeremy discovers in the concentration camp that his only protection against despair would lie in a deliberate suspension of sympathy – an attitude that consists of jiggling one's change in one's pocket and then finding out that you are 'drawn insidiously to the persecutor's premise' (p. 110), or that you have 'taken one step closer to the dreamers of the nightmare' (p. 111). This is the realization that sanctions an approach to human endeavour fundamentally premised on the fact of disbelief. The originality of *Black Dogs*, as compared with McEwan's previous novels, is that it seeks to anchor such disbelief within the historical context of a twentieth century characterized by the disintegration of value; in this, however, it stands in line with McEwan's earlier books only in that it continues a form of 'avant-garde realism' that remains enthralled by a shrunken, crippled 'reality' inherited from the Holocaust. □

(Marc Delrez, 'Escape into Innocence: Ian McEwan and the Nightmare of History', 1995)[9]

Delrez feels that 'McEwan's art colludes with the very evils it is supposed to circumscribe' because of its naturalization of evil and because 'religion and spirituality consistently are presented not only as antinomic to political commitment but also as a source of necessary alienation both from public life and, at least in the case of June, from the family values so ardently vindicated elsewhere in McEwan's work'.[10]

Jago Morrison's principal interest in the following extract is with the ways in which Jeremy attempts to make sense of the past – his own and that of others. Morrison sees the book as an example of modern fiction's concern with personal and social memory crisis.

■ One of the central themes of *Black Dogs* is Jeremy's attempts to construct a particular personal history, that of June and her turbulent relationship with Bernard. It is through the specific problems of a biography, therefore, that the vaster relationships between time, history and memory are placed in question. The characteristic McEwan move – to invest such concerns in personal experiences – can be seen in the course of Jeremy's interviews with the now elderly June in a hospice for the terminally ill. Here the concept of memory loss is introduced. Writing a biography or memoir precisely implies a task of making June produce her past 'organised' (p. 32), to create history where now there are only broken memories. In the course of this effort June quite often drifts into sleep, and it is the treatment of her awakenings that opens the novel's central agenda:

> June woke from a five-minute doze to find a balding man of severe expression sitting by her bed, notebook in hand. Where was she? Who was this person? What did he want? That widening, panicky surprise in her eyes communicated itself to me, constricting my responses so that I could not immediately find the reassuring words, and stumbled over them when I did. But already, before I had finished, she had the lines of causality restored to her, she had her story again, and she had remembered that her son-in-law had come to record it. (p. 49)

A fear is suggested here at the tendency of time and memory – and hence meaning itself – to slip out of our familiar grasp. Both they and we as readers recognise the social imperative: actively to organise experience into temporally and biographically contextualised meaning. The point, though, is that in the later stages of her illness that has become more difficult for June, something that cannot be regarded as 'given' but which requires conscious effort. The making of memory itself has become a problem. As the familiar figure of Jeremy first approaches she can only gape at him without recognition:

> She had been buried in a sleep that had itself been smothered in an illness. I thought I should leave her to collect herself, but it was too late now. In the few seconds that it took to approach slowly and set down my bag, she had to reconstruct her whole existence, who and where she was, how and why she came to be in this small, white-walled room. (p. 33)

Accentuating this question mark around the nature of memory and biography, the props McEwan gives June for psychological defence, are, cleverly, the paraphernalia of writing and scholarship: 'today she was taking longer to come to. A few books and several sheets of blank paper lay across the bed. She ordered them feebly, playing for time' (p. 33).

The dialogue between past and present is an uncertain, fluctuating thing that must be secured by writing down.

The idea of 'playing for time' is strongly suggestive of certain strategies in contemporary fiction which parody and dispel the problems of biographical and historical writing. What this novel illustrates, however, is the fact that amnesia, the loss of time, is something far closer to fear than to play [...].

A bewildering complex of disparate time-scales are suggested in the novel. All of them spiral in various ways around June's horrifying confrontation with a pair of enormous black dogs on a mountain path during her honeymoon in southern France. This incident is thus deeply enmeshed in multiple tissues of time. On a personal level, we have June's sense of a new beginning and the biological time-horizon of her recently discovered first pregnancy. The mountain landscape inscribes a powerful sense of geological age. And a vast sense of human time hangs over the area because it is a prehistoric burial site.[11] On a historical level, this is also the newly liberated landscape of post-war France, with its sense of fresh, immediate possibilities. June's physical fight for survival is further framed in memory within a fundamental teleological debate. For Bernard, the future lies in the power of historical materialism to explain and to create social change through rational analysis. For June what matters ultimately is a more essential spiritual power, promising an ultimate salvation that is outside time and history.

McEwan's basic narrative framework of a memoir-within-a-memoir is thus set further within the complex time-scales of a narrative which, on a level beyond that again, also has its own multiple time-sites of telling and remembering. The older June's 'clinical' amnesia, then, is in a sense only the most literal disclosure of the personal and social memory crisis of which *Black Dogs* is an exploration. To put this differently, the presentation of this 'clinical' amnesia in the novel is intimately intertwined with the sense of a far wider argument about the difficulty of expressing our pasts in adequate and meaningful ways. □

(Jago Morrison, 'Unravelling Time in Ian McEwan's Fiction', 2003)[12]

David Malcolm also explores the ways in which Jeremy tries to make sense of the past he has unearthed. He focuses on the relation between individual and public history, but in particular on the role that violence plays in each.

■ There are two other major groups of motifs in *Black Dogs* that seem related in some way to June and Bernard's dispute. It has already been noted how characters' lives and experiences are closely related to public and historical events. For example, Jeremy and Jenny's lovemaking is interrupted by Bernard's excited telephone call about the fall of the Berlin Wall (pp. 68–9). But one of the clearest ways in which private and public are interwoven is embodied in another major strand or motif that runs throughout *Black Dogs*. The novel continually presents violence and a rejection of civilization. Violence is clearly there in Jeremy's youth, in the sadistic-masochistic relationship of his sister and her husband, in their treatment of each other and of their daughter (pp. 15–16). The whole episode connected with Jeremy and Bernard's visit to the Berlin Wall bubbles with violence (pp. 95–9). The unimaginable violence of Majdanek (p. 109–12), the French father's brutal violence towards his child (p. 129) and Jeremy's response (p. 131), the hideous black dogs themselves (p. 151) – all embody a brutal savagery that, Jeremy suggests, will recur in Europe sometime in the future (p. 174). Even Bernard's killing of an insect becomes, for June, representative of a monstrous human cruelty (p. 76). As is often the case in McEwan's fiction, the child is an important focus in *Black Dogs*: here as a victim of brutality. Jeremy's niece Sally and the boy in the French restaurant both embody this. It is also worth noting that June is pregnant with her first child when she is attacked by the dogs.

Violence is closely connected with an abandonment of civilization. This is how Jeremy sees his friends at the novel's start: as young men who are turning from their parents' intellectual culture towards something more brutal and racy (p. 13). The skinheads who attack Bernard have cut themselves loose from decency and humanity. They have become animal-like in appearance and behaviour (pp. 96–7) [the abusive French father is also called 'an animal' by Jeremy, p. 130]. Majdanek is the antithesis of the city and the life near which it stood (p. 109). The black dogs, June feels, reverse the common expectations of our culture and civilization by attacking her (pp. 147–8). Sometime in the future, she believes, they will come back and convulse Europe again (pp. 172). Of course, in the novel things are not quite as simple as that. When June and Bernard begin their love affair, they reject the norms of their time and place; they turn from civilization, and, the novel suggests, are right to do so (p. 56). Majdanek is orderly and well made (features often connected with good civilizations), yet is also monstrous (p. 110–11). Bernard is saved from a beating by the wild, street ferocity of the young woman in Berlin, not by the power of sensible argument (pp. 98–9). Jeremy resorts to fairly savage violence to express his disapproval of the French father's striking his child (p. 131). □

(David Malcolm, *Understanding Ian McEwan*, 2002)[13]

Malcolm concludes that while *Black Dogs* may not seem unified, despite its brilliance in parts, it does perhaps 'achieve a kind of coherence by suggesting that both rationality and nonrationality can lead to violence'.[14] Consequently, the novel is perhaps more than anything else concerned with the ways in which people resort and respond to violence. If June would see this as the manifestation of evil, and Bernard would see its roots in social inequalities, McEwan's novel overall suggests that violence is more random and unpredictable than this. Jeremy's role as historical inquirer, flawed though he is, seems less to involve a discovery of (partial) truth than an examination of change. His task as private historian is not to explain why things are as they are, but to investigate how they came about; and, above all, to chart the change in people brought about by their experiences. For example, Malcolm discusses the opening to the novel after the preface:

■ The novel proper starts with [Jeremy] considering and reflecting on a snapshot of his parents-in-law in 1946, taken just before their journey to Italy and France. He notes details of their appearance and speculates about the circumstances surrounding the photograph. He is clearly fascinated [...] by June and Bernard's past. Bernard has stayed essentially unchanged, he notes, in the forty years or more since the photograph was taken; June, however, has changed almost beyond recognition. The detail in which he describes her young self shows an interest in the sheer pastness of a distant time, its substantial differences in clothing, artefacts, moral-social attitudes, and modes of behaviour (pp. 25–6). Jeremy's interest in his parents-in-law is, however, not just a matter of dress. Their political concerns – they have just joined the Communist Party and are full of optimism about the future of the world and the benign changes that they are sure will soon come with capitalism's demise – are also set out. These early passages are representative of many others in the novel. Jeremy pursues his parents-in-law into their pasts, lovingly recording details of dress and mentality, noting differences between past and present yet also trying to understand how the present grew out of that particular past.

A few pages later he returns to the photograph and reflects on the strange 'innocence' of faces in the photograph, an innocence which he sees as coming from a seeming unawareness of the future passage of time and its changes (p. 37). Looking from June to the photograph, Jeremy formulates for himself the whole motive of his memoir gathering. 'The question I really wanted to ask was, How did you get from that face to this, how did you end up looking so extraordinary – was it the life? My, how you've changed!'(p. 38). □

(David Malcolm, *Understanding Ian McEwan*, 2002)[15]

Jeremy proceeds to locate innocence in ignorance of the future, reminding the reader of McEwan's previous novel: 'It was the innocence that was so appealing, not only of the girl, or the couple, but of the time itself [...]. The innocent time! Tens of millions dead, Europe in ruins, the extermination camps still a news story, not yet our universal reference point of human depravity. It is photography itself that creates the illusion of innocence. Its ironies of frozen narrative lend to its subjects an apparent unawareness that they will change or die. It is the future they are innocent of' (p. 37). Of course, that ignorance of the future always makes the present a time of innocence. McEwan is thus suggesting that, in the hopes surrounding the fall of the Berlin Wall and the end of the Cold War, there is an innocence that time will erode (and indeed was starting to erode in Yugoslavia as McEwan was writing).

Yet, the novel's importance, like Jeremy's, lies in the asking of questions. For example, it asks the reader to make a choice between two moral positions. Bernard states his own standpoint, which includes the view that the few may be sacrificed to secure the happiness of the many:

> What are those lines of Isaiah Berlin's that everybody quotes, especially these days, about the fatal quality of utopias. He says, if I know for certain how to bring humanity to peace, justice, happiness, boundless creativity, what price can be too high? To make this omelette, what price can be too high? Knowing what I know, I wouldn't be doing my duty if I couldn't accept that thousands may have to die now so that millions can be happy for ever. (pp. 88–9)

In answer to this, Jeremy replies on June's behalf:

> She didn't go from one fantasy utopia to another. It was a search. She didn't claim to have all the answers. It was a quest, one which she would have liked everyone to be on in their own way, but she wasn't forcing anyone. How could she? She wasn't mounting an inquisition. She had no interest in dogma or organised religion, it was a spiritual journey. Isaiah Berlin's description doesn't apply. There was no final end for which she would have sacrificed others. There were no eggs to break ... (p. 91)

These are the opposed views of those who advocate the greater claims of the collective and those who assert the rights and sanctity of the individual. But this is not an easy choice. Bernard and Jeremy have this discussion beside the Berlin Wall, whose demolition is considered to be the end of tyranny in the name of communism, and yet what it immediately gives rise to is the swastika-daubed skinheads who attack Bernard when he tries to defend the Turkish communist waving his red flag. In this scene and elsewhere, the book challenges the reader to take sides, to hold opinions and defend convictions, while at the same time asserting that there are no definitive answers to moral problems, only perspectives, positions, and further questions.

CHAPTER EIGHT

Rationality Is Its Own Kind of Innocence: *Enduring Love* (1997)

As noted in the Introduction, after the publication of *Amsterdam*, McEwan said that he thought the novels he'd written over the last ten years all belonged together: 'beginning with *The Child in Time* and really ending with *Enduring Love*: novels of a sort of crisis and transformation, rites of passage of great intensity for characters'.[1] This was indeed how *Enduring Love* was received, as another macabre story of obsession and suspense, opening with one of the most compelling beginnings in recent British fiction: a height from which it could only descend in the rest of the narrative. Merritt Moseley thought it one of the best novels of 1997, Anita Brookner (born 1928) called it a 'brilliant novel' and 'marvellous fiction', while Amanda Craig bemoaned its reliance on popular science – 'half-baked ideas' – and Jason Cowley thought it overdetermined and overly schematic.[2] A. S. Byatt (born 1936), however, has placed this careful structure in the context of the novel's thematic concerns: 'it juxtaposes a mad version of the plottedness of human relations, the divine design, the instant recognition of the beloved and destiny, with a human love which is vulnerable, can be destroyed by madness and certainty'.[3] While both Joe and Clarissa at points in the novel say that they had always believed their love would endure, it is Jed Parry's love that is the most impervious to time and change and that reveals Joe and Clarissa's own love as indeed human, and therefore vulnerable.

McEwan has described the several effects on the reader he was trying to achieve in the pivotal opening chapter:

■ its narrator is a failed scientist and a successful journalist [similar to Stephen Lewis, failed modernist novelist but successful children's author in *The Child in Time*], with a particular cast of mind – a highly organised mind – and I wanted immediately to suggest this kind of mind. It's a chapter that relies very heavily on a very disciplined sense of the visual, and of the relationship of the different figures. There are characters converging across a field ... Joe's way of describing those is in terms of their distance, their points of the compass, there are lots of precise visual details to suggest someone who has a fairly confident grip on the world, the sort of grip that I would associate with someone who embraces a strong materialist view of it. So the characterisation of Joe was central to that.

Secondly, I'd read that de Clérambault's syndrome – this strange psychotic delusional state – is often triggered by an intense moment. [...]

More broadly, I suppose that I wanted to – cynically, if you like – hook the reader. Again in that architectural sense, this is the first room I wanted the reader in, and I wanted the door locked behind them. And I suppose too that I wanted to suggest, in Joe's way of analysing and describing what's happened, something out of game theory and evolutionary psychology, a Darwinian way of looking at the world. That is, to talk about who lets go first as something that involves morality, involves instinct, involves an adaptationist account of why we are what we are, quite distinct from the deist account that Jed is going to espouse. □

(Margaret Reynolds and Jonathan Noakes (eds), *Ian McEwan: the Essential Guide*, 2002)[4]

On the novel's publication most critics focused on its opening scenes as a powerful starting point, and indeed Joe's narrative foregrounds these moments as originary – 'The beginning is simple to mark' (p. 1). The start does indeed seem like a portentous moment, echoing the opening words of the Bible: 'In the beginning ...'. *Enduring Love* begins with lovers eating under a tree, while the reader is given a godlike perspective on events (through the eyes of the bird circling above), and Parry thus appears as the evil presence in this Edenic setting, before the 'Fall': 'I've never seen such a terrible thing as that falling man', the first chapter concludes (p. 16).[5] However, in interview, McEwan has explained that the balloon accident was not the genesis of the book (McEwan has since written the introduction to David Hempleman-Adams's *At the Mercy of the Winds* (2001), the story of the first man to fly to the North Pole by balloon):

■ I'd already gathered quite a lot of the book from different quarters. I was looking for a device to bring together complete strangers, and to bring them together in a kind of emotional heat. Something like a car accident might have been right, but I wanted something unusual. I heard this true story about a man and his son who were hauled away by a balloon they were trying to tether in some field in Germany. What immediately struck me was the dilemma of knowing that if you all hang on, you can bring this balloon down to earth. But as soon as anyone breaks rank, then madness follows. The issue is selfishness. And that seems to me to be the underlying basic moral factor about ourselves. We're descended

> from generations of people who *survived*, who acted successfully. But who also cooperated successfully; so we clearly need to save our own skins and look out for own interests, but we're social animals and we need other people dearly. The issue is constantly with us. I think I could place everyone I know somewhere on that scale of 0-to-10 – are they slightly more self-absorbed? Some people are completely selfless; they only give. It's self-destructive, possibly. [...] This novel was written after a long period of reading in a number of fields in science. It wasn't ever conscious research. I'm always fascinated by the subject. I think we've been very fortunate – we've had a golden age in science, for 15 years. The number of highly literate scientists writing for an intelligent lay public is extraordinary. There's a kind of science writing that seems to bridge the gap between informing laymen but also informing other sciences. To take an immediate example – Steven Pinker's book on language certainly addresses not just lay people like myself but other scientists outside his immediate field. Similarly, my own particular intellectual hero is E. O. Wilson. He's a biologist. He wrote 'The Diversity of Life' [1992], and that was just genius. The thing that really interested me was the extent to which scientists are now trespassing into other areas. [...] there is a subject matter which would have been completely ruled out of court 15 years ago as a matter of scientific inquiry, and now it's central. It's called human nature. That interface between biology and social sciences, between biology and psychology, is increasingly clear. And by, from the other end, a new spirit perhaps in anthropology that is now exploring not how exotically different we are from each other, but how exotically similar we are.[6] Which seems to me a really fascinating problem – to go to a hunter-gatherer tribe and discover that the emotional range, the expression of emotion, certain kinds of social institutions, exist right across the board whether in Manhattan or North Kalahari. I think that tells us a great deal more about what we are than Margaret Mead ever did with her tales of the mischievous young Samoans.[...] one of the things you'll find in all humans is that people stand around and talk about each other and judge each other and take great delight in examining their motives.[...] We identify ourselves by it, our groupings, and we bring to bear all that emotional intelligence, talking about someone's motives or how they crossed the line of acceptability or how they didn't pull themselves back from disaster. Novels, in a focused and more articulate way, do many of the same things. □
>
> (Dwight Garner, 'Salon Interview', 1998)[7]

For Adam Mars-Jones, the novel is undermined by Joe's development as an unreliable narrator. When Joe is questioned by the police after the restaurant shooting he says his sorbet was 'apple' (p. 181), yet ten pages earlier he has said it was 'lime' (p. 171). Mars-Jones objects not to this as error but to its enactment of Joe's single-paragraph question about self-interest opposed to objectivity: 'But exactly what interests of mine were served by my own account of the restaurant lunch?' (p. 181). Mars-Jones thinks this is late in the day to make Joe out to be an unreliable narrator, crudely indulging the novel's main theme: humans are innately unreliable (e.g. 'our sense data came warped by a prism of desire and belief, which tilted our memories too' [p. 180]).[8]

Mars-Jones concludes that though the book begins superbly, it merely fizzles out at the end into a hackneyed confrontation, followed by academic paraphernalia: a case history, cod references and unnecessary appendices.[9]

Sven Birkerts compares the novel's structure, beginning with a crisis and then chronicling the aftermath, with Russell Banks's novel *The Sweet Hereafter* (1992), Rosellen Brown's *Before and After* (1992) and Philip Roth's *American Pastoral* (1997); but he might of course have made comparison with many of McEwan's other novels, especially *The Child in Time*. Birkerts concludes that, though the novel is a *tour de force*, McEwan's accomplishment is less memorable for its style than its presentation of Parry's syndrome, with its unremitting intensity, totally immune to Joe's rebuffs and entreaties.[10]

Like Mars-Jones, another critic who argues that McEwan has allowed the melodramatic conventions of genre fiction to run away with the plot is James Wood. For him, *Enduring Love* follows too closely the classic trajectory of a Hollywood thriller, obscuring McEwan's deeper interest in the competing ways in which rationalism and irrationalism construct the world:

> ■ The plot almost exactly matches the ideal scheme commanded by Syd Field, in his how-to manual, *Screenplay: The Foundations of Screenwriting* [1984]. The Hollywood formula, according to Field, is tripartite: set-up; confrontation; resolution. Field suggests that the classic thriller involves a subject who is the victim of a danger which is revealed to us in the set-up; in the second act, the victim has to confront this danger; and in the third act, the victim must go from being a victim to an aggressor – he must react to, and conquer, danger.
>
> McEwan's novel proves Field durable. In the first chapter (superbly described – the best passage in the book), Joe Rose, who narrates the novel, witnesses a terrible accident in which a man dies. This is the 'set-up'. One of the other witnesses of this accident, Jed Parry, conceives a violent love for Joe. He begins to stalk Joe, to phone him four times a week, and to hang around outside his house. He issues what seems like a verbal threat. As is familiar from the movies, no one really believes Joe. The police are indifferent. Clarissa, Joe's girlfriend, feels that Joe is exaggerating. But Jed Parry gets violent: he sends two men into a restaurant to shoot Joe. They get the wrong table. Still the police are unconvinced. So Joe, in Field's terms, becomes an aggressor. He goes it alone. He buys a gun. At this point, the book becomes a little ludicrous, as

convention encourages. Driving back from the gun-purchase, Joe is phoned on his cellular by Jed Parry. Jed has taken Clarissa hostage in their Maida Vale flat. Joe arrives at his house and shoots Jed, who is put in an asylum for the rest of his life.

It is a pity that McEwan felt a need to serrate his plot to this blade-like acuteness. For a thicker story, which is McEwan's real interest, gets cut away in the process, and is rather mocked by the narrative excitements. McEwan wants to examine how the irrational might undermine a man's rationalism; and how two people who supposedly love and know each other – Joe and Clarissa – can interpret the same experience quite differently, and quite selfishly. □

(James Wood, 'Why it all adds up', 1997)[11]

Indeed, Joe observes that 'Selfishness is also written on our hearts' (p. 14), which is an example of his 'clear thinking'. And while Wood is probably quite right to suggest that one of the central concerns of the book is the competing ways in which people make sense of reality, McEwan seems overall to endorse Joe's rationalist approach to problem-solving. Importantly, the book also explores the significance of cultural and moral relativism. This is most apparent when Joe discusses with the Logan children whether it can be moral to eat horsemeat, to burp, to say you're going to kill someone, or even to do it (pp. 119–20). Joe has earlier concluded that 'A good society is one that makes sense of being good' (p. 15), but whether goodness can be defined according to utilitarian or scientific criteria is another matter.

McEwan himself has described the development of the story in very different terms from Wood's:

■ Jed Parry was one of those characters who emerged on the page, step by step, and as he did so, I wrote myself into my theme, I think. I was never clear in my mind at the beginning quite where this was heading – it was one of those novels really undertaken as a voyage of exploration and Jed Parry was very much at the centre of this. It surprised me, the extent and depth of his obsession and became really the linch-pin of the whole. [...] I take a rational, well-organised man, and put him through a kind of burning fire, if you like. He faces the most irrational thing I could imagine at that point that would sustain itself through the novel, which is a man who not only has fallen in love with him and believes that Joe loves him back but is persuaded, as are a number of schizophrenics, that he's receiving messages and the endorsement of God in this pursuit and that he must bring this materialist, this atheist, into the lap of God. So, it's a real trial for his rationality and also for his marriage. [...] It was important to me to sow in the readers' mind a little bit of doubt about Joe's sanity and so, you know, there were a few clues along the way, because I wanted Joe to be doubted by everybody, not just his wife, not just the police but the reader too and I wanted a man at the centre of this who was a clear thinker, who appears to be right but then perhaps is wrong, but in fact is right [...]. I wanted, in other words, to write a book somewhat in praise of rationality which I think gets a very poor showing in western literature. Novels often end with a sort of hidden message that well, it's the one who trusted her heart or his intuition that saw him through. Well I think that there are many situations or most situations in life where in fact clear thinking and the rational sees you through. □

(Ian McEwan in interview, *Book Club*, 2000)[12]

As David Malcolm discusses, the rational is a function of knowledge, and *Enduring Love* illustrates how reason can only work with its own perspective on events, testing its conclusions against available evidence. If reason is based on incorrect information, it can lead to terrible consequences in a world that requires action as well as contemplation. That choice cannot always be based on certainty is the problem faced by the men holding down the balloon in Chapter 1. If they all hang on, they may keep the balloon from floating away, but if one of them lets go, all those who retain their grip on the ropes will be dragged skywards. To be certain of the right course of action, requires knowledge of the beliefs and behaviour of others. Malcolm writes:

■ There are a number of examples of dubious certainty and uncertainty in the novel. Jed is convinced Joe loves him; he does not. Mrs Logan is convinced her husband is an adulterer; he is not. The ex-hippies Joe meets reel off pseudoeducated banalities about the environment as if it were gospel (pp. 196–7). There are also a number of moments of deep uncertainty in the novel. Does Jed really exist, wonders Clarissa, or at least in the form Joe gives him (e.g. p. 86)? Why is Joe's and Jed's handwriting so similar, she wonders (p. 100)? For a short time, at least, the reader, too, perhaps wonders. Is Joe making all this up? Is Jed some kind of projection of his own guilt, a spirit, a real figure, called up to punish himself? The reader is in suspense for part of the novel, not knowing for sure quite what is going on. The climax of this strand in the story takes place in the police station after the shooting in the restaurant (pp. 174–82). The policeman who takes statements from the witnesses gives a weary list of the subjects on which the witnesses cannot agree. It is significant that Joe responds to the policeman's list, which suggests that knowledge is a fairly dubious concept altogether, with a sense of 'familiar disappointment' (p. 180). Objectivity and 'disinterested truth' are hard to get at, but – the conclusion of his reflection here is important too – that does not make it less admirable to try, even though 'it couldn't save us from ourselves' (p. 181).

In the end, as the reader looks back at the novel, he/she is confronted with four possibilities related to the subject of knowledge. These are as follows. First, Joe is right. Facts are facts, and scientific knowledge will steer one best through the maze of human life. Second, Joe is an outright liar, and the narration is an extensive piece of self-justification to conceal or fictionalise the way he has made a mess of his relationships with Jed and Clarissa. Third, all forms of knowledge are equal – Jed's metaphysical ecstasy, Clarissa's ill-defined feelings, Joe's traditional scientific knowledge. Or fourth, knowledge is an uncertain thing, difficult to achieve, subject to revision, but is attainable, and the best way to it is through Joe's rationalism, materialism, and traditional science (although that way is not going to make him popular with his lover, even if he does save her from a madman). The novel comes out on the side of the last possibility. Joe may be frustrating to Clarissa, but – barring the possibility that the whole novel is meant to be read as an extensive piece of lying – his stubborn rationality is the best bet in the chaos of human impulses. □

(David Malcolm, *Understanding Ian McEwan*, 2002)[13]

There is an irony here, in that McEwan's espousal of Joe's position seems to challenge the ability the novel claims to have, as an art form rooted in the imagination, to make sense of the world. Joe himself deliberates this issue: '[In the nineteenth century the] dominant artistic form was the novel, great sprawling narratives which not only charted private fates, but made whole societies in mirror image and addressed the public issues of the day. Most educated people read contemporary novels. Storytelling was deep in the nineteenth-century soul' (p. 48). Joe describes how the professionalism of science and the complexities of modernism in art changed this; but, he argues, storytelling remained important, and in some cases decisive, in determining whether or not theories gained acceptance. Relativity theory was 'too beautiful to resist' (p. 49), Dirac's theory of quantum electrodynamics was 'unattractive, inelegant [...]. Acceptance was withheld on grounds of ugliness' (p. 50). Joe concludes that, in the twentieth century, 'It was as though an army of white-coated Balzacs had stormed the university departments and labs' (p. 50).[14] This connects very directly with Clarissa's research interest in the Romantic poet John Keats (1795–1821), and reminds the reader of his famous dictum 'Beauty is truth, truth beauty' from 'Ode on a Grecian Urn' (1820). So, while rationalism and knowledge are valorised in *Enduring Love,* McEwan is deeply interested in the stories people tell in order to make sense of the world.

Also interested in McEwan's emphasis on storytelling, Roger Clark and Andy Gordon discuss the role Jean Logan plays in the book:

■ Like the main characters, she too is trying to make sense of the tragic death of her husband in the balloon accident. Just like them, too, she does so by interpreting signs – reading – in order to construct a narrative. After the police return her husband's car to her, she finds the remains of a picnic and another woman's scarf in Logan's car and concludes that her husband was having an affair and that his death was caused by him 'showing off to a girl' (p. 123); otherwise, she says, 'this story doesn't make sense' (p. 122). Like many of the interpretations examined so far, Jean Logan's reading of the situation, and the narrative she constructs in the extremity of her grief, ultimately proves to be a misreading.

Joe unearths the truth – which may be a further indication that his approach, though flawed, may not be without value and validity. It turns out that Logan, on his way to a medical conference in London, had given a lift to an Oxford professor and the young female student with whom the professor was having an affair. The picnic belonged to these two and the scarf to the student. Because of the illicit nature of the affair, the professor and the student deliberately refrained from coming forward as witnesses. Hearing *this* story, Jean Logan can recognize her story as wrong. It might well be that McEwan makes the Oxford don a professor of logic in order once again to suggest that some narratives have more credibility than others – this, after all, is the true story.

In terms of its engagement with epistemological issues, then, *Enduring Love* sets up a number of competing ways of making sense, many of which contradict one another, as in the case of Jean Logan outlined here, in order to suggest that it may in the end be the case that the desire for things to make sense is articulated through acts of storytelling; however, this does not mean the truth is forever unavailable, rather that more and less accurate versions of events are always in the process of being constructed. □

(Roger Clark and Andy Gordon, *Ian McEwan's* 'Enduring Love', 2003)[15]

The most extreme example of deluded storytelling in the novel is of course Jed's narrative of his relationship with Joe. In her book on McEwan, Christina Byrnes provides a useful review of the history of de Clérambault's syndrome:

■ This pathology was first described long ago. Jacques Ferrand wrote a treatise in 1623 on 'Maladie d'Amour' or 'Mélancholie Erotique'. In 1639 Bartolomy Pardoux, a Paris physician, discussed the pathology of love in his book *Diseases of the Mind*. De Clérambault referred to these cases as 'les psychoses passionelles' [psychoses of passion] and contributed a monograph on the subject bringing together most of the published clinical material. Cases had been described by Hippocrates, Erasistratus, Plutarch, Galen, Gideon Harvey (physician to Charles II), Winslow, Clouston and Kraepelin.[16] A revival of interest in this syndrome in America, France and Russia [...] is due to the increase in the frequency of criminal charges brought against stalkers. In an article, labelled 'Obsessional Harassment and Erotomania in a Criminal Court Population', there is the following information:

> Recognising that 'stalking behaviour causes anguish and fear for the victim, and sometimes culminates in profound and lasting physical injury', the New York State Legislature amended the law on menacing and harassment [in 1992].[17]

Many variations of this syndrome are described and some are regarded as primary while others are secondary to schizophrenic and other psychotic illnesses or to organic damage to the brain. The classical case, described by de Clérambault and referred to in *Enduring Love*, which involved a woman's belief that the curtains in Buckingham Palace signalled King George V's undying passion for her, is quoted in all the textbooks. Although most of the cases are women who become obsessed with a man of higher social standing then themselves, Paul Mullen and Michelle Pathe state: 'Pathologies of love occur in men and women, the homosexual and the heterosexual, in both western and non-western cultures.'[18] They attempt to draw the boundaries between the infatuation of falling in love, the state of being in love, and the pathological erotic fixation, in spite of the lack of response from the beloved. These last border on erotomania proper which they accept as a genuine psychosis. They comment that:

> The boundary issues are particularly acute in instances where there has been some form of real relationship, however fleeting, between the individual and the object of his affection... . The lives of the victims were disrupted by telephone calls, letters and in most cases repeated approaches. Several were physically assaulted... . The act of love, even if unrequited, is itself still accompanied by a feeling of great happiness, regardless of whether it occasions pain and sorrow. For those whose lives are empty of intimacy the rewards of even a pathological love may be considerable.[19]

McEwan's research is impeccable and extensive. It supports his wish to distance homosexual strivings, spiritual revelation and stalking behaviour into a character who is incontrovertibly proved to be psychotic. [...] The novel ends with Appendix 1 which claims to be a reprint from the *British Review of Psychiatry*. The case history (like the preface to *Black Dogs*) seems to be a précis of the story and the discussion takes up the professional tone of a psychiatric paper, emphasising the parallels between the case presented and the body of facts available on de Clérambault's syndrome[20] in the professional literature, and discusses outcome and the known effects on the patient's immediate environment. It concludes with a list of twenty references from British, French, American, Canadian and Scandinavian journals of psychiatry, criminology, social science and medicine, dealing with the syndrome. All these references are authentic except for the relevant paper by T. Gillett, S. R. Eminson and F. Hassanyeh, 'Primary and Secondary Erotomania: Clinical Characteristics and Follow Up', *Acta Psychiatrica Scandinavia*, vol. 82 (1990), 65–69. This is changed by McEwan to R. Wenn and A. Camia (1990), 'Homosexual Erotomania', *Acta Psychiatrica Scandinavia*, vol. 85 (1990), 78–82.[21] Like the name of Johnny B. Well [a play on the Chuck Berry song 'Johnny B. Goode'], the drug pusher, the names of Dr Wenn and Dr Camia are a joke, an anagram of Ian McEwan. This is particularly interesting given the following:

> I devised what they call in Hollywood a back story for Wenn and Camia: that they are a couple of homosexuals, who are only interested in homoerotic behaviour. If you look at their other published paper, it is called Homosexual erotomania, and was published in *Acta Psychiatrica Scandinavia*, which is a real journal and the most obscure that I could find. I submitted the fictional paper for publication but now I feel terribly guilty because the journal I sent it to has written back saying that it is considering it for publication. □
>
> (Christina Byrnes, *The Work of Ian McEwan*, 2002)[22]

Cressida Connolly observes that McEwan's depiction of Jed's illness is so disturbing and compelling because it in many ways so closely resembles ordinary romantic attachment. His letters and pleas are those made by unrequited lovers every day, and it is in his proximity to 'ordinary behaviour' that Jed becomes most unsettling.[23] This is precisely the conclusion that the novel comes to at the end of the first appendix when the text quotes Paul Mullen and Michelle Pathe: 'the pathological extensions of love not only touch upon but overlap with normal experience, and it is not always easy to accept that one of our most valued experiences may merge into psychopathology' (p. 242).

Lastly, Jago Morrison considers the degree to which Jed is presented as the product of Joe's own obsessions and of his own impulse to storytelling. Morrison begins by using the most famous work of the French philosopher Paul Ricoeur, *Time and Narrative* (published in English 1984–87), in which Ricoeur analyses the different Western theories of time-consciousness in theology, philosophy and art.

■ For Paul Ricoeur in *Time and Narrative*, the function of narrative in relation to the everyday living of social and personal lives is to reflect and to affirm the coherence of temporal experience. Thus, according to Ricoeur, 'time becomes human to the extent that it is articulated through a narrative mode, and narrative attains its full meaning when it becomes a condition of temporal existence.'[24] Between the vast scheme of cosmic time, the meaning-laden scale of the historical, and the private, fluctuating experience of personal time, there is the potential for discordance. The task of narrative is to cement a continuum between those three orders of time perception. It could be argued that narrative in Ricoeur's scheme has a fundamentally conservative function. Arising out of 'a pre-understanding of the world of action, its meaningful structures, its symbolic resources'[25] and mediating between those and the experience of the reader, narrative over and over rehearses and reproduces the hegemonic time frame. It ensures a comfortable continuum between our understanding of the cosmic or absolute, our sense of our historical placing, and the texture of our everyday experience.

[...] The challenge posed by Parry to the security of the protagonist Joe can certainly be read on three levels, broadly mirroring the analysis proposed in *Time and Narrative*. First, Parry's stalking and harassment disrupt the fabric of Joe's personal life, in terms of his habitual work-patterns and day-to-day routines. That threat on the one hand erodes his capacity to escape this level of consciousness into that other fundamental temporal experience, a necessary, undistracted state of intellectual concentration, 'the high-walled infinite prison of directed thought' (p. 48). Second, Parry's insistent intrusion precipitates pivotal crises in the larger narratives of Joe's family life and particularly in his professional life, the level at which personal experience interfaces with the public sphere. The stable relationship with Clarissa breaks down, and Joe finds himself compelled to re-assess the direction and value of his vocation as a writer. Finally, on a third and higher level, Parry's powerful imposition of a Christian teleology functions as a direct challenge to the temporal constitution of Joe's large scientistic and evolutionary belief system.

The response Joe's narrative initially articulates towards this complex onslaught, moreover, can be seen as an attempt at a closer marriage between the levels of his temporal consciousness. That appears most obviously in the move to abandon his career as a journalist – a mere mediator of knowledge – in favour of a re-entry into the metanarrative of scientific research, 'carrying my own atomic increment to the mountain of human knowledge' (p. 75). The continuum between his science-defined cosmic understanding and the narrative of his professional life is thus to be cemented more firmly. As a journalist, Joe's meditation on the role of narrative in science has raised some uncomfortable questions, not only about the sanctity of scientific knowledge in relation to the history of the cosmos, but also about the status and meaning of his own career in relation to the history of science. The attempt to abandon that and to re-enter the research community offers an easy refusal of both those sets of questions, precisely because it offers the possibility of re-establishing a narrative coherence between the different levels of his temporal world.

The ultimate failure of Joe's attempt at ontological self-defence, through the failure of his research bid, leads to the necessity for the alternative strategy that dominates McEwan's text – the more violent narrativization of Parry himself. It is in this sense that *Enduring Love* is 'about' de Clérambault's syndrome. Through the syndrome, the novel identifies the power of medical-scientific discourse as a guarantor of temporal and epistemological security. In a social sense, the appended documents are significant because they cast Parry into a ratified linear-narrative framework that carries the force of juridical and disciplinary power. On a personal level, moreover, what de Clérambault offers Joe is a surrogate solution to his own sense of temporal dislocation:

> The name was like a fanfare, a clear trumpet sound recalling me to my own obsessions. There was research to follow through now and I knew exactly where to start. A syndrome was a framework of prediction and it offered a kind of comfort. I was almost happy. [...] It was as if I had at last been offered that research post with my old professor. (p. 124)

Nevertheless, it is within this process that the affinity between the urges of narrativization and those of obsession is gradually and inexorably suggested in the text. In his journalistic role, Joe's own discursive practice involves a deployment of narrative as mediation: 'People say I have a talent for clarity. I can spin a decent narrative out of the stumblings, back-trackings and random successes that lie behind most scientific breakthroughs. It's true, someone has to go between the researcher and the general public, giving the higher-order explanations that the average laboratory worker is too busy, or too cautious, to indulge' (p. 75). In the course of the text, however, that professional penchant for the ordering and rationalization of the ordered becomes radically extended. While Joe labours with the enigmatic and allusive discourse of Parry's letters, cutting and pasting them into the deepening narrative of a threat (which he can then take to the police), the parallel suggestion is developed of the symbiotic relationship between Parry's intrusion and the neurosis implicit in Joe's own consciousness. For Joe, Clarissa's perception of Parry is cast in precisely those terms. 'He was the kind of phantom that only I could have called up, a spirit of my dislocated, incomplete character, or what she fondly called my innocence' (p. 102). Parry needs to be assimilated and contained within the narrative of criminality, and later of psychiatric disorder, before he can be policed and contained on a bodily level. On one level, the novel is the story of Joe's success in that endeavour. What emerges in his attempts to articulate Parry's deviancy is, nevertheless, as strong a conviction of his own obsessionality:

> Three times I crossed the street towards him with my hidden tape recorder turning, but he would not stay.
>
> 'Clear off then!' I shouted at his retreating back. 'Stop hanging around here. Stop bothering me with your stupid letters.' Come back and talk to me, was what I really meant. Come back and face the hopelessness of your cause and issue your unveiled threats. Or phone them in. Leave them on my message machine. [...] I daydreamed violent confrontations that always fell out in my favour. (pp. 143–4) □

(Jago Morrison, 'Narration and Unease in McEwan's Later Fiction', 2001)[26]

The book's central plot does of course end precisely in this manner, which is one of the ways in which McEwan signals his support for Joe's rationalism despite the phantasies running beneath it. After this violent confrontation, *Enduring Love,* suitably for a book that relies so heavily on tripartite structures, concludes with three endings. Each of these endings brings to the fore the belief-system of one of the central characters. The final one, Appendix 2, ends with Jed's restated conviction that 'faith is joy' (p. 245): faith in God, in himself, and in Joe. The penultimate ending, Appendix 1, offers a scientific case-history, in which Jed's behaviour is fixed into a clinical syndrome, the discovery of which has earlier allowed Joe some catharsis: enabled Joe to explain adequately for himself what has happened, and why. His normality and indeed his faith in science are endorsed by the documented history of de Clérambault's syndrome, turning his individual experience into a 'case', thus not only helping to depersonalize Joe's individual experience but also authorising his understanding of its meaning (Jed becomes 'my de Clérambault', p. 207). Clarissa's perspective thus seems unrepresented, unless the ending before the appendices expresses it in some way. If Clarissa's belief system, emphasised not only by her comments on love and feeling to Joe but also by her interest in Keats, is taken to exist somewhere between the brute physicality of Joe's materialism and the metaphysical certainties of Jed's faith, then the endorsement of love and human relationships in Chapter 24 seems closest to her set of values. Completing the terrible cycle of events that began with Joe and Clarissa's picnic under the oak on page 1, the book here also ends with a picnic, at which Logan is proven innocent of the accusation of adultery and in which children feature most prominently (it is also important here that Joe and Clarissa later 'successfully' adopt a child, p. 242). Indeed, a child's question concludes the narrative. Rachael asks Joe to tell Leo 'the thing about the river' (p. 231). What Joe has told Rachael is that the 'smallest possible bit of water that can exist [is] Two atoms of hydrogen, one of oxygen, bound together by a mysterious powerful force' (p. 225). Millions of these particles then make up the river, he says. The analogy here is evidently with the smallest human unit in society, the family, in which two people are bound together by the mysterious force of love – and alongside them is a third, their child. This at least is the benign reading, but of course McEwan allows the interpretation that takes Joe's story to allude to the force that has bound Jed to Joe and Clarissa; which also is love. The ending of *Enduring Love* before its appendices presents a scientific explanation; but that explanation is a metaphor. To suggest Clarissa's perspective, which is drawn from art and literature, it can be noted that it is also a story. What Rachael asks Joe to tell Leo thus suggests a common ground for fiction and science in their joint reliance on narrative.

As with much of *Enduring* Love, the final passage is in fact in dialogue with other sections of the novel. For example there is Jed's earlier response to Joe's scientific articles, in which, if God is (a metaphor for) love, Clarissa's voice can also be heard:

> You write that we know enough about chemistry these days to speculate how life began on earth. Little mineral pools warmed by the sun, chemical bonding, protein chains, amino acids, etc. The primal soup. We've flushed God out of this particular story, you said, and now he's driven to his last redoubt, among the molecules and particles of the quantum physicist. But it doesn't work, Joe. Describing how the soup is made isn't the same as knowing why it's made, or who the chef is. It's a puny rant against an infinite power. (p. 135)

CHAPTER NINE

Their Reasonable Laws: *Amsterdam* (1998)

Though it won the Booker Prize, *Amsterdam* is usually considered one of McEwan's lesser novels. The book has been called a fable, a psychological thriller, and a morality tale, but it only begins to cohere when it is seen as McEwan's first sustained foray into comedy. Divided into five sections, or acts, it has the rhythm of a play and the feel of a film script in the making. The novel takes its epigraph from Auden's 'The Crossroads': 'The friends who met here and embraced are gone, \ Each to his own mistake'. The meeting this alludes to is that between four men at the funeral of Molly Lane, who has died after a long illness: the composer Clive Linley, the newspaper editor Vernon Halliday, the Foreign Secretary Julian Garmony, and Molly's overprotective husband George. The four have all been Molly's lovers and the storyline rests on their jealousy and their veiled contempt for each other, fuelled by the selfish weaknesses and hubris that undercut their pompous, high-minded beliefs.

Most reviewers of *Amsterdam* were positive, seeing this short novel as an exquisite social satire or moral fable. There were reservations from some quarters, however. For Adam Mars-Jones, the overly contrived ending merely reveals the characters to be the puppets one has suspected all along.[1] For Anita Brookner, McEwan is adept at pacing his nightmare, but *Amsterdam* amounts to little more than a brief bad dream. She explains its shortcomings in terms of scantily defined characters, few landscapes, and few women characters.[2]

But for most critics the book succeeded as a burlesque of the recently deposed Conservative government led by Prime Minster John Major. Beset by infighting over Europe and by controversy concerning Major's 'Back to Basics' campaign, the government was again rocked in October 1996 by a parliamentary inquiry into allegations that Neil Hamilton, a former Conservative junior minister, had accepted bribes to ask questions in Parliament. By January 1997, Major had lost his parliamentary majority.

McEwan has said of the political backdrop to the book:

■ The press and political culture have been trapped in something of a time-warp. A near-Victorian morality has held sway in newsrooms and sex scandals are run against an implicit set of moral values, which actually nobody in the country is living by. I think perhaps there has been a change, that that's now crumbling. ... It was as if the political culture and the press had each other by the throat where neither could move. I think if that does crumble completely we'll all be amazed that it lasted so long, so long after the trial [in 1895] of Oscar Wilde [1854–1900] and the rehabilitation of Oscar Wilde. □

(Ian McEwan, *Bold Type* Interview, 1998)[3]

These scandals and double standards resulted in the widespread currency of the expression 'politics of sleaze'. Allegations against the government brought to a head the question of whether a ruling party that prided itself on family values and free enterprise had become untenably corrupt – which is clearly the case in *Amsterdam,* and applies to the press and the arts as well as government. For Dominic Head, a substantial point of the novel is that 'it may be in the nature of an unselfconscious professionalism to dispense with ethical foundations'.[4] He continues:

■ In *Amsterdam* (1998), Ian McEwan offers a satirical portrait of those who 'had flourished under a government they had despised for almost seventeen years' (p. 12). In a sense, this is a deliberation on compromise, on left-intellectual achievement in an (apparently) hostile political context. Despite the author's first-hand knowledge of this stratum of the intelligentsia, there is no sense of explicit self-analysis: the narrative tone is detached, befitting the clinical dissection of amorality in the two principals. □

(Dominic Head, *Modern British Fiction*, 2002)[5]

In interview, McEwan himself has discussed his novel as one in which he says goodbye to 18 years of Conservative rule.

■ [Bold Type:] *Speaking of British institutions, what effect or influence have the political changes in Britain over the last few years had on the British literary community?*

[Ian McEwan:] I don't like to think that governments have that large an impact in a democracy. But clearly, changes in government are seen to mark cultural changes, and certainly this is going to be a very different time from the Thatcher–Major years, but I don't think it's time enough yet for novelists to react. Government actions need to percolate down more, or the spirit of the age needs to percolate up, for this to become a little clearer. My overwhelming sense, still, is of an era that has just come to an end. And really *Amsterdam* is my farewell to that time. And I'm very glad to say goodbye to it.

Amsterdam *was a different kind of novel from your recent work. It's much shorter, for instance, than* Enduring Love. *What inspired the change?*

For a long time I wanted to get back to the kind of form, the short novel, that could be read in three or four hours, that would be one intact, complete, absorbing literary experience. I wanted you to be able to hold the whole structure in your mind so that you could actually see how it works. Part of my ambition for *Amsterdam* is that the reader would share in the plotting of the book. It's a fairly elaborately plotted novel; it's meant to take pleasure in its own plotting, and I hope the reader is drawn into that. I always had it in mind as almost a kind of a theatrical experience. Its original subtitle was a comi-tragedy, and it was therefore in five acts, which remain in place. There were any number of ways I could have padded it out, but in fact successive drafts involved a process of making it leaner and leaner until I really couldn't lose any more of it.

It's also a departure in other ways.

It's also a departure in it that it's a social satire, heavily influenced by the early novels of Evelyn Waugh. And it is quite distinct from my novels written over the last ten-year period, which I think all belong together, beginning with *The Child in Time* and really ending with *Enduring Love*: novels of a sort of crisis and transformation, rites of passage of great intensity for characters. And although it's somewhat dark in its humour, *Amsterdam* is meant to be lighter in tone, and much more based in a recognizable, shared social reality.

Was the writing process much different, too?

It was a real pleasure to write *Amsterdam*. If I had to characterize my mood, I wrote in a state of glee. It was a very different kind of writing experience from *Enduring Love*, which was full of almost nightmare intensity – which in itself was exhilarating. But this had a quality of ... I kept thinking, 'If nobody else likes it, I don't give a damn, because I really am having fun.' One of my principal pleasures was writing in the world of work. I liked evoking both the work of a newspaper editor and the work of a composer. I have a great deal of regard for the short stories of [Rudyard] Kipling [1865–1936], for example, which are so steeped in the different kinds of work that people do. I admire it in John Updike [born 1932]. He's very good at getting into the process of particular kinds of work. □

(Ian McEwan, *Bold Type Interview*, 1998)[6]

There is a range of disparate references here: to Updike, Kipling and Waugh. We may conclude, then, that this is a far cry from the Kafkaesque world of McEwan's early writing; and two of the writers cited, Waugh and Updike, might previously have been more closely associated with a tradition that includes Martin Amis rather than Ian McEwan. *Amsterdam* sits uneasily in McEwan's novels precisely because it lacks a sense of real seriousness. It deals with weighty moral and political issues but is not prepared to contemplate the possibility that its chosen characters could engage with them in terms other than the egotistical and the corrupt. Despite this, David Malcolm concludes that *Amsterdam* is in part a psychological study and a morality tale:

■ part psychological novel and part social satire, it is also, in part, a moral fable (rather like the chapters of *The Daydreamer* [McEwan's 1994 novel for children]). *Amsterdam* has the briefness, the relatively simple characters, the clear moral and social dilemmas that are associated with the genre. Clive and Vernon are each confronted with a moral dilemma, and each makes a disastrous decision. Clive's moral dilemma is simpler. On balance, his symphony cannot outweigh the imperative to try to interrupt a rape. Vernon's dilemma is more complex. Garmony is a nasty piece of work who might well make the world worse. But the reader suspects that this is finally a secondary reason for Vernon's deciding to publish the pictures; the primary one is a desire to save his own career by raising his paper's circulation. And for their shabbiness and worse, Vernon and Clive are duly punished – fired, disgraced, ridiculed, ultimately the victims of each other's pique. The moral could scarcely be clearer if the narrator set it out: 'Thus perish the hollow men'. Alas, one cannot say that the good are rewarded in *Amsterdam*, because there are no good. The only possibly admirable character is Garmony's surgeon wife, Ruth, but even she colludes with the Conservative Party media manipulators as her public service is used as a political weapon (pp. 121–5). The police fake their evidence (pp. 152–4); the critic who mocks Clive's music and Vernon's moral stature visits a pedophile brothel (pp. 164–5). The men who come out on top are as corrupt as the losers: Frank Dibben at *The Judge* and the pompous George. The world of the great and the good is a foul place in *Amsterdam*. □

(David Malcolm, *Understanding Ian McEwan*, 2002)[7]

For John Brannigan, the novel is perhaps most concerned with the mid-life crises of those who have realized that their best work, and the best part of their lives, is behind them. The importance of Molly in this respect must be as a signifier of their own mortality and as a premonition of what awaits them at the end of the book: a drug-induced dementia followed by death (it is worth noting that Molly's 'tingling in her arm', p. 3, is echoed at their deaths in Clive's 'My arm's so hot', p. 168, and Vernon's 'pain in his upper arm', p. 173).

■ It is the loss of memory which Clive and Vernon fear most, the incapacity to access and rehearse the past, and in their dying reveries, it is the ghostly figure of Molly whom they both envisage arriving to nurse them. *Amsterdam* thus dramatizes the power of the dead over the living, and equates living with the power to remember. That Clive unwittingly plagiarizes Beethoven's [1770–1827] *Ode to Joy*, in what he thinks of as his elegy to the dead century (p. 20), and on another occasion as a 'representation of himself' (p. 156), reveals a creative mind which is as exhausted by the burden of cultural tradition and history as the landscape he roves over for inspiration is eroded by walkers and trampled by tourists. (pp. 80–3) □

(John Brannigan, *Orwell to the Present*, 2003)[8]

McEwan is therefore suggesting that a state of exhaustion has crept up on the British establishment. If we take his reference to Waugh seriously then this would seem to imply that euthanasia is the appropriate cure for the self-aggrandizement, moral corruption and possibly even senility of a governing generation that has betrayed the legacy it has inherited from the past. William H. Pritchard also invokes Waugh, and Kingsley Amis, as precursors to the McEwan of *Amsterdam*:

■ In the novel's splendid opening sequence, at the crematorium chapel where Molly Lane is being paid her last respects, Clive and Vernon, both former lovers of Molly, reminisce as they put off speaking to the dead woman's highly managerial husband. Both Clive and Vernon dislike George Lane, and that dislike has only been heightened by his authoritative surveillance of the dying woman's swift decline. ('Brain-dead and in George's clutches,' remarks Clive, mordantly.)

The brisk, concentrated touches with which the scene is put before us have a more than personal authority in their perceptiveness, as Clive registers how the crematorium crowd in daylight looks 'terrible, like cadavers jerked upright to welcome the newly dead.' Julian Garmony, the right-wing Foreign Secretary whom Clive is summoned to meet, displays the politician's characteristic 'eye movements, the restless patrol for new listeners or defectors, or the proximity of some figure of higher status.' The mourners are of a generation that grew up in an England of 'full employment, new universities, bright paperback books, the Augustan age of rock-and-roll, affordable ideals,' so they were already safe when the state, under Margaret Thatcher, withdrew its largesse and 'became a scold.'

Throughout much of the book, Clive and Vernon share the focus of attention, appropriately in a novel that builds to the disposition of their twin fates. Clive sees himself, not without some justification, as the heir of Ralph Vaughan Williams [1872–1958]; he has written a book in reaction to modernism's 'old guard' and its attempt to banish melody and harmony. In that book, 'Recalling Beauty,' Clive describes a composition by one of modernism's zealots: 'a publicly subsidized "concert" in a nearly deserted church hall, in which the legs of a piano were repeatedly struck with the broken neck of a violin for over an hour. An accompanying program note explained, with references to the Holocaust, why at this stage in European history no other forms of music were viable.' Clive has been commissioned to write a symphony from which the committee hopes a single tune can be incorporated into the millennial celebrations. Already two deadlines behind, he is approaching completion of the work and is fixed on the 'irresistible melody' he will produce as 'the dead century's elegy.'

If it sounds like McEwan is setting up his composer as fatuously taken in by his own importance, such is not wholly, or solely, the case. Clive's reflections on the arduousness of writing a symphony are informed with musical know-how, and his attempts to compose the melody – especially during a revelatory moment while hiking in the Lake District – are fully and convincingly imagined. In thinking of his task as analogous to Beethoven's composing the 'Ode to Joy,' Clive is surely overreaching, setting himself up for a fall. But McEwan makes you believe that the composer possesses real talent.

On the other hand, Vernon Halliday, editor of a downmarket London broadsheet called *The Judge*, is 'within his profession ... revered as a nonentity.' He is fighting to raise the circulation numbers and keep his job. His great opportunity for doing both comes when Molly's husband offers him deeply compromising pictures of Julian Garmony (who likes to 'dress up') taken by Molly. But when Vernon tells Clive about this opportunity, his friend is disgusted and accuses him of insulting Molly's memory, thus precipitating the serious coming asunder of her two ex-lovers.

If all this sounds highly plotted (and I've left much out), it is. *Amsterdam* is a well-oiled machine, and McEwan's pleasure in time-shifting, presenting events out of their temporal order (flashing back in Clive's mind, say, to a conversation he had the day before) is everywhere evident. Vladimir Nabokov [1899–1977], asked whether sometimes his characters didn't break free of his control, replied that they were galley slaves, kept severely under his thumb at all times. McEwan follows this prescription in spades.

In a moment that typifies the book's cruel wit, Vernon, with Clive's approval, humiliates an obnoxious critic named Lanark by telling him that he's recently seen Lanark's name on a list of distinguished people, including judges and government ministers:

'Lanark flushed with pleasure. "All this stuff about a knighthood is complete nonsense."

"It's certain to be. This concerns a childrens' home in Wales. Top-notch pedophile ring. You were videoed going in and out a dozen times. We were thinking of running a piece ... but I'm sure someone else will pick it up." '

This is the book at its best. But when the cruel wit is turned on the two central figures, especially on Clive, I wondered whether he (or McEwan) had quite deserved or earned it. Although we suspect that comeuppances are in store for both Clive and Vernon, it is hard to credit – after some of the sharp and clever things Clive has said and thought earlier – that on the verge of finishing his symphony he thinks 'quite simply, that it might not be going too far to say that he was ... a genius,' and that geniuses were few and far between in his country: 'There had been no Beethovens here.' The long narrative knife is clearly out. And is it quite conceivable that the agent of Vernon's editorial fiasco (the published pictures of Garmony backfire) should be the politician's wife, who happens also to be a crack surgeon? Her televised defense of her husband shows her emerging 'from the operating theater, tired but happy, after performing open-heart surgery on a 9-year-old black girl named Candy.'

If such narrative happenings are too neat to be true, if the dispatching of characters and the tying-up of ends in the book's final chapters constitute striking effects rather than moral exploration and understanding, they are no less entertaining for that – entertaining in the mode of earlier nasty British satirists like Evelyn Waugh and Kingsley Amis. □

(William H. Pritchard, *New York Times Book Review*, 1998)[9]

Nicholas Lezard also understands the book in this way, noticing that, for the first time, McEwan has contempt for the characters in one of his novels. As a satire on cynical heartlessness it appropriately adopts the vernacular of comedy: 'it was *The Judge's* photograph what did for him' (p. 174) and 'It's a spoiler' (pp. 124 and 173).

■ There is a distinct whiff of Evelyn Waugh in this book, not only in its style but in its subject matter. It begins at the funeral of one Molly Lane, a character who therefore only exists as a memory or, later, a hallucination; three of her former lovers are wondering how to bring themselves to talk to her cuckolded widower. The characters are a newspaper editor, a composer, and the (Tory) Foreign Secretary, all tantalisingly plausible; and that most if not all of the characters are in some way eminent adds a charge to the book's deeper subject matter: deception, both of others and of the self.

The composer's self-delusion is the most amusingly delineated: 'There were moments in the early morning ... when Clive ... had once more a passing thought, the minuscule fragment of a suspicion that he would not have shared with a single person in the world ... the thought was, quite simply, that it might not be going too far to say that he was ... a genius. A genius.' [The last ellipsis is McEwan's.]

The world of newspapers is deftly done, with shades of *Scoop* [1938; a novel by Evelyn Waugh]: 'It's time we ran more regular columns. They're cheap, and everyone else is doing them. You know, we hire someone of low to medium intelligence, possibly female, to write about, well, nothing much. You've seen the sort of thing. Goes to a party and can't remember someone's name. Twelve hundred words.' [...]

It's a measure of the sinewy precision of his style that it is only on a second reading that you realise how much McEwan despises his characters: this is how it sucks you into its moral dilemmas – or rather, makes you think at first that what are really non-dilemmas are matters for great ethical wrangling. It's a much neater trick than making you believe that simple things are in fact complicated. It is, though, smoke and mirrors. The larger ethical issue of voluntary euthanasia, which ripples beneath the surface and gives the novella its title, is eventually dodged except for supplying the final twist. Which is a little corny but is a way of telling us not to take it too seriously. □

(Nicholas Lezard, 'Morality Bites', 1999)[10]

In contrast to, say, Martin Amis, McEwan has always been seen as a serious novelist: one who believes in character, the efficacy of politics, and the presence of morality in individual action. *Amsterdam* has thus presented problems for critics who have attempted to read it in similar ways to his other works. As a satire, it is also one in which the author's own position is hard to describe, define or divine. It may be best read, then, as a divertissement, a diversion between the far more serious works *Enduring Love* and *Atonement*. Which is to say that it can be read profitably on its own terms, but resists the scrutiny successfully applied to his other novels. This would seem to be the conclusion of Christina Byrnes, who nonetheless endeavours to read the book in terms of an overall theoretical approach to McEwan's *oeuvre*. Below, in an extract from a study extracted in earlier chapters in which she reads all of McEwan's work from a psychodynamic perspective, Byrnes examines the novel in terms of sadomasochistic dynamics, maturational crises and depression.

■ He revisits some of the territory explored in the late 1970s from the perspective of twenty years of successful writing and the divorce which ended the relationship behind both of the early novellas. John Keenan writes: 'In *Amsterdam* the tone is light, but the accent nevertheless is on discord, betrayal, selfishness and death'.[11] The classical McEwan themes are reworked once more, with the difference that they are played by conspicuously successful, middle-aged men, who have acquired wealth and fame, have lived through marriages, divorces and many love-affairs and have the power to influence current events. [...]

Although Molly's body is respectably cremated, the equivalent of the bad smell from the sarcophagus in the cellar [in *The Cement Garden*] emanates, albeit symbolically, from the remains and poisons the friendship among her lovers. The theme of incest can be discerned in the claustrophobic relationships between the male characters who move like satellites trapped in her orbit, once shared her sexual favours and still nurse rivalries and ambivalence towards her. Secrecy, betrayal and the corruption of innocence is again to the fore. Sado-masochism is evident in the destructiveness and envious spoiling of each other's lives and the characters' thoughtless, or perhaps unconscious, inviting of disaster by trusting Molly and each other with incriminating secrets, which they use like weapons against each other. The sado-masochism in *Amsterdam* is not specifically sexual. It expresses itself in cutting remarks, the hurling of verbal excrement, the exposure of rivals in the shame of public humiliation and character assassination: 'I see you once said in a speech that Nelson Mandela deserved to be hanged' (p. 15) and again: 'The very last time I saw Molly she told me you were impotent and always had been' (p. 16). According to Erich Fromm destructiveness is always linked with sado-masochistic tendencies: 'In sadism the hostility is usually more conscious and directly expressed in action, while in masochism the hostility is mostly unconscious and finds an indirect expression.'[12]

Jack [in *The Cement Garden*] failed in the tasks of adolescence, Colin [in *The Comfort of Strangers*] in the tasks of manhood and Clive, Vernon and Garmony come to grief in their middle age after much conspicuous success: '*Amsterdam* contains acute insights into how essentially moral men can be poisoned by public life.'[13] McEwan attributes this to:

> The overreaching ambition, the self-delusion and the self-importance that afflicts men of about my age as they become successful and respected ... everyone makes space around them. The arena is empty for them to damn themselves.[14]

From the point of view of psychodynamic interpretations, these three novellas [*Amsterdam, The Cement Garden* and *The Comfort of Strangers*] emphasise the differences between the maturational crises of adolescence and mid-life. Parents have disappeared from the stage and such children as are mentioned are adult. The characters come face-to-face with the realities of ageing, illness, loss of competence in the world and the approach of death. McEwan told William Leith: 'I used to think, madly, in my teens and early twenties, "I know it happens to everybody, but I don't think it's going to happen to me. I have a feeling I'm different [... and] might just escape" '.[15] Sex and death are experienced differently than they were in youth. Masturbation had occupied the bulk of Jack's waking life and energy and haunted his dreams:

> In a large armchair at the side of my bed sat my mother staring at me with huge, hollow eyes [...] 'I'm not doing anything', I said, and noticed as I glanced down that there were no clothes on the bed and that I was naked and masturbating in front of her.[16]
>
> When Vernon awakes, alone in his bed:
>
> His nakedness against the sheet, the wanton tangle of bedclothes by his ankle and the sight of his own genitalia [...] sent vague sexual

> thoughts across his mind [...] he rolled onto his side and wondered whether he had it in him to masturbate. (p. 100)

A guilty preoccupation has now becomes a boring activity. The loss of virginity, which in *The Cement Garden* forms the climax of the whole novella, happened too long ago to deserve a mention and both wives and mistresses are busy with their own careers.

The long-term consequences of sexual promiscuity are hinted at in the fact that Molly dies of a disease of the central nervous system which may have been tertiary syphilis. The sexually transmitted nature of her illness is strongly hinted at in the fear of infection that both Clive and Vernon give way to after her death. It is well known that syphilis is infectious only in the primary and secondary stages and becomes latent for many years before the neurological symptoms make their appearance.[17] Shortly after Molly's funeral, both her ex-lovers experience symptoms which often herald the beginning of tertiary syphilis and Clive shows at least one episode of poor discernment together with the feeling that he is a genius. Loss of judgement combined with delusions of grandeur is typical of neuro-syphilis. Of course, fleeting mental and physical symptoms are not uncommon in stress or trauma. It seems McEwan has left Molly's diagnosis open to speculation.

[...] McEwan's once passionate commitment to democracy now sounds a sour note. Freedom of the press, which once had been his cherished ideal and which provides the checks and balances in a free society, is depicted as gross abuse of power in the office politics of *The Judge*.[18] Sleaze and corruption poison public and private life and lead to disillusionment and cynicism. Depression is palpable in the loss of dependable solace, not only from intimate relationships but even from the landscape:

> the unimaginable age of the mountains and the fine mesh of living things that lay across them would remind him that he was part of this order and insignificant within it, and he would be set free. Today however... . The open spaces that were meant to belittle his cares, were belittling everything: endeavour seemed pointless. Symphonies especially... . Passionate striving. And for what? Money. Respect. Immortality. A way of denying the randomness that spawned us, and of holding off the fear of death. (pp. 78–9)

It is small wonder that McEwan has changed his mind about euthanasia. He told Michael O'Donnell that in his Utopia there would be no option for oblivion. He now seems less willing to countenance waiting passively for death amid degeneration and dementia. In spite of the subjects dealt with in *Amsterdam*, McEwan insists:

> Not many things in life get better as you get older. But in a writer's life, perhaps there's a little plateau that you hit somewhere in your mid-40s to your mid-50s. You've still got the physical stamina to write a novel without too much pressure, thoughts of mortality... .[19]

Perhaps he has pushed the depression into the characters and the reader. McEwan's moral sense, so often defended by him in early interviews, is seen again here: 'It's about two old friends... . It's the story of how they each make a disastrous moral judgement'.[20] By now, however, he has narrowed the issues down to 'conflicts ... around selfishness and altruism'.[21] Robert Hanks points out that McEwan's Utopia bears 'a striking resemblance to the [world] we already inhabit'.[22] Adam Mars-Jones points out that:

> As time passes, the traps McEwan lays for his creatures become less arbitrary ... and more stringent, more philosophically loaded ... . In the two rudimentary moral mazes he constructs for these characters, the author seems to leave a clear thread, indicating the right course of action and all but garrottes them with it subsequently. □
>
> (Christina Byrnes, *The Work of Ian McEwan*, 2002)[23]

Amsterdam attempts to scrutinize the morals of the well-off portion of a generation brought up with 'full employment, new universities, bright paperback books, the Augustan age of rock-and-roll, [and] affordable ideals' (p. 12). It suggests that a nanny state has fostered selfish children and that the politics of sleaze and greed that came to characterize almost twenty years of Conservative government were the result. A witty diversion, *Amsterdam* reads like a potboiler, and though below McEwan's best, it can be enjoyed as his first real satire: 'a novel, play, entertainment, etc., in which topical issues, folly, or evil are held up to scorn by means of ridicule and irony' (*Collins English Dictionary*).

CHAPTER TEN

Storytelling as Self-justification: *Atonement* (2001)

Near the end of *Enduring Love*, Jean Logan asks 'who's going to forgive me? The only person who can is dead' (p. 230). This is a question at the heart of *Atonement*, but it is given a further dimension by McEwan's decision to make it also central to Briony Tallis's act of writing the novel.

Atonement received some of the best reviews of McEwan's career and suggested a writer at the height of his powers. Martyn Bedford comments that while *Enduring Love* had a superb opening but subsequently disappointed him and the Booker-Prize-winning *Amsterdam* was a work in danger of being over the hill, *Atonement* rekindled his admiration for McEwan, who has rediscovered his vitality through adopting the persona of Briony Tallis.[1] For John Updike, the book is 'beautiful and majestic';[2] for Frank Kermode (born 1919) it is easily McEwan's finest novel.[3]

If *Amsterdam* had suggested a possible falling off, *Atonement* proved that McEwan, perhaps oddly for a writer with so many novels under his belt, was still looking for a voice, or at least a new direction (the two novels have at least one thing in common: they both look to early twentieth-century writers, Waugh in the case of *Amsterdam*, Henry James and many female novelists in the case of *Atonement*, for their cues). After comparisons of his early work with Golding and Kafka, with *Amsterdam* McEwan drew strikingly on new influences, but *Atonement* was another kind of experiment: one which drew on a range of writers from the early nineteenth to mid-twentieth centuries, and evinced an interest in character and historical fiction that earlier works had, in comparison, only flirted with. After the satire of *Amsterdam*, in *Atonement* McEwan returned to the serious intent of his earlier work. He explains his approach to *Atonement* in a way that might perhaps throw the satire of *Amsterdam* into question, or at least reveal how differently McEwan approached these two novels:

■ If violence is simply there to excite, then it's merely pornographic. I think treating it seriously – which means doing it without sentimentality – you're always going to bring to it a certain quality of investigation, so it's not only the violence you show, you're writing *about* violence. You're showing something that's certainly common in human nature. You're not necessarily taking sides, it's not necessary always to produce a moral attitude, but in the greater scheme of things you are bound to place the reader in some form of critical attitude towards the circumstances. There is always a larger intent.

For example, if you're writing about the retreat to Dunkirk, as I do in *Atonement*, you can't avoid the fact that tens of thousands of people died in that retreat, and yet we have a rather fond memory of it in the national narrative, and you want to play off something of the sentimentality of the 'miracle' of Dunkirk against the reality for ordinary soldiers [McEwan's father was one of the 320,000] as they made their way towards the beaches. Many of the images that I used in the Dunkirk episode I drew from the Bosnian conflict. I used photographs from that to remind myself of how soldiers and civilians, hugely intermingled, would suffer the most appalling consequences.

I talked of sentimentality. I think it is the recurring element of popular culture's treatment of violence. There are no consequences. Someone gets hit over the head with a bottle and they fall, the camera moves on, the plot moves on. Anyone who's hit on the head with a bottle is likely to suffer a lifetime of consequences. Blindness might be one of those, because the visual regions are at the back of the head. In other words, you've got to make your reader do what Conrad did in his famous preface to *The Nigger of the Narcissus* (1897), you've got to make your reader *see*. So, when people accuse me of being too graphic in my depictions of violence, my response is, 'Well, either you *do* violence, or you sentimentalise it.' If you're going to have to, you've got to show it in all its horror. It's not worth doing it if you're simply going to add it there as a little bit of spice. I'm not interested in that at all. □

(Margaret Reynolds and Jonathan Noakes (eds), *Ian McEwan: the Essential Guide*, 2002)[4]

Atonement draws on the many precedents of Jane Austen, E. M. Forster, Elizabeth Bowen (1899–1973), Henry Green (1905–73), Rosamond Lehmann (1903–90) and Ivy Compton-Burnett (1892–1969), and perhaps most of all, Henry James (1843–1916), whose *What Maisie Knew* (1897), along with *The Go-Between* (1953) by L. P. Hartley (1895–1972), stands behind McEwan's story of an adult's world seen through the eyes of a child. One of McEwan's strongest novels, *Atonement* also echoes Clarissa's recreation of Bourton in her memories in Virginia Woolf's *Mrs Dalloway* (1925), and its method of shifting perspectives strongly recalls Woolf's writing. In the same interview with Reynolds and Noakes, McEwan explains his concern in *Atonement* with the tradition of the English novel, which was much commented upon by reviewers:

■ Part of the intention of *Atonement* was to look at storytelling itself. And to examine the relationship between what is imagined and what is true. It's a novel full of other writers – not only Briony of course, who's stalked, haunted by the figures of Virginia Woolf, Elizabeth Bowen, Rosamond Lehmann, but Robbie too has a relationship, a deep relationship with writing and storytelling.

The danger of an imagination that can't quite see the boundaries of what is real and what is unreal, drawn again from Jane Austen – another writer who is crucial to this novel – plays a part in Briony's sense that her atonement has consisted in a lifetime of writing this novel. She's condemned to write it over and over again. Now she's a dying woman, she has vascular dementia, her mind is emptying, and finally she writes a draft which is different from all the others. She fails, as she sees it, to have the courage of her pessimism, and rewrites the love story so that the lovers survive.

What really then is the truth? Well, as she says, when the novel will finally be published, which can only be after she's dead, she herself will become a character, and no one will be much interested in whether she is real or not, she will only exist within the frame of the novel. So I wanted to play, but play seriously, with something rooted in the emotional rather than the intellectual. I wanted to play with the notion of storytelling as a form of self-justification, of how much courage is involved in telling the truth to oneself. What are the distances between what is real and what is imagined? Catherine Morland, the heroine of Jane Austen's *Northanger Abbey* [1817], was a girl so full of the delights of Gothic fiction that she causes havoc around her when she imagines a perfectly innocent man to be capable of the most terrible things. For many, many years I've been thinking how I might devise a hero or heroine who could echo that process in Catherine Morland, but then go a step further and look at, not the crime, but the process of atonement, and do it in writing – do it through storytelling, I should say. □

(Margaret Reynolds and Jonathan Noakes (eds),
Ian McEwan: the Essential Guide, 2002)[5]

In one of the most perspicacious reviews published at the time of *Atonement*'s first release, Frank Kermode considers how McEwan has experimented with narrative point of view, and explores the book's structure and form in the light of the views on the novel expressed by Henry James. He notes that McEwan's novel, as Briony's re-creation, appears to have been reworked in the light of the magazine editor C.C.'s comments; which raises questions about Briony's aesthetic considerations as a novelist alongside her moral ones in writing the story. For example, the Meissen vase appears to have begun as a Ming vase, from the evidence of the story she sent to *Horizon*. Briony's detailed description of the vase, and its history, thus presumably owes as much to a literary sense of 'authenticity' as it does to a factual one (p. 24).

■ Minor resemblances between this novel by Ian McEwan and Henry James's *What Maisie Knew* have already been noticed and are of some interest. James left a quite full record of the development of his story, which described modern divorce and adultery from the point of view of a young girl. It had its roots in Solomon's offer to satisfy rival maternal claimants by cutting the disputed child in half, but it grew far more complicated in the years between the first notebook entry on this topic and the completion of the novel about 'the *partagé* child.' First there was a plan for a 10,000-word story, which, in prospect, set delightful technical problems: about 'the question of time' – 'the little secrets in regard to the expression of duration' – and about the need to use the '*scenic method*'. In the notebooks James prays that he not be tempted to 'slacken my deep observance of this strong and beneficent method – this intensely structural, intensely hinged and jointed preliminary frame'. Only when the frame was built was he ready to start what he called the 'doing'.

Ian McEwan's new novel, which strikes me as easily his finest, has a frame that is properly hinged and jointed and apt for the conduct of the '*march of action*', which James described as 'the only thing that really, for *me* at least, will *produire* L'OEUVRE'. Not quite how McEwan would put it, perhaps, but still the substance of his method, especially if one adds a keen technical interest in another Jamesian obsession, the point of view. His central character is a 13-year-old girl called Briony, aleady a maker of stories and plays, and so already a writer of fictions that have only their own kind of truth and are dependent on fantasies which readers are invited to share, with whatever measure of scepticism or credulity they can muster. [...]

Briony's play, *The Trials of Arabella*, written for the house party, but for various reasons not then performed, was the fantasy of a very young writer enchanted by the idea that she could in a few pages create a world complete with terrors and climaxes, and a necessary sort of knowingness. The entire novel is a grown-up version of this achievement, a conflict or coalescence of truth and fantasy, a novelist's treatment of what is fantasised as fact. Briony is the novelist, living, as her mother is said to have perceived (or the author, or Briony, says she has perceived), in 'an intact inner world of which the writing was no more than the visible surface.' We merely have to trust somebody to be telling something like the truth. In the scene where Robbie and Cecilia make love in a corner of the darkened library (a key scene, terribly difficult for *anybody* to write) Briony, entering, sees her sister's 'terrified eyes' over Robbie's shoulder. Who is saying she is terrified? Who is saying Cecilia 'struggled free' of her heavy partner? Surely she was carried away by lust and henceforth became Robbie's devoted lover? We can only suppose that Briony, writing at the very end of the complex affair, is imagining what she would have made of the scene at 13. She must have read the scene wrongly, for we learn that the lovers were actually 'in a state of tranquil joy' as they 'confronted the momentous change they had achieved'. At this moment Cecilia is overwhelmed by the beauty of a face she had taken for granted all her life. Can she also have had terrified eyes? Or could Briony have taken for terror an expression that meant something quite different? [...]

McEwan's skill has here developed to the point where it gives disquiet as well as pleasure. Perhaps to be disquieting has always been his ambition; the first stories were in various ways startling. By now he is such a virtuoso that one is tempted to imagine that the best readers of this book might be Henry James and Ford Madox Ford [1873–1939]. It is, in perhaps the only possible way, a philosophical novel, pitting the imagination against what it has to imagine if we are to be given the false assurance that there is a match between our fictions and the specifications of reality. The pleasure it gives depends as much on our suspending belief as on our suspending disbelief.

For example, we are told that Briony, while still a wartime nurse, sent a novella called *Two Figures by a Fountain* to *Horizon*. It was not accepted, but the editor, Cyril Connolly [1903–74] (or anyway someone who signs himself simply as 'C.C.') wrote her a letter running to over a thousand words, with favourable comment on sentences we have already admired [in Part one, Robbie is also said to have had a rejection slip initialled by T. S. Eliot from *Criterion*, p. 82]. The implication is that the present novel is an expansion of that early work. We can even spot changes from novella to novel (for example, Cecilia goes 'fully dressed' into the fountain) and might attribute the improvements to C.C.'s kindly advice. He wonders if the young author 'doesn't owe a little too much to the techniques of Mrs Woolf'. The novella, he claims, lacks the interest of forward movement, 'an underlying pull of simple narrative'. He thinks the vase should not have been Ming (too expensive to take out of doors; perhaps Sèvres or Nyphenburg?) The Bernini fountain she mentions is not in the Piazza Navona but in the Piazza Barberini (the error is corrected in the novel). He complains that Briony's story ends with the damp patch left beside the fountain when Robbie and Cecilia have gone. (It is still there in the longer version but it is there only a beginning.) Elizabeth Bowen, it seems, read the novella with interest, but thought it cloying, except when it echoed [Rosamond Lehmann's] *Dusty Answer* [1927]. The author is invited to drop by at the office for a glass of wine whenever she has the time. Had she, by the way, a sister at Girton six or seven years ago? Given her hospital address, is she a doctor or an invalid?

In the first place parody, this brilliant invention does quite a lot of what James called structural work. It is funny because although it sounds rather like him, Connolly would never have written such a letter; it lives, like the book as a whole, on that borderline between fantasy and fact that is indeed the territory of fiction. McEwan has examined this territory with intelligent and creative attention, and it could probably be said that no contemporary of his has shown such passionate dedication to the art of the novel. □

(Frank Kermode, 'Point of View', 2001)[6]

Taking up this distinction between characters and 'people', Claire Messud discusses the aspect to *Atonement* that is of most importance to McEwan in terms of morality: the recognition of others' consciousness. This is for McEwan essential to the apprehension of an equal humanity, and underpins the novelist's attempt to represent social interaction. Briony's inability to do this as a child is evident in her response to opening Robbie's letter: 'The very complexity of her feelings confirmed Briony in her view that she was entering an arena of adult emotion and dissembling from which her writing was bound to benefit … . It was wrong to open other people's letters, but it was right, it was essential, for her to know everything' (p. 113). In a world of her own creation, the novelist can know everything, but this can never be true of life, and it is one of the ironies of Part One that Briony is so convinced she has discovered a sex 'maniac' that she, and the others around her who are also taken up with their own thoughts, miss the signs of Marshall's two attacks on Lola, others taking the blame in both cases. In this, Briony perhaps has more excuse than the adults. The narrator (Briony herself therefore) describes her thus: 'At this stage in her life Briony inhabited an ill-defined transitional space between the nursery and adult worlds which she crossed and recrossed unpredictably' (p. 141). This is also an aspect taken up by Messud:

■ Briony hovers at the end of childhood but lives her fantasies with an adult fierceness, wondering to herself, '[Was] everyone else really as alive as she was? For example, did her sister really matter to herself, was she as valuable to herself as Briony was? Was being Cecilia just as vivid an affair as being Briony?' (p. 36). Although she knows rationally that this must be so, she is also enamoured of herself *as a writer*, and believes that writing imbues her with great powers. […] Hers is a childish and arrogant faith, dangerously let loose upon the household that surrounds her. That communication is composed of vast gaps and desperate, distant signals is something Briony will learn through suffering – her own, eventually, but more immediately other people's. […] Briony is old enough to recognize the complexity of what she witnesses [between Cecilia and Robbie] but perhaps not old enough to see that it is a matter of reality, not story.

She could write the scene three times over, from three points of view; her excitement was in the prospect of freedom, of being delivered from the cumbrous struggle between good and bad, heroes and villains. None of these three was bad, nor were they particularly good. She need not judge. There did not have to be a moral. She need only show separate minds, as alive as her own, struggling with the idea that the other minds were equally alive. (p. 40)

And yet by her very construction of events Briony passes judgement, determines 'good' and 'bad': as the evening unfolds, her interpretation of each action and interaction around her is shaped by her understanding of what she has seen, and although she believes absolutely in the inevitability of the story she constructs, we can see that it is partial, in both senses of the word. □

(Claire Messud, 'The Beauty of the Conjuring', 2002)[7]

For John Updike, the quality of the prose in the novel, its conspicuous ornate beauty and descriptive richness can be seen as itself part of Briony's atonement. For Updike McEwan overlays his plot from Jane Austen with modernist writing, such as detailed imagery of water and vegetation, and with divergent perspectives, flashbacks, overlapping narratives, replayed scenes. Most importantly, the novel is beautifully written – almost over-written – a feature that becomes significant once it becomes apparent that this is Briony's writing, not simply the author's.[8] At one point Briony declares to herself that 'There was nothing she could not describe', and this ability to describe, to fashion the world in words, is both Briony's gift and her curse. In childhood, as a burgeoning writer with no subject matter, she creates a story around Robbie and Cecilia, but fails to distinguish her make-believe from reality. She invests too strongly in her own fiction and is unable to recognise that her 'characters' have their own, better informed, perspectives. Mistaking the plausible for the actual, and steeped in 'The Trials of Arabella', Briony faces the storyteller's difficulty of imaginative empathy, as Martyn Bedford outlines when he says that Briony's crime is not that she lies, but that she confuses fact and fiction through her talent for artistic creation, forgetting that Robbie and Cecilia are real people as well as source material for her imagination.[9]

Revealing how McEwan differs from James but is still to be seen as writing in the tradition of the experimental realist novel, Geoff Dyer compares *Atonement* to novels of the mid-twentieth century, and especially the work of D. H. Lawrence (1885–1930), in which polite society's underbelly, or unconscious, is laid bare:

■ *Atonement* does not feel, at first, like a book by McEwan. The opening is almost perversely ungripping. Instead of the expected sharpness of focus, the first 70 or so pages are a lengthy summary of shifting impressions. One longs for a cinematic clarity and concentration of dialogue and action, but such interludes dissolve before our – and the participants' – eyes.

Unlike Martin Amis, say, or Salman Rushdie, McEwan is an invisible rather than a flamboyant stylist. Even so, the pallid qualifiers and disposable adverbs (a 'gently rocking' sheet of water, the 'coyly drooping' head of a nettle) come as a surprise. The language used to distil the scene – a gathering of the Tallis family at their country house on a sweltering day in 1935 – serves also as a wash that partially obscures it.

Various characters come and go but the novel, at this point, seems populated mainly by its literary influences. Chief among these is Virginia Woolf. The technique is not stream of consciousness so much as 'a slow drift of association', 'the hovering stillness of nothing much seeming to happen'. [...]

The consequences of the go-between blundering in like this [Briony's sudden entrance into the library] are liberating and incriminating in unequal measure. What Lawrence called the 'dirty little secret' of sex besmirches the Tallises' world, or – as Lawrence insisted – reveals how besmirched that world really is. [...] McEwan seems to be retrospectively inserting his name into the pantheon of British novelists of the 1930s and 1940s. But he is also, of course, doing more than this, demonstrating and exploring what the mature Briony comes to see as a larger 'transformation ... being worked in human nature itself'. The novels of Woolf and Lawrence did not just record this transformation; they were instrumental in bringing it about. McEwan uses his novel to show how this subjective or interior transformation can now be seen to have interacted with the larger march of 20th-century history. □

(Geoff Dyer, 'Who's afraid of influence?' 2001)[10]

As Hermione Lee notes, *Atonement* has a political dimension in its concerns with literary history and the Second World War. Briony's meditation on responsibility and imagination is not just a re-creation of her own part in private lives but a commentary on a wider society shattered by the events and decision-makers of the mid-century. McEwan also explores the role of the novelist as much as the individual agent, in a world where there appears to be no higher authority. The book poses several questions: when one's own understanding and morality are the only touchstones, without God, how can the individual find atonement? Similarly, the book suggests, from whom can history, or God, the presiding author of the universe, find atonement for the horror of the war? And how can the novelist, as Briony becomes, find atonement in a 'fictional' world of her own creation?

As Lee mentions, the broken vase stands as a Jamesian symbol of all that cannot be made whole again, except by artifice.

■ *Atonement*, we at last discover, is the novel Briony Tallis has been writing between 1940 and 1999. This quite familiar fictional trick allows

McEwan to ask some interesting questions about writing, in what is a highly literary book. The epigraph is a quotation from *Northanger Abbey*, where Catherine Morland is reproached by Henry Tilney for imagining Gothic horrors in a well-protected English setting. (In a nice echo, the Tallis-home-turned-hotel is called Tilney's.) All through, historical layers of English fiction are invoked – and rewritten. Jane Austen's decorums turn to black farce. Forster's novels of social misunderstanding – the attack on poor Leonard Bast [from *Howards End*, 1910], Adela Quested's [from *A Passage to India*, 1924] false charge of rape – are ironically echoed.

When Briony starts writing *Atonement* as a novella, in 1940, she thinks it should be modern and impressionistic, like Virginia Woolf. But she gets a rejection letter from Cyril Connolly at *Horizon* telling her that fiction should have more plot. The advice comes from a friend of Connolly's, one Elizabeth Bowen. So her rewritten novella – the Part One of *Atonement* – recalls [Bowen's] *The Last September* [1929], with its restive teenage girl in the big house. Then Briony writes the war, and all the slow, deliberate literariness of Part One falls away.

Atonement asks what the English novel of the twenty-first century has inherited, and what it can do now. One of the things it can do, very subtly in McEwan's case, is to be androgynous. This is a novel written by a man acting the part of a woman writing a 'male' subject, and there's nothing to distinguish between them.

If fiction is a controlling play, a way of ordering the universe in which the writer is away in her – or his – thoughts, then is it a form of escapism, lacking all moral force? Is it just another form of false witness, and so always 'unforgivable'? And are some forms of fiction – modernist, middle-class, limited to personal relations – more unforgivable than others? A political critique edges in.

But I wasn't sure how much the life of establishment England (with its diplomats planning mass bombings, its rapacious businessmen, its repression of women, its maintaining of feudal class systems) was being held responsible for the carnage visited on the poor bloody infantry at Dunkirk. Robbie suggests it: 'A dead civilisation. First his own life ruined, then everybody else's.'

In Part One, there is a significant tussle between Cecilia and Robbie by the fountain, for a precious Meissen vase, given to an uncle in the First World War by the French villagers whom he had saved. The vase is broken, but mended so that the cracks hardly show (another literary bow, this time to [Henry James's] *The Golden Bowl* [1904]). Just so, in Briony's accusation, 'the glazed surface of conviction was not without its blemishes and hairline cracks'.

In war-time, one of the servants breaks it irrecoverably. The 'making one' of the vase was a fix, and couldn't hold. Yet a great deal does survive at the end of the novel: family, children, memory, writing, perhaps even love and forgiveness. Or perhaps not; it depends which of the controlling novelist's endings we decide to believe in, as we hold his fragile shape of the unified fictional work in our mind's eye, and are made aware how easily it can all fall apart. □

(Hermione Lee, 'If your memories serve you well ...', 2001)[11]

In one of the most perceptive reviews that greeted the publication of *Atonement*, James Wood, who has been a stern critic of McEwan in the past, argues that the novel works best as a detailed evocation of English life in the mid-twentieth century. Consequently, Wood sees the twist at the end of *Atonement* as an unnecessary embellishment of the narrative: one that too carefully makes explicit the questions raised by the rest of the book:

■ In its second and third parts (each about sixty pages long) *Atonement* leaves behind the Tallises' country house, but it cannot leave behind the shadow of Briony's false incrimination. In Part Two, we have advanced by five years, and are following Robbie Turner as he retreats, with the rest of the British Expeditionary Force, through northern France to Dunkirk. We gather that he has been in prison, that he and Cecilia have been corresponding, and that a remorseful Briony, now eighteen, wants to retract her statement to the police so that Robbie's name might be cleared. Cecilia, we learn, has not spoken to her parents or brother since 1935 (they sided with Briony against Robbie); and of course there has been no communication between Cecilia and her younger sister.

But in some ways this information is incidental to McEwan's extraordinary evocation of muddled warfare. I doubt that any English writer has conveyed quite as powerfully the bewilderments and the humiliations of this episode in World War II. After more than twenty years of writing with care and control, McEwan's anxious, disciplined richness of style finally expands to meet its subject. This section is vivid and unsentimental, and most importantly, though McEwan must have researched the war, there is no inky blot of other books: his details have the vividness and body of imagined things, they feel chosen rather than copied.

There is marvellous writing. Robbie has been wounded; he feels the pain in his side 'like a flash of colour.' Day after day, the British soldiers make their weary, undisciplined way to Dunkirk. They can see where they are supposed to be going, because miles away a fuel depot is on fire at the port, the cloud hanging over the landscape 'like an angry father.' They are not marching, but walking, slouching. Order has broken down, and a tired anarchy rules. McEwan captures the fatigue – which invades even eating – very well: 'Even as he chewed, he felt himself plunging into sleep for seconds on end.' Into this obscure, thudding chaos, discrete and vile happenings explode and then disappear. Occasionally the Luftwaffe's planes strafe the straggling infantrymen. And one day Robbie turns to hear behind him a rhythmic pounding on the road:

> At first sight it seemed that an enormous horizontal door was flying up the road towards them. It was a platoon of Welsh Guards in good order,

> rifles at the slope, led by a second-lieutenant. They came by at a forced march, their gaze fixed forwards, their arms swinging high. The stragglers stood aside to let them through. These were cynical times, but no one risked a catcall. The show of discipline and cohesion was shaming. It was a relief when the Guards had pounded out of sight and the rest could resume their introspective trudging. (pp. 240–1)

As the soldiers near Dunkirk, Robbie crosses a bridge and sees a barge pass under it. It is like the boat in Auden's [In 1935, Robbie has a copy of Auden's *Poems*, p. 82] 'Musée des Beaux Arts': ordinary indifferent life continues while Icarus falls. 'The boatman sat at his tiller smoking a pipe, looking stolidly ahead. Behind him, ten miles away, Dunkirk burned. Ahead, in the prow, two boys were bending over an upturned bike, mending a puncture perhaps. A line of washing which included women's smalls was hanging out to dry.' Finally, when the soldiers come upon the beach, they taste the salt – 'the taste of holidays' – and then they see the remarkable formlessness of an army waiting to be shipped back to England. Some of the men are swimming, others playing football on the sand. One group is attacking a poor RAF officer, blaming him for the Luftwaffe's superiority. Others have dug themselves personal holes in the dunes, 'from which they peeped out, proprietorial and smug. Like marmosets. ...' But the majority of the army 'wandered about the sands without purpose, like citizens of an Italian town in the hour of the *passeggio*.'

In a novel so concerned with fiction's relation to actuality, this amazing conjuring cannot but fail to have the weird but successful doubleness of the novel's first section: it has a grave reality, while at the same time necessarily raises questions about its own literary rights to that reality. Was Dunkirk really like this? Stephen Crane's evocation of Antietam was so vivid that one veteran swore that Crane (who did not fight) was present with him [This refers to the evocation of the American Civil War battle of Antietam (1862) in the novel *The Red Badge of Courage* (1895) by Stephen Crane (1871–1900)]. Like Crane's descriptions, McEwan's gather their strength not from the accuracy of their notation but from the accumulation of living human detail, so alive that we are persuaded that such a thing might have occurred even if no one actually witnessed it. The soldiers dug into their own little holes in the dunes, like marmosets, has just such a fictive reality, so that it becomes irrelevant to us were a veteran to say: 'this never happened.' McEwan has made it seem plausible, because alive. This is what Aristotle meant when he said that a convincing impossibility is preferable in literature to an unconvincing possibility. Yet this great freedom shows how dangerous fiction can be, and why its transit with lies has historically been subversive and threatening. Again, McEwan wants us to reflect on these matters. He has Robbie ponder: 'Who could ever describe this confusion, and come up with the village names and the dates for the history books? And take the reasonable view and begin to assign the blame? No one would ever know what it was like to be here. Without the details there could be no larger picture.' It is fiction, and McEwan's fiction, which provides 'the details' that history may miss. But – and this is a gigantic but, surely, which this novel acknowledges – those details may be invented, may never have happened in history.

In Part Three, we see Briony working as a trainee nurse at a London hospital. We learn that she is terribly sorry for what she did in 1935 and that, in a gesture of atonement, she has forsworn Cambridge, and dedicated herself to nursing. Late in the section, she visits her estranged sister in Clapham, and finds her living with Robbie, who has briefly returned from his army service in France. Again, McEwan writes superbly well, especially in his evocation of Briony's nursing experiences. Soldiers arrive, looking identical in their dirt and torn clothes, 'like a wild race of men from a terrible world.' One of them has had most of his nose blown off, and it falls to Briony to change his dressings. 'She could see through his missing cheek to his upper and lower molars, and the tongue glistening, and hideously long. Further up, where she hardly dared look, were the exposed muscles around his eye socket. So intimate, and never intended to be seen.' There is great tenderness in this description of the poor soldier's eye muscles, 'so intimate and never intended to be seen.' We may even think of another moment, earlier in Briony's life, when she also witnessed something 'intimate and never intended to be seen.' But the mark of the true writer, the writer who is really looking, really witnessing, is that notation of the soldier's exposed tongue as 'hideously long' – something worthy of Conrad.

Atonement ends with a devastating twist, a piece of information that changes our sense of everything we have just read. It is convincing enough, but its neatness seems like the reappearance of the old McEwan, unwilling to let the ropes fall from his hands. In an epilogue, set in 1999, we learn that Briony, now a distinguished old novelist, wrote the three sections – the country house scene, the Dunkirk retreat, and the London hospital – that we have just read. Moreover, Robbie and Cecilia were never together, as the third section suggested. Robbie was killed in France in 1940, and Cecilia died in the same year in London, during the German bombing. The conjuring that we have just witnessed has been Briony's atonement for what she did. She could not resist the chance to spare the young lovers, to continue their lives into fiction, to give the story a happy ending.

This twist, this revelation, further emphasizes the novel's already explicit ambivalence about being a novel, and makes the book a proper postmodern artifact, wearing its doubts on its sleeve, on the outside, as the Pompidou does its escalators. But it is unnecessary, unless the slightly self-defeating point is to signal that the author is himself finally incapable of resisting the distortions of tidiness. It is unnecessary because the novel has already raised, powerfully but murmuringly, the questions that this final revelation shouts out. And it is unnecessary

> because the fineness of the book as a novel, as a distinguished and complex evocation of English life before and during the war, burns away the theoretical, and implants in the memory a living, flaming presence. □
>
> (James Wood, 'The Trick of Truth', 2002)[12]

Atonement is importantly a book about, as well as a work of, imagination. At the start of the novel, Briony is a precocious 13-year-old girl with a desire for intrigue. Because she has no secrets she creates in compensation the signs of their presence: 'hidden drawers, lockable diaries and cryptographic systems' (p. 5). A solitary child with an uneventful life, she steeps herself in the plots of novels and plays such that she discovers in their envisioning of alternative realities, what she calls a powerful new 'source of secrets' (p. 6). Briony's mother is depicted at the same time as thinking that 'Her daughter was always off and away in her mind, grappling with some unspoken, self-imposed problem, as though the weary, self-evident world could be re-invented by a child' (p. 68).

In Briony, McEwan presents an image of the child and the writer together, in that Briony's story is fictionalised by Briony herself, but also in the sense that the child and the novelist both specialise in fashioning worlds of their own imagining, are both 'daydreamers' in the novel's terms. The 13-year-old Briony believes that observing and conjecturing upon Robbie Turner's sexual advances to her sister has 'made her into a real writer'. But, in McEwan's implied presentation of literary history in the novel, this is a deeply problematic approach to realism, of the kind Henry James could be said to have critiqued, as it involves the presumption that we can know others by inhabiting, in the words of the novel, 'some god-like place from which all people could be judged alike ...'. Briony aspires to such omniscient sympathy but concludes that, 'If such a place existed, she was not worthy of it. She could never forgive Robbie his disgusting mind' (p. 115).

Subsequently, Briony's desire to craft fiction gives rise to the story she fabricates for the police of Robbie's assault on her cousin Lola. The passage that describes this reads: 'Her eyes confirmed the sum of all she knew and had recently experienced ... . The truth instructed her eyes. So, when she said, over and over again, I saw him, she meant it' (p. 169). This is one of the most insistent messages of McEwan's later fiction from *Black Dogs* onwards, and which he summarizes in *Enduring Love* simply as 'believing is seeing'. Which is perhaps to say that he thinks imagination fails when it works more with the products of opinion than observation.

Sixty years later, after she has come to describe herself as 'unforgiveable' (p. 285), Briony is still reimagining the events of the distant past from others' perspectives in an attempt to make amends for her own childhood mind with what she calls its 'joyful feeling of blameless self-love' (p. 177). At a time when Robbie and Cecilia are both long dead, Briony considers there is no one else to whom she can atone, and no other way than through imagination, the source of her 'crime'.

Finally, John Mullan discusses the role that weather plays in the novel, concentrating on the way McEwan uses the heatwave to suggest high-running passions. McEwan has in fact used high summer as a setting fairly often. Both *The Cement Garden* and *The Child in Time* accentuate the heat over long summer days, while, in his first short-story collection, aside from 'The Last Day of Summer', 'First Love, Last Rites' opens with 'From the beginning of summer ...' and 'Butterflies' begins by asserting in its first paragraph 'I have never known it so hot in England.' As Mullan notes, in *Atonement* at least, McEwan is tapping into a familiar strain in the English novel:

■ 'I love England in a heatwave,' says Leon Tallis in *Atonement*. 'It's a different country. All the rules change.' There is dramatic irony in his complacent small talk. Restraints have already begun to collapse. Robbie and Cecilia have become fumbling lovers and have been interrupted by the appalled Briony. The weather is suffocating. In 'an aroma of warmed dust from the Persian carpet' the characters try to eat their sweltering roast dinner. Very English. Before the evening is out, the shocking and mysterious act of violence at the novel's heart will have been committed. And Briony will have committed her crime of false testimony.

Heat hangs over the first part of McEwan's novel and shapes its action. Emily Tallis lies nursing her migraine and thinks of 'the vast heat that rose above the house and park, and lay across the Home Counties like smoke, suffocating the farms and towns'. Later she jokes that 'hot weather encouraged loose morals amongst young people'. They were right. Unknown to her, sexual passion and resentment are brewing. 'Fewer layers of clothing, a thousand more places to meet. Out of doors, out of control', she goes on. Wise heads they were, to want to keep their English daughters indoors. [Mullan then remarks on the fact that hot weather has seemed to fascinate English novelists like Forster and Greene, and notes the importance of a heatwave to Austen's *Emma* (1816)] ...

The country house summer swoon of *Atonement* recalls the long heat of L.P. Hartley's *The Go-Between* [This is conscious on McEwan's part and he also made reference to the novel in Briony's letter from *Criterion*, but had to remove it when he was told Hartley's book was published in the 1950s]. Animation is suspended, the habits of every day are halted. Sometimes disastrously, heat releases the English from reserve and novelists have often used it for episodes of sexual awakening. The unnatural stirrings of adolescent sexual instinct in McEwan's first novel,

The Cement Garden, naturally take place during a heatwave. The extraordinary chapters of Hardy's *Tess of the D'Urbervilles* [1891] set at Talbothays Dairy, charting the growing attraction between Tess and Angel Clare, rely on hot weather. In 'Ethiopic' heat, the air of the novel becomes 'stagnant and enervating'. 'And as Clare was oppressed by the outward heats, so was he burdened inwardly by the waxing fervour of passion for the soft and silent.'

Perhaps there are also memories of the old-fashioned children's story (of Enid Blyton [1897–1968, whom McEwan read avidly as a child] or Arthur Ransome [1884–1967]) in long days of fictional heat. *Atonement* trades effectively on the importance of weather to recollection, the idea that summers were always hotter in the past. The structure of the novel – the events of its first part compulsively recollected in the following three parts – makes the hot, suffocating days of its opening seem to belong to another time: distant, past, yet palpably there in the memorable, inescapable sense of the weather. □

(John Mullan, 'Elements of Fiction: turning up the heat', 2003)[13]

Critics have noted that *Atonement* is a self-aware fiction in terms of the literary antecedents it invokes and evokes. While its story of the relationship between two sisters and many other aspects of the novel derive from Austen, *Atonement* is a story in the country-house tradition for its first section, a war memoir in its second, and a home-front story of reconciliation in its third, where it draws on writers like Lehmann but also war reminiscences such as *Testament of Youth* (1933) by Vera Brittain (1893–1970). *Atonement* is also a complex novel in terms of form. It places itself in a realist tradition of deep, rich characterization and social breadth, but displays a modernist concern with consciousness and perspective. Ultimately though it emerges as at least in part a postmodernist novel, because it questions its own fictive status, exposing itself as a construct; yet, it also stretches beyond this by foregrounding questions of morality that belong to a pre-postmodern humanism.

Some reviewers disapproved of the postmodernist shift at the end of *Atonement*, where the third-person narrative suddenly proves to have been intradiegetic, attributed not to an anonymous authorial voice but to Briony, a character within the story. This 'trick' as it has been pejoratively described is extremely important to the novel. In terms of form it represents the shift in literary history that McEwan is concerned with, from Austen to James and Woolf, and in terms of content it underlines the difficulties for a disbelieving Western world to atone for the twentieth century's violent past, beyond bearing personal witness to its tragedies, both small and large.

CONCLUSION

And Now, What Days Are These?: *Saturday* (2005)

> Ah, love, let us be true
> To one another! For the world, which seems
> To lie before us like a land of dreams,
> So various, so beautiful, so new,
> Hath really neither joy, nor love, nor light,
> Nor certitude, nor peace, nor help for pain;
> And we are here as on a darkling plain
> Swept with confused alarms of struggle and flight,
> Where ignorant armies clash by night.
>
> Matthew Arnold, 'Dover Beach'

> the New York attacks [of 9/11] precipitated a global crisis that would, if we were lucky, take a hundred years to resolve.
>
> *Saturday*, pp. 32–3

With *Atonement* McEwan cemented his claim to be the foremost British novelist of his generation. While his novels have received mixed responses, every one of them has been hailed by some reviewers and has provoked in-depth analyses from critics. As a body of work, his fiction to date has been a remarkably consistent series of stories and novels concerned with many of the foremost issues and events of modern times: from gender relations to post-imperial nationalism, the politics of Britain's elite to extended philosophical and social comment, the history of postwar Europe to the genealogy of the English novel. His fictions have been considered extreme in their depiction of violence and sexuality but have been repeatedly praised for their sensitive treatment of individual lives and the human condition. The present Guide began in 1975 with McEwan's debut collection *First Love, Last Rites* and now concludes in 2005 with his novel *Saturday*.

Set on 15 February 2003, McEwan's ninth novel is a day-in-the-life narrative that follows one character from the early hours of Saturday morning to the dawn of Sunday. It is an introspective, contemplative book in which there is little incident in comparison with most contemporary novels. Its circular structure is easy to describe. A 47-year-old neurosurgeon called Henry Perowne, suddenly waking around 3.45 a.m. for no reason he can perceive, feels in a state of euphoria in the moments before he watches a burning jet plane's emergency landing at Heathrow from one of the bedroom windows of his house in Fitzrovia. Later, Perowne chats with his 18-year-old son Theo, a blues musician, then makes love with his wife Rosalind, and ventures out to play a game of squash with his American anaesthetist at his club, on the way to which he watches the anti-war marchers protesting against the oncoming second Gulf War and has a minor car accident. After his squash game, one visit to his sick mother and another to see his son's blues band, Perowne returns home for a family reunion at which his daughter Daisy and his father-in-law John Grammaticus, both poets, will be present. The gnawing sense of fear and threat that has grown at the back of Perowne's mind is realised when the family are held at knifepoint by Baxter, the driver of the other car in the morning's accident. Several hours after Baxter is thrown downstairs and incapacitated by Perowne and Theo, Perowne is called by the hospital to operate upon the badly injured man who threatened him in the morning and his whole family in the evening. Following a successful operation, Perowne returns home in the small hours of Sunday morning. Here, bringing the story full circle by strongly echoing the first scene of the novel, several pages are given over to his meditations on life and his precarious happiness as well as on the perilous state of world affairs.

If there is a significant development in the novel, it is from Perowne's untroubled peace and tranquility as he wakes on Saturday morning to his feelings twenty-four hours later: 'At the end of this day, this particular evening, he's timid, vulnerable … . All he feels now is fear. He's weak and ignorant, scared of the way consequences of an action leap away from your control and breed new events, new consequences, until you're led to a place you never dreamed of and would never choose – a knife at the throat' (p. 277).

Reviews of *Saturday* were almost all positive. Mark Lawson in the *Guardian*, David Sexton in the *Evening Standard*, Peter Kemp in the *Sunday Times* and Ruth Scurr in *The Times* were all highly complimentary. Scurr concluded that McEwan excels 'artistically, morally and politically' (29 January 2005, 'Books Review' section, p. 15) while Kemp thought that 'written with superb exactness, complex, suspenseful, reflective and humane, this novel about an expert on the human brain by an expert on the human mind reinforces [McEwan's] status as the supreme novelist of his generation' (30 January 2005, 'Culture' section, p. 42). Notes of caution were sounded in *The New Statesman* by Sophie Harrison who found Perowne a somewhat smug, and consequently unsympathetic, character. However, McEwan arguably presents Perowne's smugness as a metonym for the material West's indifference to world affairs, as he muses, for example on 'progress' alongside 'hunger, poverty and the rest' while listening to Schubert in his Mercedes (p. 77). Overall, McEwan is most interested in the ways in which the liberal Western citizen can engage with the contemporary world: 'This is the growing complication of the modern condition, the expanding circle of moral sympathy … . The trick, as always, the key to human success and domination, is to be selective in your mercies. For all the discerning talk, it's the close at hand, the visible that exerts the overpowering force' (p. 127). But globally significant events like 9/11 and the Iraq war are 'visible' to most people in a way that previous events were not, and Perowne is insufficiently alive to his involvement in the world until he is confronted with violence and the opportunity for mercy close to home: the opportunity to operate on the man who has threatened his life and family.

As mentioned in the Introduction, in among the many literary references to writers such as Philip Larkin and Henry James, one poem by Matthew Arnold is a touchstone in the novel, and its recitation by the pregnant Daisy causes her assailant Baxter to turn away from his cruel sexual game towards a renewed interest in life (pp. 220–2). 'Dover Beach' is one of Arnold's most well-known mid-nineteenth-century poems of reflection and doubt, where the speaker is caught 'between two worlds' (as Arnold famously has it in his poem 'The Grande Chartreuse'), just as Perowne is caught between the precarious happiness that marks his Saturday and the looming darker world of Sunday, a tomorrow where his deepest fears may be realised or even eclipsed, just as any anxieties at the beginning of the twentieth century were probably no match for the horrors of Hitler, Stalin, Mao and Saddam Hussein. But McEwan is also interested in the Matthew Arnold of *Culture and Anarchy* (1867–68), where Arnold argued for the centrality of art and literature in life. This is something Perowne is unable to see until Arnold's poem has a profound effect upon Baxter. Perowne is a rational, prosaic figure who sees the beauty of music in his son's guitar playing but has until now been unable to appreciate the worth of literature and its imagined worlds. He is thus in stark contrast to Briony in *Atonement*, and McEwan in *Saturday* is quite markedly portraying a figure who is different in almost every respect from his previous protagonist. On the other hand *Saturday* follows on from *Atonement* inasmuch as it picks up on the subject of the contemporary world with which that book closed. Indeed this is McEwan's first novel to engage fully with the present just as *Atonement* was in broadbrush terms his first historical novel.

The issue that hangs over the book is the Iraq War. The pro-war Perowne is a dove when he discusses the impending attacks with his no-nonsense American squash partner, Jay Strauss, but a hawk when he gets into an argument with his daughter Daisy (p. 193), newly arrived from Hyde Park and the march against the war, thought to be the largest civil protest in the history of the islands. Perowne's belief in the war is akin to a negative vote because he is not sure what the invasion of Iraq will bring about other than the deposition of Hussein, of whose brutal regime he has heard stories at first hand from an Iraqi Professor of Ancient History: 'it's only terror that holds the nation together, the whole system runs on fear, and no one knows how to stop it. Now the Americans are coming, perhaps for bad reasons. But Saddam and the Ba'athists will go' (p. 64). By the close of the book, Perowne is far less sure that the war is for the best. The attack that Baxter has mounted against his family has left him fearful and enervated, unsure of the right thing to believe. His sense of separation from the violence of the world has been shattered and Perowne ends the book a still contented but now anxious man.

Music and literature are the two art forms that impinge on Perowne at several points in the narrative, through the influence of his children. He believes 'fiction is too humanly flawed, too sprawling and hit-and-miss to inspire uncomplicated wonder at the magnificence of human ingenuity, of the impossible dazzlingly achieved. Perhaps only music has such purity' (p. 68). With this last thought Perowne echoes the view of the eminent Victorian critic Walter Pater (1839–94), who argued that all art aspired towards the condition of music ('The School of Giorgione' in *The Renaissance*, 1873); and Pater's exacting and exquisite prose style, so influential on the early James Joyce, can also be detected in McEwan's writing in his most recent novels. Perowne is a pragmatist who is sceptical about the uses of imagination, and especially of fiction in which 'anything can happen': 'This notion of Daisy's, that people can't "live" without stories, is simply not true. He is living proof' (p. 68). That Perowne is mistaken here is one of the messages of the book. He is living a fiction to the extent that he considers himself apart from the violence of the streets, which he spies from his bedroom window, or the horrors of the world, about which he reads in the papers. He is even largely indifferent to the peace protesters: 'The largest gathering of humanity in the history of the islands, less than two miles away, is not disturbing Marylebone's contentment' (p. 126). The confrontational incident with Baxter following a minor car accident breaks Perowne out of his own 'anosognosia', about which he is still ignorant as he walks to get the car that he will drive towards his own moment of crisis and violence: 'How restful it must once have been ... to be prosperous and believe that an all-knowing supernatural force had allotted people to their stations in life. And not see how the belief served your own prosperity – a form of anosognosia, a useful psychiatric term for a lack of awareness of one's own condition' (p. 74). Perowne thus travels to his squash game in his silver Mercedes in the firm belief that he is cocooned from the world, driving parallel with the anti-war protesters but disengaged from their cause. Perowne's position in the metal shell of the car itself intimates this sense of isolated protection in a vehicle that is about to 'crash': 'his own word "crash", trailing memories of the night as well as the morning, fragments into a dozen associations' (p. 105).

It was suggested by some critics that the subject of *Saturday* is happiness, but this is less a matter of McEwan's narratorial reflection than Perowne's mental musings: 'for the professors in the academy, for the humanities generally, misery is more amenable to analysis: happiness is a harder nut to crack' (p. 78). For most of the day, Perowne thinks everyone around him is content and his own 'wellbeing' is indeed so complete that it 'needs spectral entities to oppose it' (p. 78). Whether the reader views this as complacency or as normalcy probably depends on their own attitudes and empathies, but McEwan pointedly places this train of Perowne's thought on the threshold of his moment of crisis, which symbolically takes place at a crossroads, where his thoughts will shift from 'the motorist's rectitude, spot-welding a passion for justice to the thrill of hatred' (p. 82) towards a very different kind of thrill when he is confronted with the deliberate and directed violent hatred of Baxter: 'the blow that's aimed at Perowne's heart and that he dodges only fractionally, lands on his sternum with colossal force, so that it seems to him, and perhaps it really is the case, that there surges throughout his body a sharp ridge, a shock wave, of high blood pressure, a concussive thrill that carries with it not so much pain as an electric jolt of stupefaction and a brief deathly chill' (p. 92).

Perowne is here temporarily jolted out of his serene equanimity and catapulted into another world, even though he thinks he escapes Baxter when he finds an opportunity to flee in his Mercedes. The residual aggression from the confrontation is directed into the squash game he plays with Jay Strauss ('He has to beat Strauss', p. 107), which accretes meanings around it to do with everything that has happened to Perowne that morning as well as the belligerence of the Iraq invasion. Perowne 'finds himself tending towards the anti-war camp' (p. 100) as Strauss straightforwardly argues that 'Iraq is a rotten state' needing to be 'liberated and democratised' (p. 100). The two men, successfully cooperative in the medical theatre but extremely competitive here, do battle on the court where there is only 'the irreducible urge to win, as biological as thirst' (p. 113), reminding the reader that McEwan is as interested in (social) scientific theories of behaviour as Perowne: 'Among the game theorists and radical criminologists, the stock of Thomas Hobbes keeps on rising. Holding the unruly, the thugs, in check is the famous "common power" to keep all men in awe – a governing body, an arm of the state, freely granted a monopoly on the legitimate use of violence' (p. 88). This is not just a comment on the American military intervention into Iraq but to the police force on the nearby London streets keeping the hundreds of thousands of protesters in check while they express 'their preference for peace and torture', as Perowne thinks (p. 126). By contrast, Perowne's daughter Daisy characterizes her father's attitude as: 'let the war go ahead, and if in five years it works out you're for it, and if [it] doesn't, you're not responsible' (p. 188).

At the end of his day, Perowne has had many moments of happiness, in bed with his wife, watching his son, and at work (p. 258). He ends the day looking out of his bedroom window again, bringing to mind Gabriel Conroy at the end of Joyce's 'The Dead' but also the narrator of Arnold's 'Dover Beach', caught in reverie of the past and contemplation of the future. Like the figures conjured by those two literary allusions, Perowne at the end of his daily cycle is at a present moment of self-doubt that reflects the times and echoes the position of an imaginary person similar to himself a hundred years before at the beginning of the previous century's cycle: 'If you described the hell that lay ahead, if you warned him, the good doctor – an affable product of prosperity and decades of peace – would not believe you. Beware the utopianists, zealous men certain of the path to the ideal social order. Here they are again, totalitarians in different form, still scattered and weak, but growing, and angry, and thirsty for another mass killing. A hundred years to resolve' (pp. 276–7). For once, following his leap of empathy with Baxter, Perowne has been able to immerse himself in an imaginative sympathy with someone in his position a century earlier, and this is partly because he recognised that Baxter has been moved by 'the magic' of a poem in a way that he 'never has, and probably never will' (p. 278). The ability to be moved by the world and by others, whether real or imagined, is perhaps the dominant subject of McEwan's most recent fiction, and the different ways in which it is explored in the contrasting novels of *Atonement* and *Saturday* indicate the range of McEwan's writing, in terms of the many poles around which fiction moves: time, place, character, literature and history.

It was mentioned in the Introduction that McEwan has also published a novel for children, *The Daydreamer*: a sequence of seven interconnected stories about transformations, journeys and adventures, told by an adult (mis)remembering the metamorphoses of his childhood imagination. Though fiction of a different kind from the other works discussed in this Guide, the book exemplifies several of McEwan's abiding preoccupations: with children becoming adults and adults returning to childhood, with the transformations of imagination, and with grotesque imagery. In *The Daydreamer*, the conceit of the seven interlinked stories is that daydreaming is an out-of-body experience where the imagination takes the mind far from the individual's physical environment. Each of the stories thus concerns a different kind of physical metamorphosis imagined by the mind: the daydreamer's projection into another kind of body, such as a doll or a cat, a baby or a grown-up, or others' transformations from mother's boy into bully or old lady into burglar. The middle chapter of the book concerns a vanishing cream where the body is cloaked in invisibility, but it is in the final story that McEwan confronts his familiar theme of childhood's uneasy relationship with the adult body. In the daydreamer's twelfth year he begins 'to notice just how different the worlds of children and grown-ups were' (p. 130). It is here that McEwan makes explicit his debt to one of his principal influences, Kafka, by transforming the first sentence of 'Metamorphosis' (1915): 'The following morning Peter Fortune woke from troubled dreams to find himself transformed into a giant person, an adult' (p. 135). By alluding to Gregor Samsa's overnight metamorphosis into a giant insect, McEwan is suggesting both the importance of childhood and (day)dreaming to the inventions that underpin fiction and also the gulf between 'the worlds of children and grown-ups', physically bridged by the transformation of adolescence. Which is also to say that though it is a book for children, *The Daydreamer* may profitably be read in terms of themes that have preoccupied McEwan throughout his fiction since the short stories and consistently in his novels for adults from *The Cement Garden* to *Saturday*.

Kafka's 'Metamorphosis' is given to Daisy Perowne in *Saturday* because it is 'ideal for a thirteen-year-old girl' (p. 133). When her father reads the story he is intrigued but 'ill-disposed towards a tale of impossible transformation'. The story marks the beginning of Perowne's literary education but his daughter concludes that 'he's a coarse, unredeemable materialist. She thinks he lacks an imagination' (p. 134). Briony Tallis suffered all her life because of an overactive childhood imagination, but on balance Henry Perowne is perhaps a less sympathetic character precisely because, despite his ability to help those who come under his care in the operating theatre, over the course of his life he has often lacked the ability to empathise with others through imaginative identification.

From one perspective *Saturday* is a book about the 'war on terror' that, in terms of international politics, has replaced the Cold War McEwan looked at in his mid-career novels, but from another perspective it is fundamentally and principally about consciousness (for examples, see the references to consciousness in the first sentence and on the last page). The novel is in fact concerned with mental states and processes generally – the reader spends most of the novel listening to Perowne's thoughts, Perowne's mother has Alzheimer's, and Baxter has a degenerative brain disorder, Huntington's disease, that results from an inherited gene.

His critics have thus come to see McEwan as a writer who is simultaneously interested in personal responsibility and global issues. He has developed into a fine stylist and also an author adept at anatomizing life and death in a compassionate and contemplative way of which he would have been incapable at the beginning of his career. To illustrate this one need only consider the differences between the uncomplicated treatment of Jack's father's death at the start of *The Cement Garden*, a mere plot device, and Perowne's emotionally sophisticated reflections on his mother's imminent demise in *Saturday*.

McEwan's own life experiences have undoubtedly allowed him to make this transition and now to write with conviction and artistic integrity, such that *Saturday* is his most autobiographical work to date (Perowne's house is modelled on McEwan's own and the parallels between the surgeon and the writer are numerous). McEwan has also deepened his abiding interest in science and it is likely that he will continue to be one of those for whom the continuation of a 'two cultures' schism in British intellectual life between art and science is deeply regrettable. McEwan studies is itself likely to develop this seam of inquiry into his work as issues such as consciousness, evolutionary psychology, madness and mental degeneration are explored in greater detail. Finishing with *Saturday*, this review of essential criticism on McEwan leaves its subject at a fascinating point in his own evolutionary development as a writer. He has come to be seen as Britain's foremost contemporary novelist and each of his future works is likely to be judged by this yardstick.

As readers of McEwan's fiction, we can only anticipate that novels of a similar stature to *Atonement* and marked by the technical virtuosity of *Saturday* will follow in the next phase of his career. Alongside the appearance of important new works it is also to be expected that the critical corpus on McEwan will grow at a substantial rate, developing on from analyses that foreground the central concerns of McEwan's fierce early stories to differently inflected inquiries that provide a more rounded review of all the fiction in the light of the interests of McEwan's later, subtler novels.

Notes

INTRODUCTION

1 Dwight Garner, interview with Ian McEwan, 'Salon Interview', *Salon* (31 March 1998), http://archive.salon.com/books/int/1998/03/cov_si_31int.html
2 John Mark Eberhart, 'In a better light', *Kansas City Star*, http://www.kansascity.com/mld/kansascity/entertainment/columnists/john_mark_eberhart/5968903.htm
3 Ibid.
4 Ian McEwan, 'Only love and then oblivion. Love was all they had to set against their murderers', special report: Terrorism in the US, *Guardian*, Saturday 15 September 2001. McEwan wrote two articles for the *Guardian*, on 12 and 15 September.
5 Michèle Roberts, review of *Enduring Love*, *The Times* (23 August 1997).
6 *Bold Type*, 'Interview with Ian McEwan', http://www.randomhouse.com/boldtype/1298/mcewan/interview.html 1998

CHAPTER ONE

1 In this, McEwan appears to follow on from Beckett, one of whose best-known stories is the morbid and hilarious 'First Love'.
2 John Mellors, *London Magazine* (August–September 1975), pp. 112–13.
3 Robert Towers, *New York Review of Books* (8 March 1979), p. 8.
4 'Solid Geometry' was eventually filmed and broadcast by another television company, with Ewan McGregor in the central role, in 2003.
5 John Haffenden, *Novelists in Interview* (London: Methuen, 1985), pp. 169–73.
6 Ian Hamilton, 'Points of Departure', *New Review*, 5:2 (Autumn 1978), pp. 17–18.
7 Kiernan Ryan, *Ian McEwan*, Writers and their Work (Plymouth: Northcote House, 1994), pp. 7–9.
8 [*Malcolm's note*:] Christopher Ricks, 'Adolescence and After: An Interview with Ian McEwan', *Listener*, 12 April 1979, pp. 526–7.
9 David Malcolm, *Understanding Ian McEwan* (Columbia: South Carolina University Press, 2002), pp. 21–2, 32.
10 Jack Slay, *Ian McEwan*, Twayne's English Authors Series (Boston, MA: Twayne, 1996), pp. 18–20.
11 Lynda Broughton, 'Portrait of the Subject as a Young Man: the Construction of Masculinity Ironized in "Male" Fiction', in Philip Shaw and Peter Stockwell (eds), *Subjectivity and Literature from the Romantics to the Present Day* (London: Pinter, 1991), pp. 139–43.

CHAPTER TWO

1 Julian Moynahan, 'In an Advanced Modern Manner', *New York Times Book Review* (26 August 1979), pp. 9, 20.
2 Hermione Lee, 'Shock Horror', *New Statesman* (20 January 1978), pp. 86–7.
3 Caroline Blackwood, 'De Gustibus', *Times Literary Supplement* (20 January 1978), p. 53.
4 V. S. Pritchett, *New York Review of Books* (24 January 1980), pp. 31–2.
5 Hamilton (1978), p. 19.
6 Haffenden (1985), pp. 171–2.

7 Angela Roger, 'Ian McEwan's Portrayal of Women', *Forum for Modern Language Studies*, 32:1 (1996), pp. 12–13.
8 Roger (1996), p. 14.
9 [*Byrnes's note*:] Anon, 'Taciturn Macabre and Unseen Truths', *The Birmingham Sun* (30 November 1983), p. 8.
10 [*Byrnes's note*:] Erich Fromm, *Fear of Freedom* (London: Routledge & Kegan Paul, 1942), p. 136.
11 Christina Byrnes, *The Work of Ian McEwan: A Psychodynamic Approach* (Nottingham: Paupers' Press, 2002), pp. 57–8.
12 Kiernan Ryan, 'Sex, Violence and Complicity: Martin Amis and Ian McEwan', in Rod Mengham (ed.), *An Introduction to Contemporary Fiction* (Cambridge: Polity, 1999), pp. 209–11, 213.
13 [*Brown's note*:] Edward Soja, *Postmodern Geographies* (London, 1989), pp. 190–248.
14 [*Brown's note*:] *The Rolling Stones Complete*, London, 1981, song no. 77, no page number [the track first appeared on *Let it Bleed* (1969)].
15 Richard Brown, 'Postmodern Americas in the Fiction of Angela Carter, Martin Amis and Ian McEwan', in Ann Massa and Alistair Stead (eds), *Forked Tongues?: Comparing Twentieth-Century British and American Literature* (Harlow: Longman, 1994), pp. 104–5.

CHAPTER THREE

1 See respectively, Robert Towers, 'In Extremis', *New York Review of Books* (8 March 1979), p. 8 and Paul Ableman, 'Regressive', *Spectator* (30 September 1978), pp. 23–4.
2 Anne Tyler, *New York Times Book Review* (26 November 1978), pp. 11, 92.
3 Blake Morrison, 'Paying Cellarage', *Times Literary Supplement* (29 September 1978), p. 1077.
4 Christopher Williams, 'Ian McEwan's *The Cement Garden* and the Tradition of the Child/Adolescent as "I-Narrator"', *Atti del XVI Convegno Nazionale dell'AIA: Ostuni (Brindisi) (14–16 Ottobre 1993)* (Fasano di Puglia: Schena Editore, 1996), pp. 219–20.
5 Hamilton (1978), p. 21.
6 Randall Stevenson, *The British Novel Since the Thirties* (London: Batsford, 1986), p. 185.
7 John Carey, *Pure Pleasure* (London: Faber, 2000), pp. 146–8.
8 Carmen Callil and Colm Tóibín, *The Modern Library* (London: Picador, 1999), p. 113.
9 Haffenden (1985), pp. 170–1.
10 Roger (1996), pp. 14–16.
11 David Sampson, 'McEwan/Barthes', *Southern Review*, 17:1 (March 1984), pp. 76–7.
12 Haffenden (1985), p. 171.
13 [*Slay's note*:] Michael J. Adams, 'Ian McEwan', in Larry McCaffery (ed.), *Postmodern Fiction: A Bio-Bibliographic Guide* (New York: Greenwood Press, 1986), p. 460.
14 Slay (1996), pp. 46–8.
15 Ian McEwan, 'Mother Tongue: A Memoir', in Zachary Leader (ed.), *On Modern British Fiction* (Oxford: Oxford University Press, 2002), p. 41.
16 Ibid., pp. 41–2.

CHAPTER FOUR

1 Ian McEwan, 'An Interview with Milan Kundera', in Malcolm Bradbury (ed.), *The Novel Today* (London: Fontana, 1990), p. 215.
2 John Leonard, 'Books of the Times: *The Comfort of Strangers*', *New York Times* (15 June 1981), p. 14; Richard Martin, '*The Comfort of Strangers*', *American Book Review* (November 1982), p. 23; Richard P. Brickner, *New York Times Book Review* (5 July 1981), p. 7; Eliot Fremont-Smith, 'Dearth in Venice', *Village Voice* (15 July 1981), p. 32.

3 Malcolm Bradbury, *The Modern British Novel, 1878–2001*, rev. edn (Harmondsworth: Penguin, 2001), p. 438. The final quotation comes from *The Comfort of Strangers*, p. 134.
4 Haffenden (1985), p. 170.
5 Ibid., pp. 177–81.
6 Ryan (1994), pp. 35–7.
7 Judith Seaboyer, 'Sadism Demands a Story: Ian McEwan's *The Comfort of Strangers'*, *MFS: Modern Fiction Studies*, 45:4 (Winter 1999), p. 958.
8 [*Seaboyer's note*:] Fredric Jameson, *Postmodernism, or, the Cultural Logic of Late Capitalism* (Durham: Duke University Press, 1991), p. 415.
9 Seaboyer (1999), pp. 959, 961, 965–7.
10 Roger (1996), pp. 17–19.
11 For a discussion of these issues in relation to feminism see Jessica Benjamin, *The Bonds of Love: Psychoanalysis, Feminism, and the Problem of Domination* (New York: Pantheon, 1988).

CHAPTER FIVE

1 Ian McEwan, *or Shall We Die?*, in *A Move Abroad* (London: Picador, 1989), p. 24. McEwan's 1983 oratorio, commissioned by the London Symphony Orchestra, with music by Michael Berkeley, was based on a Hiroshima documentary script by Jonathan Dimbleby and on the testimonies of two survivors.
2 See Judy Cooke, 'Time Stands Still', *Listener* (17 September 1987), p. 24, Boyd Tonkin, 'In at the Birth', *New Statesman* (18 September 1987), p. 28, Michael Neve, *Times Literary Supplement* (4 September 1987), p. 947 and Gabriele Annan, 'Worriers', *New York Review of Books* (4 February 1988), pp. 17–19.
3 Ian McEwan, 'Preface', in *A Move Abroad* (London: Picador, 1989), pp. xxv–xxvi.
4 Margaret Reynolds and Jonathan Noakes (eds), *Ian McEwan: The Essential Guide* (London: Vintage, 2002), p. 11. McEwan is referring at the end to Dr Benjamin Spock (1903–98), an American paediatrician whose theories encouraged mothers to show greater attention towards, and allow greater freedom of expression for, their children.
5 Bradbury (2001), p. 481.
6 D. J. Taylor, 'Ian McEwan: Standing Up for the Sisters', in *A Vain Conceit: British Fiction in the 1980s* (London: Bloomsbury, 1988), p. 59.
7 Concern with the subject now referred to as the 'Condition of England' was sparked by Thomas Carlyle's essay on 'Chartism' (1839). In fiction, the long-standing discussion notably includes E. M. Forster's *Howards End* (1910) and H. G. Wells's *Tono-Bungay* (1909), two 'Condition of England novels' contemporary with C. F. G. Masterman's influential study entitled *The Condition of England* (1909).
8 Allan Massie, *The Novel Today 1970–89* (London: Longman 1990), p. 51.
9 Adam Mars-Jones, *Venus Envy: On the Womb and the Bomb*, Chatto Counterblasts 14 (London: Chatto & Windus, 1990), p. 24.
10 Ibid., pp. 24–8.
11 See Bowlby's Chapter on 'Mourning of Adults', in *Loss* (Harmondsworth: Penguin, 1991).
12 Rosa González-Casademont, 'The Pleasure of Prose Writing vs Pornographic Violence: An Interview with Ian McEwan', *The European English Messenger*, 1:3 (Autumn 1992), p. 44.
13 Reynolds and Noakes (eds) (2002), p. 13.
14 Ellen Pifer, *Demon or Doll: Images of the Child in Contemporary Writing and Culture* (Charlottesville and London: University of Virginia Press, 2000), pp. 201–3.
15 Reynolds and Noakes (eds) (2002), p. 10.
16 [*Slay's note*:] Roberta Smoodin, 'The Theft of a Child and the Gift of Time', *The Los Angeles Times Book Review* (20 September 1987), p. 19.

17 [*Slay's note from the original article in Critique*:] As Claire recounts her story, the narration slips into the past, with the narrator telling the story as it happened forty-four years ago; however, Claire's intrusions upon the story bring us back to the immediate present. Interestingly, then, there are two simultaneous presents: the present of Claire and Douglas and their courtship, and the present of Claire relating the story to her son. In essence, time has warped yet again in the novel.
18 [*Slay's note*:] Even the courtship is filled with amusing references to time; for instance, Claire works in the clock section of a department store, and Stephen's father, Douglas, meets his future wife when he returns a broken clock.
19 Slay (1996), pp. 123–5. The extract first appears in Jack Slay, 'Vandalizing Time: Ian McEwan's "The Child in Time" ', *Critique: Studies in Contemporary Fiction*, 35:4 (Summer 1994), pp. 212–14. Here, Slay's section begins 'Like so many of the characters and elements in *The Child in Time*, science (especially in its associations with the entity of time), too, is seen metaphorically as a child. Thelma envisions this particular child as "on the point of growing up and learning to claim less for itself" ' (pp. 43–4).
20 Dominic Head, *Modern British Fiction* (Cambridge: Cambridge University Press, 2002), p. 235.
21 Ben Knights, *Writing Masculinities: Male Narratives in Twentieth-Century Fiction* (London: Macmillan, 1999), p. 218.
22 Ibid., pp. 218–19.
23 [*Knights's note*:] Not for nothing had McEwan just written the libretto for Michael Berkeley's anti-nuclear cantata *or Shall We Die?*
24 Knights (1999), pp. 208–9.
25 [*Edwards's note*:] The tradition can be said to begin with Wordsworth's opposition to the encroachment of the railway on the Lake District; a reminder of the shifting significance of this (it now seems) most human of industrial forms of transport in the poetic sense of the country and its landscape.
26 [*Edwards's note*:] Donald Davie, *Thomas Hardy and British Poetry* (London: Routledge & Kegan Paul, 1973), p. 66.
27 [*Edwards's note*:] Davie (1973), p. 73.
28 Paul Edwards, 'Time Romanticism, Modernism and Modernity in Ian McEwan's *The Child in Time*', *English*, 44:178 (1995), pp. 48–51.

CHAPTER SIX

1 Those who praised the novel include Anthony Burgess, 'Goodbye to Berlin and Farewell to Arms', *Observer* (6 May 1990), p. 61, George Stade, 'Berlin Affair: A thriller', *New York Times Book Review* (3 June 1990), p. 33 and Joan Smith, 'The Body Politic', *New Statesman and Scientist* (11 May 1990), pp. 35–6.
2 Michael Wood, 'Well Done, Ian McEwan', *London Review of Books* (10 May 1990), pp. 24, 26. Wood is of course referring at the end to Leonard, and the quotation he cites is from Leonard's imaginary defence of himself in court (p. 217).
3 Brown (1994), p. 107.
4 [*Ledbetter's note*:] As I complete this text, I am aware that the current discussion is to slice and divide Bosnia into three pieces, according to ethnicity. The editors of the current issue of the US magazine *The New Yorker* describe this act, technically called 'partition', as 'dismemberment' (*New Yorker*, 26 July 1993, p. 4).
5 Solingen, a city in west central Germany, was severely damaged during the Second World War.
6 Mark Ledbetter, 'The Games Body-Politics Plays: a Rhetoric of Secrecy in Ian McEwan's "The Innocent" ', *Victims and the Postmodern Narrative or Doing Violence to the Body: An Ethic of Reading and Writing* (Basingstoke and London: Macmillan; New York: St Martin's Press, 1996), pp. xii, 159, pp. 99–102.

7 Tamás Bényei, *Acts of Attention: Figure and Narrative in Postwar British Novels* (Frankfurt: Peter Lang, 1999), pp. 221–2.
8 González-Casademont (1992), pp. 42–3.
9 Maria is less impressed by this speech. She later says: ' "Does he think I'm the Third Reich? Is that what he thinks you are marrying? Does he really think that people represent countries? Even the Major makes a better speech at the Christmas dinner" ' (p. 139). It is also worth remembering that Maria in fact marries Glass and not Leonard.
10 *The Comfort of Strangers*, p. 134.
11 [*Slay's note*:] Laurie Muchnik, 'You Must Dismember This', *Village Voice* (28 August 1990), p. 102.
12 Slay (1996), pp. 135–8.
13 Ryan (1994), pp. 58–60.
14 Ibid., p. 60.
15 Merritt Moseley, 'Ian McEwan', in *British Novelists Since 1960*, Second Series, ed. Merritt Moseley, *Dictionary of Literary Biography*, Vol. 194 (Detroit: Gale, 1998), p. 213.

CHAPTER SEVEN

1 Respectively, Graham Coster, 'Evil and Novels', *London Review of Books* (25 June 1992), pp. 20–1 and Michael Wood, 'When the Balloon Goes Up', *London Review of Books* (4 September 1997), pp. 8–9, which discusses both *Black Dogs* and *Enduring Love*.
2 See the contrasting views of M. John Harrison, 'Beating the Retreat', *Times Literary Supplement* (19 June 1992), p. 20 and Amanda Craig, 'They Rape Women', *Literary Review* (June 1992), p. 4.
3 Moseley (1998), pp. 213–14.
4 Michel Delville, 'Marsilio Ficino and Political Syncretism in Ian McEwan's *Black Dogs*', *Notes on Contemporary Literature*, 26:3 (1996), p. 12.
5 Wendy Lesser, *New Republic* (16 November 1992), p. 41.
6 [*Byrnes's note*:] Andrew Billen, 'A Goodbye to Gore', *Observer* (14 June 1992), p. 29.
7 [*Byrnes's note*:] Billen (1992), p. 29.
8 Byrnes (2002), pp. 242–3.
9 Marc Delrez, 'Escape into Innocence: Ian McEwan and the Nightmare of History', *Ariel: A Review of International English Literature*, 26:2 (April 1995), pp. 18–20.
10 Ibid., p. 16.
11 This burial site is the Dolmen de la Prunarède that June takes to be a symbol of the universe's indifference to human squabbles, somewhat like the symbol of the Kawa Dol in E. M. Forster's *A Passage to India*. The dolmen is first mentioned on pp. 40–1, then again on pp. 58, 122–3 and 139.
12 Jago Morrison, 'Unravelling Time in Ian McEwan's Fiction', *Contemporary Fiction* (London: Routledge, 2003), pp. 75–7.
13 Malcolm (2002), pp. 151–3.
14 Ibid., p. 153.
15 Ibid., pp. 143–4.

CHAPTER EIGHT

1 *Bold Type* (1998).
2 See Merritt Moseley, 'Recent British Novels', *Sewanee Review*, 106 (1998), pp. 678–82; Anita Brookner, 'Desire and Pursuit', *Spectator* (30 August 1997), pp. 28–9; Amanda Craig, 'Out of the Balloon', *New Statesman* (5 September 1997), p. 43; Jason Cowley, 'Portrait: Ian McEwan', *Prospect* (December 1998), pp. 42–5.
3 A. S. Byatt, *On Histories and Stories* (London: Vintage, 2001), p. 83.
4 Reynolds and Noakes (eds) (2002), pp. 15–16.

5 A quotation from Milton's *Paradise Lost* follows shortly: 'Hurl'd headlong flaming from th'Ethereal Sky' (p. 29).
6 For a discussion of this in the novel itself, see p. 4.
7 Garner (1998).
8 Adam Mars-Jones, 'I Think I'm, Right, Therefore I Am', *Observer* (7 September 1997), p. 16.
9 Ibid.
10 Sven Birkerts, '*Enduring Love*', http://www.nytimes.com/books/98/12/27/specials/mcewan.html
11 James Wood, 'Why it all adds up', *Guardian* (4 September 1997), p. 9.
12 McEwan in conversation with James Naughtie, Radio 4's *Book Club* programme (1 October 2000), bbc.co.uk/arts/books/club/enduring/transcript.shtml
13 Malcolm (2002), pp. 178–9.
14 Joe's viewpoint seems to echo Jean-François Lyotard's argument in *The Postmodern Condition* (1979) that science legitimates itself in advanced capitalist societies through an appeal to narrative.
15 Roger Clark and Andy Gordon, *Ian McEwan's* Enduring Love (London: Continuum, 2003), pp. 47–8.
16 [*Byrnes's note*:] J. W. Lovett Doust and H. Christie, 'The Pathology of Love: Some Clinical Variations of De Clérambault's Syndrome', *Social Science and Medicine*, 12 (London: Pergamon Press, 1978).
17 [*Byrnes's note*:] Harman, Rosner and Owens, 'Obsessional Harassment and Erotomania in a Criminal Court Population', *Journal of Forensic Sciences*, 40 (March 1995), p. 82.
18 [*Byrnes's note*:] M. Pathe and P. E. Mullen, 'The Pathological Extensions of Love', *British Journal of Psychiatry*, 165 (1994), p. 239. McEwan includes a quotation and reference to this article (pp. 242–3), but gives the page references as 614–23.
19 [*Byrnes's note*:] Pathe and Mullen (1994), p. 239.
20 [*Brnes's note*:] The delusion involved in De Clérambault's syndrome is in a different category from an adolescent's romantic infatuation which might lead to a normal love relationship, because in the mind of the patient there exists an unshakeable conviction of an overwhelming passion outside him/herself and solely in the mind of a person s/he believes to be his/her admirer.
21 [*Brnes's note*:] Here are more echoes of the footage of film shot during the Conservative Party Conference in *The Ploughman's Lunch*.
22 Byrnes (2002), pp. 265–7. The final quotation is from P. H. S., 'Shrink to Fit', *The Times* (2 September 1997), p. 22.
23 Cressida Connolly, 'Over-Fished Waters', http://www.users.dircon.co.uk/~litrev/199709/connolly.html
24 [*Morrison's note*:] Paul Ricoeur, *Time and Narrative*, Vol. 1, trans. Kathleen McLaughlin and David Pellauer (Chicago: Chicago University Press), 1994, p. 52.
25 [*Morrison's note*:] Ricoeur (1994), p. 54.
26 Jago Morrison, 'Narration and Unease in McEwan's Later Fiction', *Critique*, 42:3 (Spring 2001), pp. 258–60.

CHAPTER NINE

1 Adam Mars-Jones, 'Have a Heart', *Observer Review* (6 September 1998), p. 16.
2 Anita Brookner, *Spectator* (12 September 1998), p. 39.
3 *Bold Type Interview with McEwan* (1998).
4 Dominic Head, *Modern British Fiction* (Cambridge: Cambridge University Press, 2002), p. 47.
5 lbid., p. 46.
6 *Bold Type Interview with McEwan* (1998).

7 Malcolm (2002), pp. 194–5.
8 John Brannigan, *Orwell to the Present: Literature in England 1945–2000* (London: Palgrave, 2003), p. 88.
9 William H. Pritchard, *New York Times Book Review* (27 December 1998), p. 4.
10 Nicholas Lezard, 'Morality Bites: Ian McEwan's five-finger finesse', *Guardian* (24 April 1999).
11 [*Byrnes's note*:] John Keenan, 'Foreign Affairs of the Heart', *The Guardian* (5 September 1998), p. 8.
12 [*Byrnes's note*:] Erich Fromm, *Fear of Freedom* (London: Routledge & Kegan Paul, 1942), p. 137.
13 [*Byrnes's note*:] Jeremy Gavron, 'Poisoned by Public Life', *The Financial Times* (29 August 1998), p. 5.
14 [*Byrnes's note*:] William Leith, 'Form and Dysfunction', *The Observer* (20 September 1998), p. 8.
15 [*Byrnes's note*:] Leith (1998), p. 4.
16 [*Byrnes's note*:] *The Cement Garden*, p. 95.
17 [*Byrnes's note*:] W. Mayer-Gross, E. Slater and M. Roth, *Clinical Psychiatry* (London: Cassell, 1960), pp. 448–58.
18 [*Byrnes's note*:] A national newspaper which seems to be modelled on *The Times*.
19 Garner (1998).
20 [*Byrnes's note*:] Ian McEwan, *Interview On-Line: Author Chat Transcripts*, Barnes & Noble, http://www.barnesandnoble.com/community/...5QVIOUNHO9&SOURCEID=000001313100216851
21 [*Byrnes's note*:] Robert Hanks, 'The Week on Radio: Dark Visions of Utopia' (Ian McEwan in conversation with Michael O'Donnel, BBC Radio 4, 14 March 1997), *Independent* (22 March 1997), p. 31.
22 [*Byrnes's note*:] Hanks (1997).
23 Byrnes (2002), pp. 143–9. The final quotation is from Mars-Jones (1998), p. 16.

CHAPTER TEN

1 Martyn Bedford, 'She Stripped off and Plunged In', *Literary Review* (October 2001), p. 52.
2 John Updike, 'Flesh on Flesh', *New Yorker* (13 May 2002), p. 80.
3 Frank Kermode, 'Point of View', *London Review of Books* (4 October 2001), p. 8.
4 Reynolds and Noakes (eds) (2002), pp. 22–3. It is slightly misleading of McEwan to say that what Conrad 'did' in the preface to *The Nigger of the Narcissus* was make the reader see. Conrad in fact says this is what he is aiming to do rather than *does* it: 'My task which I am trying to achieve by the power of the written word ... is, before all, to make you see.'
5 Reynolds and Noakes (eds) (2002), pp. 19–20.
6 Kermode (2001), pp. 8–9.
7 Claire Messud, 'The Beauty of the Conjuring', *Atlantic Monthly*, 289:3 (March 2002), pp. 106–7.
8 Updike (2002), p. 80.
9 Bedford (2001), p. 52.
10 Geoff Dyer, 'Who's afraid of influence?', *Guardian* (22 September 2001), p. 8.
11 Hermione Lee, 'If your memories serve you well ...', *Observer* (23 September 2001).
12 James Wood, 'The Trick of Truth', *The New Republic Online*, http://www.powells.com/review/2002_03_21.html (21 March 2002).
13 John Mullan, 'Elements of Fiction: turning up the heat', *Guardian Review* (22 March 2003), p. 32.

Select Bibliography

The best and most up-to-date bibliography on McEwan can be found at the Ian McEwan website: http://www.ianmcewan.com/bib/

TEXTS BY IAN McEWAN

NOVELS

(Details are given below of first UK editions, followed by details of editions quoted in this Guide where these are different from the first UK edition.)

The Cement Garden. London: Jonathan Cape, 1978. London: Vintage, 1997.
The Comfort of Strangers. London: Jonathan Cape, 1981. London: Vintage, 1997.
The Child in Time. London: Jonathan Cape, 1987. London: Picador, 1988.
The Innocent or The Special Relationship. London: Jonathan Cape, 1990. London: Vintage, 1998.
Black Dogs. London: Jonathan Cape, 1992. London: Vintage, 1998.
The Daydreamer. London: Jonathan Cape, 1994. London: Vintage, 1995.
Enduring Love. London: Jonathan Cape, 1997. London: Vintage, 1998.
Amsterdam. London: Jonathan Cape, 1998. London: Vintage, 1998.
Atonement. London: Jonathan Cape, 2001.
Saturday. London: Jonathan Cape, 2005.

SHORT STORIES

(Details are given below of first UK editions, followed by details of editions quoted in this Guide.)

First Love, Last Rites. London: Jonathan Cape, 1975. London: Vintage, 1976.
In Between the Sheets. London: Jonathan Cape, 1978. London: Vintage, 1997.

UNCOLLECTED SHORT STORIES

'Intersection' in *Tri-Quarterly*, Fall 1975, 63–86.
'Untitled' in *Tri-Quarterly*, Winter 1976, 62–3.
'Deep Sleep, Light Sleeper', in *Harpers & Queen*, August 1977, 82–5.

SCRIPTS

The Imitation Game (Jack Flea's Birthday Celebration, Solid Geometry, The Imitation Game). London: Jonathan Cape, 1981. London: Picador, 1982.
A Move Abroad (*or Shall we Die*? and *The Ploughman's Lunch*). London: Picador, 1989.
Soursweet, London: Faber, 1988.

SELECTED CRITICISM AND REVIEWS

BOOKS ON McEWAN

Byrnes, Christina. *The Work of Ian McEwan: A Psychodynamic Approach*. Nottingham: Paupers' Press, 2002.
Malcolm, David. *Understanding Ian McEwan*. Columbia: South Carolina Press, 2002.
Ryan, Kiernan. *Ian McEwan*. Writers and their Work. Plymouth: Northcote House, 1994.
Slay, Jack. *Ian McEwan*. Twayne's English Authors Series. Boston, MA: Twayne, 1996.

GENERAL BOOKS THAT DISCUSS McEWAN

Bradbury, Malcolm. *The Modern British Novel, 1878–2001*, revised edition. Harmondsworth: Penguin, 2001.

Brannigan, John. *Orwell to the Present: Literature in England 1945–2000*. London: Palgrave, 2003.

Callil, Carmen and Colm Tóibín. *The Modern Library*. London: Picador, 1999.

Carey, John. *Pure Pleasure*. London: Faber, 2000.

Head, Dominic. *Modern British Fiction*. Cambridge: Cambridge University Press, 2002.

Massie, Allan. *The Novel Today 1970–89*. London: Longman, 1990.

Stevenson, Randall. *The British Novel Since the Thirties*. London: Batsford, 1986.

Taylor, D. J. *After the War: The Novel and English Society Since 1945*. London: Chatto & Windus, 1993.

—— *A Vain Conceit*. London: Bloomsbury, 1988.

SELECTED ARTICLES AND ESSAYS ON McEWAN

Banks, J. R. 'A Gondola Named Desire'. *Critical Quarterly*, 24:2, Summer 1982, 27–31.

Benyei, Tamas. 'Places in Between: The Subversion of Initiation Narrative in Ian McEwan's *The Innocent*'. *British and American Studies*, 4:2, 1999, 66–73.

Broughton, Lynda. 'Portrait of the Subject as a Young Man: the Construction of Masculinity Ironized in "Male" Fiction', in *Subjectivity and Literature from the Romantics to the Present Day*, ed. Philip Shaw and Peter Stockwell. London: Pinter, 1991, 135–45.

Brown, Richard. 'Postmodern Americas in the Fiction of Angela Carter, Martin Amis and Ian McEwan', in *Forked Tongues? Comparing Twentieth-Century British and American Literature*, ed. Ann Massa and Alistair Stead. London: Longman, 1994, 92–110.

Byrnes, Christina. 'Ian McEwan: Pornographer or Prophet?' *Contemporary Review*, 266:1553, 1995, 320–3.

Cochran, Angus B. 'Ian McEwan (1948–)', in *British Writers. Supplement IV*, ed. George Stade. New York: Scribner's, 1997, 389–408.

Delrez, Marc. 'Escape into Innocence: Ian McEwan and the Nightmare of History', *Ariel: A Review of International English Literature*, 26:2, April 1995, 7–23.

Docherty, Thomas. 'Now, Here, This', in *Literature and the Contemporary*, eds Roger Luckhurst and Peter Marks. Harlow: Longman, 1999, 50–62.

Edwards, Paul. 'Time Romanticism, Modernism and Modernity in The Child in Time'. *English*, 44:178, 1995, 41–55.

Kohn, Robert E. 'The Fivesquare *Amsterdam* of Ian McEwan'. *Critical Survey*, 16:1, 2004, 59–76.

Ledbetter, Mark. 'The Games Body-Politics Plays: a Rhetoric of Secrecy in Ian McEwan's "The Innocent" ', in *Victims and the Postmodern Narrative or Doing Violence to the Body: An Ethic of Reading and Writing*. Basingstoke and London: Macmillan; New York: St Martin's Press, 1996, pp. xii, 159, 88–103.

Mars-Jones, Adam. 'Venus Envy'. Chatto Counterblasts 14. London: Chatto & Windus, 1990.

Morrison, Jago. 'Narration and Unease in McEwan's Later Fiction', *Critique*, 42:3, Spring 2001, 253–70.

—— 'Unravelling Time in Ian McEwan's Fiction', in *Contemporary Fiction*. London: Routledge, 2003, 67–80.

Moseley, Merritt. 'Ian McEwan', in Merritt Moseley (ed.), *British Novelists Since 1960*, Second Series, *The Dictionary of Literary Biography*, Vol. 194. Detroit: Gale, 1998.

Pifer, Ellen. 'Ian McEwan's *The Child in Time*', in *Demon or Doll: Images of the Child in Contemporary Writing and Culture*. Charlottesville and London: University of Virginia Press, 2000, 189–211.

Ricks, Christopher. 'Playing with Terror'. *London Review of Books*, 4:1, 21 January–3 February 1982, 13–14.

Roger, Angela. 'Ian McEwan's Portrayal of Women'. *Forum for Modern Language Studies*, 32:1, 1996, 11–27.

Ryan, Kiernan. 'Sex, Violence and Complicity: Martin Amis and Ian McEwan', in *An Introduction to Contemporary Fiction*. Cambridge: Polity, 1999, 203–18.

Sampson, David. 'McEwan/Barthes'. *Southern Review*, 17:1, March 1984, 68–80.

Seaboyer, Judith. 'Sadism Demands a Story: Ian McEwan's "The Comfort of Strangers" '. *MFS: Modern Fiction Studies*, 45:4, 1999, 957–86.

Slay, Jack. 'Vandalizing Time: Ian McEwan's "The Child in Time" '. *Critique: Studies in Contemporary Fiction*, 35:4, 1994, 205–18.

Walkowitz, Rebecca L. 'Ian McEwan', in *A Companion to the British and Irish Novel 1945–2000*, ed. Brian W. Shaffer. Oxford: Blackwell, 2005, 504–14.

SELECTED INTERVIEWS

Billen, Andrew. 'A Goodbye to Gore'. *Observer*, 14 June 1992, 29.

Cowley, Jason. 'The Prince of Darkest Imaginings'. *The Times*, 6 September 1997, 9.

Danziger, Danny. 'In Search of Two Characters'. *The Times*, 27 June 1987, 13.

Daoust, Phil. 'Post-Shock Traumatic: Profile of Ian McEwan'. *Guardian*, 4 August 1997, 6.

Franks, Alan. 'McEwan's Best Bitterness'. *The Times*, 27 June 1992, 4.

González-Casademont, Rosa. 'The Pleasure of Prose Writing vs Pornographic Violence: An Interview with Ian McEwan'. *The European English Messenger*, 1:3 (Autumn 1992), 40–5.

Grimes, William. 'Rustic Calm Inspires McEwan Tale of Evil'. *New York Times*, 18 November 1992, 25.

Haffenden, John. *Novelists in Interview*. London: Methuen. 1985, 168–90.

Hamilton, Ian. 'Points of Departure'. *New Review*, 5:2, Autumn 1978, 9–21.

Hatterstone, Simon. 'Slaughter of the Innocent'. *Guardian*, 23 June 1994, 10.

Hunt, Adam. 'Ian McEwan'. *New Fiction*, Vol. 21, Winter 1996, 47–50.

Johnson, Daniel. 'The Timeless and Timely Child'. *The Times*, 8 December 1990, 16–17.

Kemp, Peter. 'Hounding the Innocent'. *Sunday Times*, 14 June 1992, 6–11.

Lawley, Sue. 'Desert Island Discs'. BBC Radio 4, 16 January 2000.

Leith, William. 'Form and Dysfunction'. *Observer*, 20 September 1998, 4–8.

McEwan, Ian. 'An Interview with Milan Kundera', in *The Novel Today*, ed. Malcolm Bradbury. London: Fontana, 1990, 205–22.

Pilkington, Edward. 'Berlin Mon Amour'. *Guardian*, 13 June 1992, 29.

Reynolds, Margaret and Jonathan Noakes. *Ian McEwan: The Essential Guide*. London: Vintage, 2002.

Ricks, Christopher. 'Adolescence and After: An Interview with Ian McEwan'. *The Listener*, 101, 12 April 1979, 526–7.

Smith, Amanda. 'Ian McEwan'. *Publisher's Weekly*, 232, 11 September 1987, 68–9.

Tresidder, Megan. 'The Dreamer Who Creates Nightmares'. *Sunday Telegraph*, 28 June 1992, 2.

Walter, Natasha. 'Looks Like a Teacher, Writes Like a Demon'. *Observer*, 24 August 1997, 2.

Writer's Talk: Ideas of Our Time. 'Ian McEwan with Martin Amis'. Guardian Conversations, 69, ICA video, 1989.

INDEX